Jurassic Classics

In memory of my friend
Ron Haydock (1940–1977),
who gave me one of the most valuable pieces
of advice in becoming a writer:
"Don, you gotta hustle."

Jurassic Classics

A Collection of Saurian Essays and Mesozoic Musings

by

DONALD F. GLUT

McFarland & Company, Inc., Publishers

Jefferson, North Carolina, and London

ALSO BY DONALD F. GLUT
AND FROM MCFARLAND

Dinosaurs: The Encyclopedia, Supplement 1 (2000)

*Carbon Dates: A Day by Day Almanac of
Paleo Anniversaries and Dino Events* (1999)

Dinosaur Valley Girls: The Book (1998)

Dinosaurs: The Encyclopedia (1997)

The Frankenstein Catalog (1984)

Library of Congress Cataloguing-in-Publication Data

Glut, Donald F.
    Jurassic classics : a collection of saurian essays and Mesozoic
musings / by Donald F. Glut
        p.   cm.
    Includes index.
    ISBN 0-7864-0961-4 (softcover : 50# alkaline paper) ∞
    1. Paleontology.   2. Dinosaurs.   I. Title.
QE723.G58   2001
560—dc21   00-51108

British Library cataloguing data are available

Cover image © 2001 Sinclair Refining Company.

Manufactured in the United States of America

*McFarland & Company, Inc., Publishers
    Box 611, Jefferson, North Carolina 28640
    www.mcfarlandpub.com*

TABLE OF CONTENTS

CAVE WRITINGS
(A PREHISTORIC PREFACE)

For over a third of a century, I have been writing articles and essays about prehistoric "things"—dinosaurs, extinct mammals, early humans, monsters—some of them real, others hatched solely in the imagination, yet all of them connected by the singular theme of their being, or representing, or having to do, in some way, with creatures from before the dawn of recorded history.

Most of those pieces have long been extinct (*i.e.*, out of print). Others, though still in existence, have become virtually unobtainable, and some were seen by relatively few readers even when they were newly published. Therefore, I have gathered these articles from their myriad sources for a second appearance in this volume.

When I first conceived of this project, I realized only too well that some of the articles would be dated (*e.g.*, referring to "future" projects that have long since become history); that some of the paleontological information in them would no longer be considered correct (*e.g.*, the statement that pterosaurs only glided, when the current consensus among scientists is that they actually flapped their way into the sky); and that some were written so long ago that their styles would not be up to current professional standards (*e.g.*, articles from "fanzines," that is fan-produced magazines).

From the outset I decided to edit the articles where necessary—updating, supplementing, augmenting, polishing, and so on—so that each piece would be fresh and up to date, reflecting recent styles, standards, and science. It was my intention to avoid the need for explanatory insertions or footnotes that would only create confusion or interrupt the

1

flow of the text. Curious readers who wish to find out where the changes have been made (and who have a lot of free time on their hands) will have to assume the role of the true field scientist by seeking out and unearthing the originals, then making the comparisons themselves.

In addition to the older articles, I decided also to include some pieces that had never seen print. The article about *Tyrannosaurus rex* as this dinosaur has been perceived over the years by the public, the piece on the Grés à Voltzia floodplain, and the conclusion to the series on the Mesozoic Era are all presented for the first time in section one of this book.

I have prefaced each article with introductory notes. These notes are intended to set each piece in historical perspective, comment upon its origins and content, add new information where appropriate, provide a sense of continuity from one article to the next, and, in effect, constitute an entire series of new articles.

The topics of the articles are diverse, but I have tried to group them by broad themes. I have divided the book into three major sections.

PALEO WORDS, the first section, includes articles about paleontology itself and topics relating more directly to that science. Section Two, PERSONAL PETROGLYPHS, gathers topics with which I have had a personal involvement. Section Three, MESOZOIC MEDIA, deals with media-related topics. Within each section the individual works are arranged in chronological order by date of original publication.

As I began to reread and revise the articles, the value in this arrangement became even more apparent. It surprised me how some articles complemented and even supplemented each other in various ways, often expanding upon points briefly mentioned in an earlier piece. In a way, despite the sometimes very different themes of the separate works, they seemed to come together like puzzle pieces—or like the individual fossil bones that fit together to become a mounted dinosaur skeleton in a museum—forming some larger and more encompassing whole.

I hope that the articles, with their introductions, comprise an informative and also sometimes nostalgic journey back through time.

D.F.G.
Burbank, California
December 2000

ONE

PALEO WORDS

GIVING LIFE TO ANCIENT BONES

Charles R. Knight, whose name appears frequently in the text of this volume, was inarguably the most influential of all the artists to restore extinct animals, and many of those who know his work consider him still to be the best. Excelling in all media (pencil, watercolor, oils, sculpture, *etc.*), Knight, or "Toppy" as his daughter Lucy affectionately called him, set the standard with his re-creations of dinosaurs and prehistoric creatures. The effect Knight's work had upon future artists, the public's conception of extinct animals and the popular media cannot be overly stressed; indeed as will be shown in subsequent articles in this collection, many future re-creations of ancient animals—on the printed page, the motion picture screen, and elsewhere—would be visually based directly upon Knight's originals.

Knight's work also made a strong positive impression on me, when I was a young child during the early 1950s. I saw reproductions of his pictures and models in, it seemed, most of the books about prehistoric animals that I took out of the library. And his murals graced my favorite hall—the one that displayed the bones of ancient animals—in what was then called the Chicago Natural History Museum (now The Field Museum). In fact, I believe Charles R. Knight was the first artist I actually knew by name.

I had spent a number of years attempting—futilely, it turned out—to interest various art-book publishers in a book about Knight. Always the response came back negative, reflecting a rather snobbish attitude on the part of the publishers that responded, Knight then not being considered by the general art world as important enough to warrant a book.

The project seemed stillborn until one fateful night in fall, 1977, when I was attending my first meeting of the Society of Vertebrate Paleontology, that year held in Los Angeles. A group of dinosaur aficionados had crowded into a hotel room to view a showing of my huge collection of 35mm slides of fossils and life restorations of prehistoric creatures. Among the audience were vertebrate paleontologist Robert A. Long and sculptor Sylvia Massey (later Massey Czerkas, now simply Czerkas), the latter being the founder of the original, Los Angeles–based Dinosaur Society. Among the projected slides were numerous reproductions of Knight's work. As more and more comments were heard praising Knight's restorations, I mentioned that I had been unsuccessful with placing a book about the artist and his work. It was at that moment that Rob Long began to suggest—no, *insist*, and quite vociferously so—that this book *must* be done— that if it weren't, Knight could very well be "buried in obscurity"— and that Sylvia and I were the logical choices to put the project together.

The die cast, Sylvia and I subsequently began to discuss the potential project seriously. I contacted Knight's daughter Lucy Knight Steel, who then put us in touch with the artist's granddaughter Rhoda Khalt. Both Sylvia and I might be described as "hustler" types, and she managed to interest a top literary agent in the book, who promptly sold the project to E. P. Dutton, Inc. Working with the Knight family and having access to its personal letters and other documents, we completed the lavishly illustrated volume, a combination authorized biography and art book, with me handling the cave lion's bulk of the writing, in time to debut at the gala opening—on March 5, 1982, at the Natural History Museum of Los Angeles County—of a major exhibition of the artist's work, organized by Sylvia. Both the book and the exhibition possess the same title: *Dinosaurs, Mammoths and Cavemen: The Art of Charles R. Knight.*

Two separate pieces were especially edited and adapted from our book, one for publication in *Natural History* (volume 91, number 2, February 1982) and the other for *Terra* (volume 20, number 3, Winter 1982), magazines published by the American Museum of Natural History and the Natural History Museum of Los Angeles County, respectively. These articles differed in various ways from one another, as each tended to emphasize specifics pertinent to one or the other institution. The *Terra* version also included some uncredited new material written by Natural History Museum of Los Angeles County fossil-mammal specialist John M. Harris specifically regarding the La Brea mural Knight did for that museum in 1925, its exhibition and subsequent restoration. The following text was adapted from the version that appeared in *Natural History*.

Although the Charles R. Knight art exhibition successfully continues to travel the world, the book has been long out of print. Copies of the book, however, reproducing much of his work with most illustrations in full color, may still be purchased from The Dinosaur Museum, P.O. Box 277, Monticello, Utah 84535.

Charles Robert Knight was the first and, without question, the foremost artist to re-create, with both scientific accuracy and romantic beauty, creatures and environments of the prehistoric past. For nearly half a century, Knight gave to a modern world his visions of its prehistory, producing roughly 1,000 drawings, paintings, and sculptures of ancient animals and human beings. His were the first truly modern visual conceptions of the creatures that once inhabited this planet, and his depictions of them have never—even decades after he created his final piece of art—been surpassed.

Knight was born in Brooklyn, New York, in 1874, to Lucy and George Wakefield Knight. George Knight was then employed as the personal secretary to banker John Pierpont Morgan, who would later play an important role in Charles's career at New York City's American Museum of Natural History, one of the world's great museums. From his early childhood on, Knight's parents instilled in their young son an interest in, and love of, nature.

Charles was only five years old when his father took him to the American Museum of Natural History, but even at that age he was aware that there could be an artistic approach to presenting animal life to the public and had already discovered in himself an intense interest in drawing.

After the death of Knight's mother, his father married Sarah Davis, a woman with artistic abilities who recognized her stepson's talents. She sent him to the Froebel Academy, and there he began his formal art education, taking classes in drawing, mapmaking, and clay and sand modeling, in addition to more mundane subjects. Knight later enrolled at the Metropolitan Art School, where most of the students were older than he was. These more experienced students taught the young artist that he could earn money for his artwork. Knight, who was attending classes at the Art Students League, became skilled in watercolor, pencil, charcoal, crayon and oil, and utilized those skills when, at age 16, he began his professional career.

Knight was hired by a church-decorating firm to draw animals and plants for stained-glass windows. While working at this job, he spent much of his free time at the zoo in Central Park drawing animals from life. When he finally carried his personal studies over to the American Museum of Natural History, he already had a full mastery of his artistic materials. Visiting the museum almost daily, he studied the carcasses of various creatures, familiarizing himself with their musculature and skeletal structure. In the taxidermy department he carefully examined eyes, paws, noses and ears, and drew detailed close-ups of what he saw. Often the carcasses were foul-smelling, but he was learning from this firsthand course in animal anatomy. No dead tiger, kangaroo, pelican or macaw passed through his hands without being re-created on paper. What he learned in that department about muscle and bone, and what he had already learned through experience about animal psychology, helped lay the foundation for the next phase of his career.

Knight's name soon became known to the scientists at the museum. As an amateur scientist always anxious to learn more about the animals that he drew, Knight soon met many of the staff scientists who, impressed by his desire to learn, offered him continued advice and encouragement. One of Knight's closest friends at the museum was head taxidermist John Rowley. One day in 1894, Rowley told Knight that Dr. Jacob L. Wortman, the assistant curator of the museum's fossil department, was looking for someone to make a drawing of a prehistoric animal.

At Rowley's suggestion, Knight went upstairs to offer his services. Wortman, a specialist in fossil teeth, wanted him to create a life restoration, that is, an illustration that would depict the animal as it might have looked when living, of an extinct piglike animal called *Elotherium*. Knowing something about modern-day pigs, Knight studied the skeletal remains of *Elotherium*, applied to those ancient bones his educated estimate as to its musculature and attitudes, then made a restoration that both satisfied and delighted Wortman. Soon Wortman was giving Knight more assignments, inadvertently directing him into a field of work that would occupy much of his time for the next four decades.

In 1896, Knight made one of the most important contacts of his life, Henry Fairfield Osborn, a distinguished paleontologist (specializing in fossil mammals) who had just taken a position at the American Museum, where he later founded the Department of Vertebrate Paleontology. When Osborn first came to the museum, its fossil collection was meager and much of it existed on shelves in the workshops, seen only by workers who cared little about the interests of the general public. But, in addition to being a scientist, Osborn had a keen taste for artistic beauty. "Prof. Osborn

was something of a natu-
ralist and an artist at heart,"
Knight later wrote, "and had
a great appreciation of all
things living and beautiful."

Osborn promptly rec-
ognized Knight's talents
and took the young artist
under his wing. He revealed
to Knight his dream of lur-
ing the layman into the
American Museum's halls
by making the paleontological exhibits both visually
informative and exciting.
Of course, Knight would
become a prime force in
Osborn's master plan.

About this time Knight
also met William Diller
Matthew, a Canadian geol-
ogist and paleontologist
who had recently joined the
American Museum staff. In
later years, Knight wrote
that Matthew "for years was

Portrait of artist Charles R. Knight taken circa
1943–45. Courtesy Shelburne Studios, Inc.

my chief consultant and advisor on matters of pose and difficult bone
structure, and what unusual forms might indicate in the living animal."
Like Knight, Matthew soon shared Osborn's dream.

Osborn arranged for the museum to acquire more fossil vertebrate
specimens, and the galleries that were to house the new exhibits resounded
with the noises of the fossil preparators' scrapers, mallets, and drills. The
trio of Osborn, Knight, and Matthew endeavored to have the fossil skeletons mounted in lifelike poses, a revolutionary concept for the period.
One staff member, chief fossil preparator Adolph Hermann, opined that
fossil specimens were for study and not for the edification of the public.
Hermann, whose idea of mounting a skeleton was simply to string the
vertebral column along a straight length of steel rod, was, not surprisingly, opposed to the new ideas of the Osborn-Knight-Matthew team.
But he soon acquiesced, as did others at museums around the world, which
began to imitate the new mounting techniques. Knight, of course, was

also to provide the paintings of the animals in life that would grace the American Museum's paleontology galleries.

To achieve the remarkable realism displayed even in his earliest pre-historic-life restorations, Knight first studied the bones of the extinct creature. His goal was not simply to restore an animal never seen by a modern viewer, but to infuse it with life. Therefore, he applied the knowledge he had garnered from studying living animals, his philosophy being that no one can paint an animal that is "dead" before being able to paint one that is alive. Then, after questioning Osborn or Matthew about the possible appearance and habits of the animal, he extrapolated what he knew of present-day animal physiology and psychology and gave life to the ancient bones.

Once he had a fairly accurate conception of the extinct creature in his mind, he would make a miniature sculpture of the animal so that he could take it out into the sunlight and note the shadows it cast on the ground. Sculpting was relatively new to the artist, who mastered the technique so that he would have a three-dimensional model from which to make his painting. This step in his restoration process worked for Knight, and his command of the sculpting medium would soon lead him along other avenues of artistic pursuit.

Life restorations of prehistoric animals were rarities in the late 1800s, most paleontologists being content to study disarticulated fossil bones rather than see some usually hypothetical re-creation of the animal in the flesh. But Osborn was, through Knight's skills, doing his best to change such thinking. In 1896, *The Century Illustrated Monthly Magazine* (also known as simply *The Century Magazine*) published an article by Osborn, "Prehistoric Quadrupeds of the Rockies," which was illustrated with nine spectacular paintings by Knight of extinct mammals.

That article brought Knight's work to the attention of Osborn's mentor, Edward Drinker Cope, one of the pioneers in the field of paleontology during the 19th century. Cope was then associated with the Academy of Natural Sciences of Philadelphia. Under Professor Cope's direction, William Hosea Ballou had written an article on extinct reptiles for *The Century Magazine*, and the professor's disciple, Osborn, suggested that his disciple, Knight, provide the illustrations, based on Cope's own pencil sketches.

Anxious to meet the legendary Cope, Knight went to the scientist's red-brick dwelling at 2102 Pine Street in Philadelphia. Hardly a detail of the place seemed to escape his memory when he later wrote of that first visit:

> Inside everything was unique and completely dust covered. Never have I seen such a curious place—just like the kind that Dickens would have loved.

Piles of pamphlets rose from floor to ceiling in every narrow hallway, leaving just enough room to squeeze by them and no more. At the right as I entered, I looked into the front parlor. Shuttered with inside blinds, the floor was completely hidden by the massive bones of some vast creature, probably a dinosaur. Dust lay thick here as elsewhere, and the place was absolutely bare of furniture and hangings. No pictures, no curtains, nothing but petrified skeletons of extinct monsters more or less carefully disposed in every available open space. This in itself was peculiar, but it merely introduced one to the strange sights to be encountered in this almost sinister domicile. The second floor, to which I was promptly conducted, was reached by a narrow stair, the wall side of which carried small shelves holding pickled snakes and other reptiles in bottles. The back room on this floor was a long, narrow affair with a bay window overlooking a meager garden. This room, sacred to all good Philadelphians as a sitting room or back parlor, was one of the most singular places I have ever seen. It, too, was littered with various objects from end to end, all piled helter-skelter on tables, chairs and shelves. A human skull grinned at me from the mantle, and a large bronze vulture spread its menacing pinions above a cage containing a living gila monster. Bones, recent and fossil, were everywhere, all dusty, and all in apparently inextricable confusion. But Cope himself, the presiding genius among all this scientific chaos, met me with a genial and charming smile, made me sit down and talked as only Cope could talk, about the things I came to discuss.

Before long Knight and Cope were heavily engaged in their discussions of prehistoric life. Impressed by Knight's thirst for the truth about ancient subjects, Cope set up a makeshift studio for him at a drawing table in the bay window, "the only free space in the room." Here Knight spent two weeks studying Cope's simple pencil sketches and learning how Cope had arrived at his conclusions regarding his creatures' possible form and proportions. "Under his expert guidance," Knight wrote, "I felt that I had stepped back into an ancient world—filled with all sorts of bizarre and curious things, and in imagination I could picture quite distinctly just what these mighty beasts looked like as they walked or swam in search of food." Like Osborn and Knight, Cope regarded paleontology as not merely the study of brittle fossil remains, but as a science in which knowledge of the present might help to explain and give life to those denizens of the past.

Unfortunately, Cope, who had been ailing when Knight first came to visit him, never saw the fruits of their meetings. Three weeks after Knight left him, Cope died. Knight's restorations did appear in the November 1897 issue of *Century Magazine*, however, a testimony to the men's brief association. The paintings, depicting Cope's leaping dinosaurs and other saurians, graced with near photographic realism two articles

Mural depicting the Late Jurassic plated dinosaur *Stegosaurus stenops*, one of a total of 28 painted by Charles R. Knight circa 1926–31 for The Field Museum of Natural History's Hall 38. Knight regarded this series of murals as his magnum opus. Courtesy The Field Museum (neg. #59163).

featured in that issue, Ballou's "Strange Creatures of the Past: Gigantic Saurians of the Reptilian Age" and "A Great Naturalist: Edward Drinker Cope," a piece about the late scientist written by Osborn.

Through the efforts of Osborn and the talents of Knight, a new public awareness of and interest in prehistoric life was being born. People flocked to the paleontology halls of the American Museum of Natural History to see the newly acquired skeletons, mounted in exciting, realistic poses, and the life restorations by Knight, whose work was already known through the popular press. Public interest in the museum was at an unprecedented high.

By the spring of 1898, Osborn managed to bring some small aspects of the museum outside its walls and to the public directly through a catalog of models, casts, and photographs of restorations of fossil vertebrates that could be purchased by interested parties. Osborn hoped that the items

Mural by Charles R. Knight painted for Hall 38 (circa 1926–31) depicting Late Cretaceous life in what is today Kansas, including the flying reptile *Pteranodon*, mosasaur *Tylosaurus* and giant sea turtle *Portostega*. Courtesy The Field Museum (neg. #66186).

would help to spread information about extinct creatures to interested, though uninformed, people. Later, through a survey conducted by staff members of the museum's Department of Vertebrate Paleontology, it was learned that, to museum visitors, the most meaningful fossil exhibits were those accompanied by Knight's watercolor restorations.

Encouraged by the public's interest in the American Museum, a number of wealthy benefactors, John Pierpont (or simply J. P.) Morgan among them, made generous donations to the institution. Morgan had already donated to the museum a complete mastodon (the so-called "Warren Mastodon," bought from Dr. John Warren, who had been maintaining it in his Boston museum), along with many other treasures.

Making good use of Morgan's friendship and generosity, Osborn easily persuaded him to pay the bills while Knight produced a score of watercolor and sculpture restorations of prehistoric life. If the restorations were not entirely accurate in light of present-day paleontological knowledge, they were correct in regard to what was known scientifically at the time. By 1898, Osborn prepared another catalog, making available to scientific schools, colleges, and students not only reproductions of Knight's finished works, but also copies of the small preliminary models he sculpted prior to making his paintings. As for Knight's original pieces, Osborn talked Morgan into buying them and then donating the collection to the museum. With this donation, Knight's association with the American Museum of Natural History was secure and would remain so for many years.

Gradually Knight assumed celebrity status at the American Museum. Earlier in his career he had based his works largely on the mounted skeletons on display in the galleries; now newly acquired specimens were being set up to mimic the poses in his restorations. The artist had entered the realm of prehistoric-animal art only to become, so short a time afterward, its premier creator. The scientific world was rapidly coming to acknowledge that, when it came to restoring extinct creatures, Knight was the expert.

Although Charles R. Knight produced works for numerous major institutions and publications, he maintained strong connections with the American Museum for more than 40 years. The great vertebrate paleontologist Edwin H. Colbert, a former curator of vertebrate paleontology at the American Museum of Natural History and a friend of the late artist, said of him, "Knight's restorations of extinct animals are great not only because of his inherent abilities as an artist but also because of his readiness to work with scientists ... his was a constant quest for truth in art and science ... he had so much imagination that he could project himself back in time and feel that he was on a cliff with one of those monsters."

TYRANNOSAURUS REX IN THE PUBLIC EYE

During the late 1980s, Dinamation International Corporation, a company mostly known for the design, manufacture and distribution of accurate life-sized robotic prehistoric animals, decided to branch out into various publishing avenues. One of these projects was *Dinosauria*, which was to be an upscale magazine featuring lots of color photographs and illustrations, and containing substantive articles written by professional paleontologists and also laymen such as I who were somewhat knowledgeable about dinosaurs. The slick magazine was to be edited by George Olshevsky—or "Dinosaur" George, as he's sometimes called—a dinosaur expert with his own paleontology-related publishing company.

I was solicited by George and Dinamation to write an article for the premiere issue on *Tyrannosaurus rex*, that favorite among so many dinosaur fans, and how it has been portrayed in the media. If the magazine had actually come out, the article would have been under the longer title of "The Making of a Legend: *Tyrannosaurus rex* in the Public Eye."

Although the first issue of *Dinosauria* was fully edited by Olshevsky, designed, laid-out and pasted down (and dated Fall, 1989), the magazine itself, for whatever reasons, never came out. That was indeed unfortunate, as it would most likely have been— and would still be—the best popular magazine devoted to extinct animals on the market. Final proofs of the article for the first issue, however, did provide information to paleontologist John R. Horner and science writer Don Lessem (AKA "Dino Don") for one chapter of their excellent, jointly authored book *The Complete T. Rex* (Simon & Schuster 1993).

The article is presented here—for the first time in print anywhere—as it would have been in *Dinosauria* number 1, through the
courtesy of Michael Converse and Dinamation International Corporation. Because of its emphasis on the fossils and "paleo-art"
that influenced later media representations of *Tyrannosaurus*, I
have included it in this part of the book rather than in section
three.

Dinosaurs have fascinated the public for more than a century and
a half. The imagery of these incredible animals has been captured in every
conceivable artistic and entertainment medium, including prose fiction,
motion pictures, radio and television programs, comic books and strips,
theatrical presentations, music, poetry, park exhibits, display posters,
model kits, toys, clothing, and miscellaneous merchandise.

Of all the hundreds of known genera and species of dinosaurs, the
one dinosaur most frequently exploited by all these media is undoubtedly
the aptly named "king tyrant reptile," *Tyrannosaurus rex*. That *T. rex* has
enjoyed such extensive publicity is understandable, for in our collective
imagination, this dinosaur is the quintessential "monster"—a savage, giant-
sized, dagger-toothed, unstoppable flesh-eater. Enhancing his popular
appeal is the fact that this Mesozoic monarch actually existed, though the
danger he represented passed with the end of the Cretaceous period some
65 million years ago.

Today, one can safely encounter *Tyrannosaurus* either by visiting one
of his once rare mounted skeletons in a museum or by experiencing one
of those myriad media incarnations. These latter representations, however, are almost invariably out of date, which frustrates anyone with even
a smattering of dinosaur knowledge. Thus, to a general public unac-
quainted with paleontological literature and serious dinosaur books, the
media characterizations have, unfortunately, become a prime source of
misinformation about *Tyrannosaurus*.

It turns out that most, if not all, of the popular images of *Tyrannosaurus* can be traced to five famous paintings: two by Charles R. Knight,
one by Rudolph F. Zallinger, one by Neave Parker and one by Zdenek
Burian. The portrayals of *Tyrannosaurus* in those works are so powerful
and compelling, and have sired such a host of imitations, that despite
decades of subsequent research they remain immutably fixed in the public's mind.

Charles R. Knight, perhaps the greatest of all paleontological artists, was the first to restore dinosaurs scientifically. Working closely with professional scientists, he based his restorations on the most current vertebrate paleontology. He executed his first influential *Tyrannosaurus* painting during the initial decade of the 20th century under the direction of American Museum of Natural History paleontologists Henry Fairfield Osborn and William Berryman Scott. This celebrated work depicts a *Tyrannosaurus* confronting a family of the horned herbivorous dinosaur *Triceratops*. Modern paleontologists can point out a suite of errors in it, including the tyrannosaur's misplaced eye (Osborn may have followed Edward Drinker Cope in misidentifying the antorbital opening in the muzzle as the eye socket), three-fingered hand (Canadian paleontologist Lawrence M. Lambe showed in 1914 that tyrannosaurid hands had only two digits), and overly long, dragging tail (in 1970, British Museum paleontologist Barney H. Newman estimated that the famous *Tyrannosaurus* skeleton mounted at the American Museum had about ten extra feet of plaster tail vertebrae). It must be stressed, however, that these mistakes should not be attributed to Knight, who restored his *T. rex* faithfully from what was known in the early 1900s.

Photographs of this visually appealing version of *T. rex* were published in countless books and periodicals, from which they entered the reference files of artists and craftspeople the world over. Copied and recopied, Knight's image of *T. rex* proliferated in movies, comic art, and merchandise. It can be recognized in certain plastic dinosaur figures sold in stores, and it still turns up in comic-book stories about "lost worlds" and time travel.

One of the most striking incarnations of this painting can be seen in *King Kong*, the RKO Radio Pictures movie classic of 1933. Moviegoers will never forget the vivid battle between Kong, the giant gorilla-king of Skull Island, and *Tyrannosaurus*, the king of the dinosaurs. To create this sequence, sculptor Marcel Delgado modeled his dinosaur directly from Knight's painting. Special-effects wizard Willis H. O'Brien then brought ape and dinosaur to life by laboriously photographing their cast rubber figures frame by frame, moving each model a fraction of an inch between shots. When the film was run through a projector at normal speed, the figures seemed to come alive. Some of the movements O'Brien gave to his *Tyrannosaurus*, such as the serpentine lateral swishing of the tail, could not possibly have been made by the living animal, but the sequence is nevertheless dramatic and visually stunning—one of the most lifelike dinosaur scenes ever to appear on the motion-picture screen.

Knight's second *Tyrannosaurus* painting, probably the most famous

Artist Charles R. Knight's second major painting of the Late Cretaceous *Tyrannosaurus rex*. From a mural made for The Field Museum of Natural History. Courtesy The Field Museum (neg. #59442).

life restoration ever made of *T. rex*, is a mural from the series he painted between 1926 and 1931 for the Field Museum of Natural History's vertebrate-fossil Hall 38. It portrays *Tyrannosaurus* in a side view confronting an approaching *Triceratops*. Although errors persist in the restoration, the eye is correctly situated, the hand has only two fingers, and the tail is off the ground. (Another *Tyrannosaurus*, however, seen in the background, is standing in a vertically oriented pose, tail on the ground.)

Like its smaller predecessor, this version of *Tyrannosaurus* inspired illustrations in books and periodicals about dinosaurs for many years. Its oft-copied pose and contours can be spotted in numerous popular dinosaur books, especially those written for children. (Publishers presume that young readers cannot tell the difference between the original painting and an inferior copy, but children are generally the most eagle-eyed detectors of such dinosaur "swipes.")

Science-fiction books and periodicals are a fertile field for redrawn versions of Knight's second *Tyrannosaurus* painting. Edgar Rice Burroughs's fantastic heroic tales for pulp magazines, hardcover books, and paper-backs were illustrated with obvious Knight influence by such artists as J. Allen St. John and Frank Frazetta. In comic-book art, in which a series of panels tell a visual story, the "swiping" from Knight's originals is even more obvious, especially when the same picture is pirated many times in a single story or even sequence of panels.

Interestingly, a three-quarters view of the tyrannosaur from Knight's mural became almost as widely circulated and influential as the original side view. This was because the two-dimensional mural was the source for the life-size, three-dimensional, mechanized—and once again three-fingered—*Tyrannosaurus* model designed by P. G. Alen for the Sinclair Refining Company's dinosaur attraction at the 1933 Chicago World's Fair, "A Century of Progress." Quite obviously, all of the figures in the Sinclair exhibit were based on Knight's murals at The Field Museum, which was conveniently located within walking distance of the fairgrounds.

Alen's *Tyrannosaurus* figure was photographed in a three-quarters view that was subsequently rendered in oil by artist James E. Allen for *The Sinclair Dinosaur Book*, working under the supervision of famous American Museum of Natural History paleontologist Barnum Brown, who also wrote the text. This booklet was published in 1934 and circu-lated for years thereafter as a "giveaway" promotional item for the oil com-pany. Although Allen's painting correctly showed the dinosaur's two-fingered hand, the head had a rather horselike appearance, and the legs bulged much too conspicuously from the body.

James E. Allen's painting soon appeared on stamps issued by Sin-clair and in numerous other dinosaur books. Like Knight's original lat-eral view, the three-quarters version promptly made its way into reference files, and its re-creations soon surfaced in pulp magazines and comic books. Especially amusing are the occasional illustrations in which the copying artist (such as St. John), apparently unaware of the original Knight mural, attempted to reorient Allen's three-quarters view back into a side view, thereby "doubly distorting" Knight's painting!

Both the Knight mural and the Allen painting apparently influenced the cement *Tyrannosaurus* figure, made during the mid-1930s by local businessman and sculptor Emmet A. Sullivan, that still stands in Dinosaur Park in Rapid City, South Dakota—the first such park to exhibit life-size dinosaurs in the United States. Most of Sullivan's models can be traced more directly to The Field Museum murals than to the Sinclair dinosaur exhibit, but the *Tyrannosaurus* uncannily resembles his predecessor at the World's Fair, three-fingered hand and all.

During the early 1950s, Rudolph F. Zallinger's monumental "Age of

James E. Allen's painting of *Tyrannosaurus rex* for *The Sinclair Dinosaur Book* (1934), based on a three-quarter view of the Knight-inspired full-scale model at the Sinclair Dinosaur Exhibit, Chicago World's Fair (1933–34). ©Sinclair Refining Company.

Reptiles" mural, completed in 1948 for the Yale Peabody Museum of Natural History, became almost as influential as Knight's works. This 16-by-110-foot panoramic painting, which depicts the evolution of terrestrial life on Earth, has never been photographed for publication (doing so would require moving such obstructions as the museum's mounted *Apatosaurus* skeleton). But Zallinger's meticulous compositional study, or "cartoon," painted in 1943 before he started the mural, has been reproduced many times, most importantly in the fifth installment of the "World We Live In" series in the September 7, 1953, issue of *Life* magazine. (It even appears, in part, on the dust jacket of the original 1984 edition of my book, *The Dinosaur Dictionary*.)

Among the extinct animals restored in Zallinger's mural was a rather "fat" appearing *Tyrannosaurus* with microscopic forelimbs and other anatomical inaccuracies. Despite these faults, this interpretation of *T. rex* became a new standard for popular depictions of the dinosaur.

Readers of the long-running comic-book series *Turok, Son of Stone*, which debuted in 1954, could spot Zallinger's version turning up again and again, sometimes several times in the same issue. Circa 1956, when toy manufacturers began to mass produce the first plastic dinosaur toys, the Zallinger *T. rex* dominated those prehistoric menageries. (Recall the "waxy" plastic figures from the J. H. Miller Manufacturing Corporation and the "hard rubber" plastic figures from Louis Marx and Co.) These can sometimes still be found, commanding inflated collector's prices, in antique and collectible shops. Universal-International's 1957 minor science-fiction movie *The Land Unknown* also used the Zallinger painting for its prehistoric animals and its Mesozoic Era settings. The tyrannosaur, however, was distorted and tilted back into a more vertical pose to accommodate the human "actor" inside, so the final result was far from convincing. (Trivia buffs should note that the head from this dinosaur costume can still occasionally be seen, breathing flames, as "Spot" in reruns of *The Munsters*, a mid–1960s Universal television series.)

The restorations of *Tyrannosaurus* by British artist Neave Parker and Czech artist Zdenek Burian considerably influenced toys and comic-book stories of the 1970s and later. Parker's monochrome painting, one of many in a series of British Museum (Natural History) postcards initially published during the 1950s, shows *T. rex* in an impossibly upright pose (this illustration was used for the cover of my *Dinosaur Dictionary*, 1972 first edition). Burian's familiar painting, showing a *Tyrannosaurus* attacking two duckbilled dinosaurs, was first published in 1960 in the picture book *Prehistoric Animals* by Joseph Augusta. As Gregory S. Paul observed in his book *Predatory Dinosaurs of the World* (1978), the head of the *T. rex* is disproportionately small in this restoration, and no lips are shown.

I once asked Ray Harryhausen, Willis O'Brien's successor in the art of stop-motion animation, what the title dinosaur in *Valley of Gwangi* (Warner Bros.-7 Arts, 1969) was supposed to be. (Gwangi looked to me like a basic *Tyrannosaurus*, although its forelimbs were rather long, and its hands, like those of the Late Jurassic theropod *Allosaurus*, had three digits.) Ray blithely responded that Gwangi was a "combination" of both dinosaurs—a patently impossible chimera.

Legendary film producer and visionary Walt Disney is known to have preferred "his" tyrannosaurs to have three-fingered hands (as in the 1940 animated classic *Fantasia* and in the mechanical figure, from the 1964 New York World's Fair, that is now at Disneyland Park), because to him the dinosaurs "looked better that way." True to his preference, *Tyrannosaurus,* in the more recent Disney film *My Science Project*, has long forelimbs with three fingers.

Unfortunately, the media dinosaur is all too frequently regarded by its creator as a fantastic monster open to any subjective interpretation, rather than as a real animal with a very specific anatomy. "Swipes" adapted from outdated art pieces often evolve into primary sources, and errors are perpetuated *ad infinitum*. Furthermore, some media creators deliberately portray dinosaurs the "old-fashioned" way, because in their eyes their original inspiration remains the image of how dinosaurs "should" look.

Popular artists must learn to base their research on original sources—the bones themselves and the scientific papers describing them—or on the highly accurate life restorations by modern paleo-artists (including Mark Hallett, Gregory S. Paul, Stephen A. Czerkas, Robert T. Bakker, Brian Franczak, John Gurche, and Douglas Henderson). Then, perhaps, popular culture will at last experience the final extinction of such "fantasy creatures" as the three-fingered *Tyrannosaurus rex*.

A MIDDLE TRIASSIC FLOODPLAIN

In 1990, I received a phone call from paleontologist friend Robert A. Long, an authority on the Triassic period, then stationed at the University of California Museum of Paleontology in Berkeley. Rob was embarking on a series of pieces about the entire Triassic, the period during which the earliest dinosaurs first appeared, and asked me if I would care to collaborate with him. Although I rarely work with co-authors, I usually don't have to be coaxed much to co-write something with a professional scientist.

Rob's master plan for these articles, six of them in all, was quite grand. "Think in terms of Greek Mythology, Jason on the *Argo*, perhaps," he wrote me. "We'll complete six odysseys over the ancient, enormous super-continent Pangaea—covering the 35 million years of the Triassic period (each journey representing a stratigraphic stage)." Future articles would include some popular Triassic tetrapods such as therapsids (the so-called "mammal-like reptiles") and, of course, dinosaurs.

Rob, who had already done the research, sent me his very comprehensive, first-draft manuscript sampling about a Middle Triassic fossil locality—very rich in both plant and animal fossils from the so-named Anesian stage of the Triassic, about 240 million years ago, substantially predating the appearance of dinosaurs—in France named the Grés à Voltzia. He described his piece as more or less a "checklist of organisms." Rob's intent, however, was to make the Triassic come alive, as if the reader had somehow traveled back through time to experience the Triassic world firsthand. As Rob put it to me, "The specimens need to be transformed into living components of the environment. See if you agree, and if so, please play with the text."

I reorganized the text, "played with it" and produced the following article. In order to convey the feeling that the reader was "actually there," I used the present tense. In writing over Rob's original version I learned a lot about an environment that was out of my usual field of interest and knowledge, particularly in Rob's descriptions of fossil plants and invertebrates. The actual journey, as would be those of future articles, was followed by descriptions of the various plants and animals mentioned therein.

This segment of the project appears through the courtesy of Robert A. Long.

Preliminary Notes: "Grés à Voltzia" (called "Voltziasandstein" by the Germans and the "Voltzia Sandstone" by English-speaking workers) is the term given by French geologists and paleontologists to a series of sediments occurring in the North Vosges, a low mountain range in the Saverne and Sarre-Union regions of Eastern France. These sediments correlate with the uppermost part of the Buntsandstein (the Röt) of the central Germanic Basin. The unit is environmentally transitional in representing the passage from continental Buntsandstein to marine Muschelkalk deposition in the southeastern part of that basin. The Grés à Voltzia also earmarks the beginning of the Anisian stage in the region.

The Grés à Voltzia averages in thickness about 20 meters. It is subdivided into two highly distinctive horizons—the Grés à mueles (or milestone grit) of continental-littoral facies, and the capping Grés à argileux (argillaceous grit), a typical marine precursor of the Muschelkalk Sea. It is the 12-meter thick former division that merits some detailed enumeration here, for these floodplain sediments have yielded a treasury of plant and animal fossils unequaled anywhere in the Triassic.

In the extraordinary *Monograph des plantes fossiles du Grés Bigarraedé la Chaînedes Vosges*, published in 1844, Wilhelm Philipp (also Guillaume Philippe) Schimper, a native of Saverne, and his associate A. Mougeot described the Grés à Voltzia flora. Many excellent illustrations from this tome still appear today in botany and paleobotany textbooks. In 1914, on the eve of the first World War, Philipp Bill issued another splendid publication on fossils of the Grés à Voltzia, *Über Crustacean aus dem Voltziensandstein des Elsasses*, describing the extraordinary crustacean fauna.

Since World War Two, Louis Grauvogel has amassed a collection of

Grés à Voltzia fossils exceeding anything Schimper or Bill could have imagined. Numerous publications on these specimens have appeared through Grauvogel's pen. Jean-Claude Gall also wrote a fine series of papers, mostly on the invertebrates and the paleoenvironment of the Vosges sediments. More recently, Léa Grauvogel-Stamm, Louis's daughter, produced the definitive work on the plant life of the Grés à Voltzia.

The vast stretch of ground called the Grés à Voltzia floodplain extends, apparently without limit, toward the western part of this great super-continent, Pangaea. As far as some ancient eye might see—in this part of the world that will, some 240 million years hence, be called France—the somber hills of this land fade into the cool grays of an even more distant expanse of ground. These far-away mounds demarcate the eastern margin of a vast emergent land mass that extends westward as far as present-day Great Britain and southwest beyond Spain.

Spilling eastward from these hills, a network of river channels cuts through the floodplain, their waters eventually emptying into the Röt, the inland sea of the Germanic Basin. There the skies become the stage for spectacle, as incessant flashes of sheet lightning dramatically shed their brilliance upon these Gallic foothills. This celestial drama heralds the vast flooding that will soon begin on the plains of Grés à Voltzia.

The channels meander through the floodplain's "proximal domain," that region nearest the foothills and farthest from the shoreline. Levees border these channels while, beyond, parched brown vegetation extends across the ground in a flat canopy.

Beneath the wide rivers there is life.

A lone coelocanth swims below the glassy surface of the water, sharing its domain with a few other varieties of fishes, including the cleithrolepids and semionotids. Benthosuchid amphibians lurk in the muds and among the aquatic plants at the channel bottoms, their meter-long length reminders of an earlier time when these kinds of animals were the planet's dominant life forms. Among the plants, horsetails now called *Schizonuera* and *Equisetites,* quiver rhythmically as the water flows along. Oftentimes their branches soak up the fluids of the smaller rivulets, eventually choking them dry.

At last the cloud-darkened skies, streaked by mosaics of lightning, release the torrential rains. Large chunks of river bank, with many complete plants rooted tenaciously to the water-soaked sediment, are ripped away, dragged downstream by the overflowing streams and then dumped elsewhere en masse. Here, through rapid deposition, these plants may be preserved intact, their roots, stems, leaves, and reproductive structures still connected. On these muddy banks will prosper a variety of flora including herbages, small- and broad-leafed horsetails, fernlike plants such as *Anomopteris* and *Neuropteridium*, and gymnosperms including the narrow-leafed *Voltzia*, wide-leafed *Albertia*, and strap-leafed *Yuccites*. Nearby in swampy hollows live numerous torpid benthosuchids, their watery environments having been upset by the floods.

Beyond the bands of moist reeds exists a veritable wasteland. There, although vegetation does grow, the flat terrain is only sparsely wooded. Several kinds of low bushes darken the wide stretches of ground. Trees, if present at all, are rare, conifers predominant, yet with gingkos making infrequent appearances. Animal life thrives in these near-barren wastes, though mostly in the form of large populations of scorpions. In smaller numbers, spiders and millipedes scuttle across the dry earth. Apparently sharing this environment are quadrupedal reptiles called chirotheres, measuring from two to three meters in length, their presence indicated by trackways they would leave behind.

Further downstream is the "distal domain," an uneven expanse of nearly sea-level terrain that spaces the watercourses apart from each other. The ground here is pocked with other fresh to brackish bodies of water only infrequently connected with the river channels, and represented in the geologic record by thin shale lenses. In some parts of this region, these bodies are in the form of shrinking, shallow, foul pools. Elsewhere, once abandoned channels have collected some of the ocher-colored turbid water displaced by the flood. Here also there is life, as a rich and remarkable assemblage of crustaceans and several kinds of fishes make their home in these waters. Sometimes the entire domain is blanketed by extensive veneers of shallow water. These thin wet surfaces will eventually dry out, leaving behind only clusters of pools, ponds, and small lakes to be scorched, with the emergent flats, under the intense heat of day.

The freshwater lakes and brackish pools wither away with the declining fluvial-deltaic sedimentation. With them perish their short-lived faunas, which weaken at first, eventually vanishing entirely. Consequently, the lower and geologically older portion of the shale lenses will be rich with the beautifully preserved fossils of these life forms. In contrast, the higher (and younger) section will preserve no such remains, while the trace element boron, an indicator of salt-saturation, will increase upward. However, the fossils that will be preserved will provide evidence that life here is, at the very best, harsh. The organisms that live in these water-bodies are basically small and have short life spans, few ever achieving adult dimensions.

The deposits that will yield the remains of these animals are unique.

Nowhere else in the Triassic will fossils of such delicate structure be so unaltered. These animals represent an "autochothon," meaning that they perish exactly where they live. As a result, jellyfish bells will remain intact and fragile crustacean appendages will be preserved whole. Even clusters of eggs will be found still encased within their mucous sheaths.

Of all the animals in these saliferous pools, the crustaceans are dominant. Most of them have migrated inland after previously inhabiting the nearby sea. In their new domain, these arthropods will leave a splendidly preserved fossil record of the most diversified crustacean menagerie to be collected from any Triassic deposit. Their legacy will include tadpoles (notostracans), clams (conchostracans), seed (ostracodes), opossum shrimp (mysidaceans), pill bugs (idopods), syncarids, and two major groups of decapods: the true shrimps (natantians) and the crayfishes (reptantians). Two extinct arthropod groups exhibiting possible affinities with the Crustacea also live here. These are the halicynids, perhaps somewhat repulsive looking creatures by our esthetic standards, and, in contrast, the strange and exotic-looking euthycarcinoids.

Darting underwater through this magnificent convention of crustaceans are other life forms, including horseshoe crabs (xiphosurans) and jellyfishes (hydrozoans). Amorphous gobs of mucous, each the bearer of numerous insect eggs, glide ghostlike through the salty waters. Fishes, the same kinds that inhabited the "promixal domain," are also present. Infrequently they must share their world with the large-headed saurichthyids—fishes that, on rare occasions, stray in from the connecting coastal waters. The benthosuchid amphibians stay clear of this region, however, effectively barred by the very saltiness of the pools.

The river channels finally drain into the sea. Along the shore, vast mudflats covering hundreds of kilometers extend from the channel, seemingly stretching without limit in either direction. These mudflats are often hidden beneath a pellicular drape of water. When emergent, they are dotted with pools and lagoons to be inhabited later by typical marine animals. These creatures, living in dense populations, will include benthonic mollusks, brachiopods, and worms. The presence of terrestrial reptiles, later to be known only from their footprints (named *Rhynchosauroides*), attests to the shallowness of these waters.

A profound change occurs near the area that will become the top of the Grés à Voltzia beds. Here the river channels, numerous pools, and lakes dry up; consequently, aquatic life throughout the floodplain will die. For mile upon mile the terrain lacks almost any relief, its monotony interrupted only by dry watercourses and the telltale depressions of former lakes. Ripe for new conquest, this land is promptly overrun by rampant vegetation, primarily scrub growing in thick and tangled masses. The roots of an enormous number of these plants are destined for preservation in the upper sediments.

As this region will inevitably subside, the ancestral Muschelkalk, that great sea to the east, will progressively drown the entire North Vosges area under its warm, shallow waters.

Life Forms of the Grés à Voltzia (Plants)

Club Mosses

Lycopods, or club mosses, continue to prosper, though not so abundantly as they had in earlier times. *Pleuomeia*, the most characteristic of Early Triassic club mosses, has lingered into these later Anisian times, reproducing by spores carried by the winds. Once a remarkably abundant genus, *Pleuomeia* is now an "endangered species" represented by two species, *P. oculina* (with bark scarred by scalelike leaves set in spiral arrangement) and the better known *P. sternbergii* (this species only known from a few chunks of fossilized bark).

Horsetails

The tranquil surface of the waters is often pierced by vast belts of reeds. Closer inspection reveals these "belts" to be groupings of sphenopsids, members of a family of horsetails, or plants having a jointed and hollow stem. Less frequently these horsetails are also closely arranged with various kinds of low-growing conifers (including the genera *Aethophyllum* and *Voltzia*).

The margins of ponds and water veneers in the North Vosges region are especially rich with sphenopsid populations, especially those of the species *Schizoneura paradoxa*. Unlike the true and showier southern form, *S. gondwanensis*, the latter with its broad leaf bundles produced from at least a half dozen leaflets, this more conservative French species displays narrow leaf bundles comprising just two to four leaflets. More significant are the reproductive structures possessed by the northern and southern schizoneuras. In *S. paradoxa*, for example, these conelike structures (or *Echinostachys*, as they are called in the northern forms) are set on stalks and clustered on the sides of the plants' nodes. (For almost a century and a half, the long, slender female cones of the conifer *Aethophyllum* has been incorrectly reconstructed as the terminal cones of *S. paradoxa*, a mistake corrected only after the later discovery of complete fossils of this horse-tail.)

Sharing the margins of these waters with the schizoneuras is another horsetail, the perhaps less noticeable species *Equisetites mougeteoti*. Unlike the leafy *Schizoneura* forms, this species sports tiny leaves joined below in a sheath, ending in narrow toothlike projections. *E. mougeteoti* is not especially large (later species of *Equisetites* having stems measuring more than 400 millimeters across), the jointed column in its stem generally spanning only about 40 millimeters, indicating that a complete plant would measure just a meter and a half tall.

Fernlike Plants

The harsh environmental conditions of this region may explain the curious absence of undoubted ferns. Nevertheless, some unusual fernlike scrubs—growths of stunted vegetation—prosper here. Although positive identification of these plants cannot be made, they may represent kinds of aberrant ferns, seedferns, or even some unknown stock. One thing is certain, however. These scrubs are strikingly beautiful.

Several species of the large genus *Neuropteridium* are present here. Superficially suggesting some giant millipede, this scrub exhibits a massive rachis or stalk. To this are attached numerous simple pinnate (that is, resembling a feather) leaves, some of which measure as much as a meter in length. Stiff and sturdy, these leaves are covered by a thick cuticle, the latter presumably a xeromorphic (modified structurally to retard the exhalation of vapor through pores) character serving to reduce the loss of moisture. *Crematopteris* (the term given to the reproductive organ of this plant) is a long straplike structure bounded by many small, leaflike appendages.

Big and showy *Anomopteris* possesses bipinnately divided leaves (opposite leaflets subdivided into opposite leaflets) measuring almost one third of a meter long. The pinnae or leaflets in this genus are much longer and more slender than those in *Neuropteridium*.

Conifers

Identified in this region are all the major plant groups, the most abundant (also in terms of collected specimens) being the conifers. Genera with such names as *Aethophyllum, Albertia, Voltzia, Yuccites, Cycadocarpidium, Willsiostrobus, Darneya*, and *Sertostrobus* dominate the landscape. (*Sertostrobus* is known from complete plant specimens; *Cycadocarpidium* is known from female-variety cones, *Albertia* and *Yuccites* from fossilized foliage, *Willsiostrobus, Darneya*, and *Sertostrobus* from male cones.) However, what these plants enjoy in numbers and varieties, they apparently lack in size. None of these forms seems to have attained more than modest dimensions. For instance, the bush of *Aethophyllum* (the earliest known herbaceous conifer) measures less than two meters tall.

Even an untrained eye might easily distinguish among the various foliages of these different kinds of conifers:

Aethophyllum has very long, narrow leaves with parallel veins, terminating in a sharp apex.

Albertia has short, wide obvate leaves (somewhat resembling those of the modern podocarp *Agathis*) lined with many prominent parallel veins, no leaf exceeding two inches in length (the male cone of this plant being of the *Darneya* [*D. pellata*] variety).

Voltzia has a quite varied general leaf structure, some species (*e.g., V. walchiaeformis*) possessing scaly juniperlike leaves, others (*e.g., V. heterophylla*) with pinelike needle clusters, others with a kind of cypresslike appearance (the variety of associated male cone morphs, including *Darneya, Sertostrobus*, and possibly some *Willsiostrobus* species suggesting that *Voltzia* represents an artificial genus).

Yuccites (*Pelourdea* of some authors) has very long, straplike leaves often measuring about one-third meter long, with parallel veins (superficially resembling the leaves of the modern angiosperm *Yucca*), and is usually regarded as a late surviving member of the Cordaites.

This is a region of seasonal change. The biological cycle of conifers throughout these seasons has been splendidly demonstrated in the two-foot thick shale-lense deposits of the Grés à Voltzia. A great number of pollen grains preserved near the base of one lense clearly indicates the flowering season (spring). Higher in the shale section, all pollen has been supplanted by scatterings of male cone scales, while higher yet, the scales are replaced by seeds (autumn). The half-dozen kinds of indigenous conifer cones include these four male and two female varieties:

Aethophyllum has a male-variety cone generally resembling that of *Willsiostrobus*, but with very wide scales that end in a remarkably long, needlelike though highly flexible apex. Its female cones are extremely long, furry, and catkin-like in structure, and measure from five to six times longer than the male.

Yuccites has a male cone of the *Willsiostrobus* (*W. rhomboidalis*) variety.

Cycadocarpidium also has male cones like those of *Willsiostrobus*;

female cones in this genus are somewhat flower-like in structure, shorter and more compact than those of *Aethophyllum*.

Willsiostrobus has male cones that are sturdy, usually short and straight (such as *W. bromsgrovensis*), or moderately long (*W. cordiformis*). The scales of these cones are small and compacted together, either bluntly terminated (as in *W. cordiformis*) or ending in sharp projections (*W. ligulatus*).

Darneya has rather sturdy male-variety cones made up of large scales (as in *Sertostrobus*, but in which the scales are less densely clustered together). *Sertostrobus* has delicate, flexible and elongate male cones, their scales being large and loosely clustered together.

Despite the wealth of conifer types represented here, no example reveals any close affinities with modern forms. Arborescent (or treelike) conifers seem to be rare; perhaps they are even nonexistent. At present the true nature of these many and varied forms remains somewhat of a mystery. (Traditionally, most gymnosperms in this region have been referred collectively to one group, the Voltziaceae; however, this may, to some extent, be an artificial grouping of rather diverse kinds of primitive conifers.)

Life Forms of the Grés à Voltzia (Animals)

Aquatic Organisms

TADPOLE SHRIMP (NOTOSTRACANS)
Dwelling at the pool bottoms are countless numbers of tadpole shrimp or notostracans. Tadpole shrimp, then as now, are long-bodied crustaceans having numerous body segments, a low-arched carapace that protects the head and thorax, and compound sessile (or stalkless) eyes set close together.

The present species, crawling over and plowing into the soft ooze of these pools, is *Triops cancriformis minor* (the longest ranging species, known from about two dozen specimens, and surviving virtually unchanged into modern times). It possesses a carapace ranging from three to 16 millimeters in length. To swim, the creature must first flip its body upside-down. Potential dinners eyed during an underwater jaunt include other crustaceans, with their tasty soft parts, as well as the egg clusters of insects. When other foods are neither available nor preferred, the animal might eat others of its own species.

CLAM SHRIMP (CONCHOSTRACANS)

Outnumbering the notostracans in diversity and quantity—in fact, the most common of all creatures living in these waters—are the clam shrimp or conchostracans, represented by thousands of fossils, leading to the recognition of four genera and six species, some specimens found still containing eggs in their valves.

These animals can largely be distinguished from one another by the form of their carapaces. *Dictyonatella* has a carapace displaying from four to six heavy ridges. Possibly the number of these ridges are growth-related, thereby offering information as to an individual organism's age. *Eustheria* displays about a dozen such well-defined ridges; *Palaleolimnadia* has from seven to ten delicately incised ridges; and *Liolealiina* exhibits a sculpturing of multiple ridges, as well as a few strong radial or cross ridges.

Eggs belonging to these animals can be differentiated based upon two rather consistent sizes. The smaller (and more numerous) eggs are presumably on the verge of hatching. The larger (and much rarer) eggs seem to have evolved to their size as a protection against injury during distribution by the wind upon dessication of their pool environment.

SEED SHRIMP (OSTRACODES)

Various types of seed shrimp, called ostracodes, may breed beneath the pools. (Of the two known forms in this area, only the tiny *Triassinella* is adequately known, its fossils found in marine deposits, its rare occurrence in the Grés à Voltzia pools possibly being accidental). Never surpassing a millimeter in length, this genus can be recognized by its elongate, unsculptured carapace with its trapazoidal contour.

OPOSSUM SHRIMP (MYSIDACEANS)

There are strong stirrings in the pond waters. Frequently such agitations are created by great swarms, comprising several hundred individuals, of shrimplike mysidaceans (or "opossum shrimp").

Shrimpella beneckei represents the only species yet known in this region. Its long, transparent body ranges from 14 to 20 millimeters long, and possesses a short, thin carapace. The animal's thoracic appendages are feebly developed, clearly not adapted for crawling along the pool bottom. Easily acquired plankton and detritus probably sustain the animal, while its own soft parts might provide food for the cleithrolepid and semionotid fishes that occupy the same waters.

OTHER CRUSTACEANS (SYNCARIDS)

Triassocoris is a rare and poorly understood syncarid, but its possible appearance and life style may be imagined. This small creature has a body length totaling a mere 12 millimeters. More noteworthy than size is the animal's snout, which has evolved into a very long rostrum (or beaklike process). As in other syncarids, the carapace is not present, and the first thoracic element is fused to the head.

Perhaps *Triassocoris* crawls along the bottom of a pool, then, by flipping its tail fin, quite rapidly shifts to a swimming mode. The animal might even leap out of the water (as another syncarid, the modern Tasmanian mountain shrimp *Anaspides*, presumably can). Most likely, *Triassocoris* feeds upon algae, detritus, crustaceans and worms, catching food with the tendril-like appendages nearest its head. Captured, the food is then transferred to the shrimp's mouth where it is secured by the snapping beak.

ISOPODS

Fewer in number than the mysidaceans are isopod crustaceans (the modern sowbug, *Porcellionoides pruinosus*, being a familiar cosmopolitan isopod), including *Palaega*. From the approximately 100 fossils recovered, *Palaega* is known to have a body length ranging from four to eight millimeters. Its head has a shape resembling a shield; its segmented body, lacking a carapace, is ovate, flattened and moderately arched. *Palaega* can be imagined burrowing and swimming on its scavenger's quest for food.

DECAPODS

Inhabiting these pools are members of both major divisions of the order Decapoda—designated the swimmers (natantians) and the crawlers (reptantians). We may speculate that the soft parts of these animals, if properly prepared, might satisfy the culinary tastes of modern diners— for these crustaceans are related to modern forms usually served in fine restaurants with cocktail sauce and melted butter.

Among the natantians, numerous true shrimps of the genus *Antrimpos* (to be known in the Grés à Voltzia from several hundred specimens, the genus traceable back to the earliest Triassic, Induan level, Middle Sakamena beds of Madagascar) congregate in large swarms, as do *Shrimpella*. *Antrimpos*, however, is a much larger animal than the latter, its length (excluding the antennae) averaging around 50 millimeters, the biggest individuals achieving a record length of 80 millimeters. The body of this shrimp is long, narrow, and laterally compressed, and the abdominal region has developed distally into a strong swimming organ. Darting backwards through these waters, *Antrimpos* is well adapted to snaring prey that includes small crustaceans, worms, perhaps even tiny fishes.

As are other reptantians, the early crayfish *Clytiopsis* (known in the Grés à Voltzia from about eight dozen specimens; preserved elsewhere throughout the Middle Triassic, the youngest fossils known from the Lettenkeuper sediments, late Ladinian, in northern Thüringia, Germany) is basically terrestrial, walking or crawling on appendages more powerful than those of its natantian "cousin" *Antrimpos*. From 16 to 50 millimeters long, *Clytiopsis* has a long carapace with a thick granular surface. Its head is equipped with a short triangular rostrum.

Though mostly a land-dweller, *Clytiopsis* is no stranger to the water. For long stretches of time, this animal might bide motionless in the muck at the bottom of a pond. However, its long wait is rewarded with the inevitable appearance of prey. Whether it be another kind of crustacean or a very young fish, the crayfish then springs out in ambush, sometimes darting after a potential meal with a flip of its powerful, flattened tail. Utilizing its two pairs of pincer-equipped thoracic appendages (the first pair of pincers being especially large), *Clytiopsis* efficiently snares its victim and feasts.

OTHER INVERTEBRATES (HALICYNIDS)

Most repulsive appearing (by human standards, at least) of all these pool denizens are the crablike halicynids.

The genus that gave the group its name, *Halicyne*, bears a strong superficial resemblance to today's crab louse. But unlike the modern pest, this ancient creature has hundreds of times the bulk. Its formidable look includes a head shield equipped with stalked eyes set very widely apart. Five pairs of powerful, bristly legs project from its body. As these legs are similar to those of carnivorous insects, *Halicyne* may well live a predacious life style. Features of the appendages, as well as the internal structure of this animal, suggest that *Halicyne* may have affinities with the crustaceans.

EUTHYCARCINOIDS

Among the more odd inhabitants of these waters, *Euthycarcinus* is a creature that ranges in length from five to 65 millimeters. Its head is large, blunt, and has wide-set sessile eyes. The first pair of its antennae are small, the second pair huge. Both head and thorax are covered by broad dorsal shields, and the abdomen terminates in a very long, swordlike style or telson. *Euthycarcinus*, like *Halicyne*, exhibits some affinities with the crustaceans, but how close this connection is remains a mystery. No ancestors or descendants of *Euthycarcinus*, known from more than a hundred specimens, have been found, although a closely related contemporary, *Synaustrus*, is known from one specimen found in Australia.

HORSESHOE CRABS (XIPHOSURANS)

Among the non-crustacean invertebrates inhabiting these pools are horseshoe crabs, which belong to the class Merostomata. Approximately a hundred examples of these animals are known from the North Vosges, all belonging to the species *Limulitella bronni* (the genus known throughout the Triassic, mostly in the German Basin, though another species, *L. volgensis*, occurs as far east as the Vetluga Series of Russia). This seems to be an animal enjoying a vast range of size, generally from 5.7 to 120 millimeters (not including telson). The largest individual (with telson) has an estimated length of about 250 millimeters, making it the largest known Grés à Voltzia aquatic invertebrate. In addition to physical remains, *Limulitella* will leave behind several trackways preserved in Grés à Voltzia rocks.

Limulitella possesses a carapace with moderately developed lateral wings (directed more posteriorly in the middle Buntsandstein genus *Psammolimulus*). Its small, narrow abdomen apparently lacks serrations and posterior projections (present in the Buntsandstein form).

INSECTS

Clusters of insect eggs glide gracefully through the pool waters. Insects are numerous in the Grés à Voltzia. Their numbers, known only from eggs and larvae, include mayflies (Order Ephemeroptera), dragonflies (Order Odonata), and possibly true flies (Order Diptera); none of these insects, however, have yet been studied in detail.

Encased in chitinous shells and bound together in mucous sheath, insect eggs (some containing embryos) have been preserved in the fine shale layers of the Grés à Voltzia. Three kinds of egg clusters, none of them associated with any specific insect group, have been found and named, these including: 1. *Monilipartus*—represented by strings comprising 3,000 oval eggs (resembling strings of tiny pearls), measuring about 40 millimeters long; 2. *Clavapartus*—clusters of from 500 to 2,500 oval eggs, loosely combined in a mucous sheath resembling a swollen club, an entire cluster about 20–30 millimeters long; and 3. *Furcapartus*—tightly bound clusters of spherical eggs formed into a "V" shape, each branch about 15 millimeters long.

JELLYFISHES (HYDROZOANS)

Small medusid jellyfishes bob among the countless other varieties of animal life swimming in the Grés à Voltzia pools. The genus *Progonionemus*, belonging to the extant order Limnomedusae, is known from nine specimens with bells ranging from eight to 40 millimeters in diameter. The largest individuals of this form sport tentacles as long as 40 millimeters.

POLYCHAET WORMS

Four varieties of worms are known in these waters, three being poly-chaets (strongly segmented, usually marine forms, with bristle-bearing appendages called parapodia), the fourth of unknown annelid affinities. Two orders of polychaets are represented here—the Errantia and the Sedentaria.

Errantians move freely through the pond waters. Highly predacious, their heads are equipped with powerful chitinous jaws outfitted with strong and distinctive "worm teeth" (called scolecodonts, generally the only hard evidence for these creatures preserved in the fossil record). Two kinds of errantians, from scolecodonts and also preserved soft parts, are known from the Grés à Voltzia.

Long and slender *Eunicites* is made up of 150 segments (with para-podia well preserved in the two known Grés à Voltzia specimens). Excel-lently developed dental apparatus consists of a pair of large forceps-like structures and two maxillary (upper jaw) and three dentary (lower jaw) plates. Its body length is about 35 millimeters, width one millimeter. (Splendidly preserved *Eunicites* specimens are also known from Late Jurassic Solnhofen deposits in Germany.)

The very different *Homaphrodite*, known from nine specimens, has a body one and a half times the width, but less than a third the length of that of *Eunicites*. Also by contrast, its oval body has but 35 segments and the simple dental apparatus only two elements.

Sedentarians are commonly called fanworms or featherduster worms. They dwell in pools which they either secrete or build. These worms belong to the Sedentaria, an order consisting of predominantly sedentary polychaets having indistinct heads that lack jaws. The parapodia in these worms are too short for use in walking or swimming.

Spirorbis, the sedentarian known from the Grés à Voltzia, secretes a calcareous, coiled tube measuring 1.5 millimeters across and resembling the shell of a tiny snail. Many of these tubes have been found attached to plants, the valves of lamellibranches, and even fish eggs.

Triadonereis, the fourth worm genus indigenous to this area, is known from a half dozen specimens. Since none of these includes a head, the relationships of this form are unknown. From what has been preserved, this animal seems to be about 15 millimeters long. The genus will persist into the latest Anisian (the lowest level of the Middle Triassic) time, its remains found in the marine Trochitenwalk beds of Wiesloch, Germany.

FISHES

A surprisingly small number of carnivorous fishes are known in the Grés à Voltzia to take advantage of the abundant invertebrate life.

Apparently the conditions here are too severe to support either a large diversity or number of them. None of the fishes inhabiting this area attains large size (and their total number, represented by the number of fossils presently collected, could survive quite comfortably in a 10-gallon aquarium).

Ornate *Dipteronotus* is the largest nectonic genus in these waters. It is a typical cleithropelid fish in having a deep body with correspondingly deep, narrow scales. However, *Dipteronotus* differs from earlier forms (like *Cleithrolepis* and *Cleithrolepidina*) in maintaining very long spines on the upper margin of the anterior body, moderately large appendicular fins, the close proximity of the anal and pelvic fins, and the greater length of the anal and dorsal fins. Its head, not so flat as in the southern genera, is provided with very large eyes. (A review of the three specimens found at Vosges, and also a much larger collection including about 230 individuals from the Karlsruhe-Durlach region in southwestern Germany about 120 kilometers northeast of the Vosges, demonstrates various growth stages of this fish. Little individuals, from 35 to 40 millimeters long, have short anterior spines and rather shallow bodies; presumed adults, 120 millimeters in length, have longer spines and much deeper bodies.)

Small, narrow-bodied semionotid *Pericentrophus* is the most common fish in these waters, its growth range extending from 10 to 30 millimeters in length. As in usual semionotids, the bones of the upper jaw do not contact the opercular bones, the tail is symmetrical (top and bottom portions of the tail fin the same size), the fleshy upper tail lobe is small, and the scales are comparatively thin. Compared to other semionotids, this genus has a rather short snout.

Beautiful *Dorsolepis* (known from a fragmentary specimen from Karlsruhe-Durlach, missing its head, and also from isolated fins from the North Vosges) seems to have an oval, laterally compressed body with very well-developed dorsal fins, a long, slender upper tail fin, and measures between 40 and 100 millimeters long. Apparently this is a late-surviving relict—a living fossil in its own ancient time—of the typical Late Paleozoic palaeonisciform family Platysomidae.

A small saurichthyid fish swims in the Vosges waters, although its native environment is probably elsewhere (known only from a single specimen at this locality). Named *Saurichthys daubreei*, this fish has an enormous head, about one-third the length of its body, which is in contrast to those proportions in other *Saurichthys* species. Since big-headedness is often a juvenile feature, and as this fish measures only 80 millimeters long, *S. daubreei* may be a very young individual.

Certainly no juvenile is *Systolichthys*, a big (600 millimeters long), huge-headed saurichthyid, discovered in the upper Muschelkalk (Ladinian level of the Triassic) deposits of Montral-Alcover, near Barcelona, Spain. Possibly the Grés à Voltzia form is an early example of this genus.

A coelocanth is also present in these waters (its presence to be recorded by a single, almost complete but poorly preserved skeleton and some isolated scales), measuring some 120 millimeters in length.

AMPHIBIANS

Deathtraps await prey in freshwater pools that parallel the nearby streams. The traps are in the form of jaws, about one-third of a meter long, lined with an array of sharp teeth. Here beneath the surface, the big

Three carnivorous *Cynognathus* individuals (cynodonts) confront the herbivorous *Kannemeyria* (a dicynodont), "mammal-like reptiles" from the Karroo series of South Africa that lived about the same time as (or slightly earlier than) the fauna and flora of the Grés à Voltzia in France. Mural painted by Charles R. Knight in 1931. Courtesy The Field Museum (neg. #75016).

amphibian *Eocyclotosaurus*, the top aquatic carnivore in the Grés à Voltzia food chain, patiently anticipates its next meal. While some of its genus also wait for their dinner, others squat sunning themselves on the leaves that separate the many bodies of water of this "distal domain."

Eocyclotosaurus is among the last descendants of the benthosuchid line that was so common earlier in the Triassic in what is now Russia. As do its more primitive Russian relatives, this genus possesses a rather slender snout, frontal bones that contact the eye openings, and a pair of double openings on the anterior palate. *Eocyclotosaurus* is a more derived form, however, in the near closure of the notches of its skull's otic region.

This amphibian (as apparent from two skull impressions found in the Grés à Voltzia) measures from 250 to 275 millimeters long. Extrapolating from head to body ratios of other (more completely known) labyrinthodont amphibian skeletons of about one-third to more than a meter in length, *Eocyclotosaurus* seems to weigh from about 13.5 to 18 kilograms. Surely, as far as other animals in its environment are concerned, this is a neighbor best avoided.

Terrestrial Organisms

INSECTS

With vertebrate life restricted to water habitats, it is not surprising that all terrestrial niches of the Grés à Voltzia floodplain are dominated by insects. Countless numbers of them thrive here (known from thousands of collected specimens, the most completely studied being the giant protodragonfly *Triadotypus guillaumei*, known from a partial wing, and the primitive stonefly *Pseudodiptera gallica*).

Triadotypus seems to have been a monster indeed with a wingspan exceeding 300 millimeters (one Carboniferous-age giant, *Meganeura*—the largest of all known insects—having a wingspan of 760 millimeters). The genus represents one of the last members of the Paleozoic order Protodonata, a group comprising typically large to enormous, highly predacious insects with wing venations rather similar to those of true dragonflies (Order Odonata), and with powerful legs developed for seizing prey.

Smaller than the giant protodragonfly is *Pseudodiptera*, which measures some 20 millimeters across its wings. This genus belongs to the Order Mecoptera and represents the extinct Order Paratrichoptera, a group that first appeared millions of years back during the Late Permian period and will vanish by the end of the later Jurassic.

Among the other insects of the Vosges are mayflies (known from a few adult specimens, presently unstudied; Order Ephemeroptera), cockroaches (known from whole specimens and numerous wings; Order Dictyoptera), beetles (known from many elytra or wing cases; Order Coleoptera), and true bugs (known from entire individuals and many wings; Order Hemiptera).

SCORPIONS

Darkness brings ominous activity to the semiarid wastes of the Grés à Voltzia. Stones quiver and slide as things unseen, secretly hiding underneath, begin to stir. There is movement also in the parched crevices of ground. Here the night belongs to the scorpions which take control of their domain, teeming in large numbers as they begin their nocturnal hunt across the barren landscape.

The scorpion (mostly unstudied) presents a striking image. Its trapezoidal head shield is developed into an odd anterior expansion equipped with two eyes. The tail consists of wide segments and terminates in a large, poison-bearing barb or stinger. Delicate pincers keep ready to seize prey.

These creatures (to date of this writing unnamed, based upon preliminary studies) may represent a new and undefined genus of the otherwise Paleozoic Era family Eoscorpiidae. (Collected are almost 15 complete specimens ranging in length from 17 to 65 millimeters, plus numerous isolated tergites or upper body-segment plates.

SPIDERS

True spiders (of the Order Araneida), apparently all small, ranging from two to seven millimeters in body length, inhabit the Grés à Voltzia. These creatures (known from about a dozen examples, mostly unstudied) seem to represent the only species known in the Triassic, their rarity probably due to their very fragile structure and spiders' general avoidance of the kinds of habitats likely to preserve their fossilized remains.

MILLIPEDES

Millipedes (belonging to the Class Diplopoda and apparently the subclass Helminthomorpha; known from about a dozen specimens, largely unstudied) also inhabit the floodplain, their body length averaging between 50 and 60 millimeters. As is the case with spiders, these many-legged creatures will be rare in the fossil record (other Triassic millipedes having been found in South Africa and Siberia).

REPTILES

Gazing down over the expanse of the Grés à Voltzia floodplain, over the dry wastes and sea-splashed mudflats, a reptile exists (to date, only one kind known from physical remains, the few preserved bones—including ribs, vertebrae, and a femur—of this unidentified form having been discovered in a chunk of stone small enough to fit inside a coffee mug). It must be a small animal, a mere 10 millimeters long.

More is revealed of the elusive reptiles by their footprints, preserved as trace fossil called ichnites. These tracks reveal that some fairly large reptiles inhabit the floodplain. A dozen *Rhynchosauroides*-type prints preserve in time a few routine moments in the lives of several fairly big members of the Lepidosauria (a group that will include lizards, snakes, and rhynchocephalians), splashing across a coastal mudflat. The length of one hind print, about 100 millimeters, will show that the trackmaker is approximately 1,500 millimeters (or an impressive five feet) long.

Further upstream, quadrupedal, five-toed chirotheres also leave their tracks as evidence of their activity, posture, and size. Their hind foot prints range from 50 to 100 millimeters long, indicating that these archosaurians (or "ruling reptiles") possess moderately erect limbs, and range in length from 800 to 1,800 millimeters (about 2.5 to 6 feet).

Reptiles now stride across the Triassic landscape.

Some time must pass, however—in fact, some 13 million years— before a new group of archosaurs, the dinosaurs, appears and eventually claims this Earth as its own.

THE WORLD OF
THE MESOZOIC

During the early 1990s, in the wave of dinosaur mega-interest jump-started by the phenomenally successful movie *Jurassic Park*, various publications began to spring up devoted exclusively to dinosaurs and sometimes also other prehistoric creatures.

One of these was the tabloid newspaper *The Dinosaur Times*, edited by writer and renaissance man Ed Summer, and aimed at an audience primarily composed of children. Unlike most such publications geared toward young people, however, this one, Summer determined, would not "talk down" to its readers but, instead, treat them maturely and with respect. Indeed, many of the paper's youthful audience would be more knowledgeable about dinosaurs than many of its adult readers.

Vertebrate paleontologist Michael K. Brett-Surman (of the National Museum of Natural History, Smithsonian Institution, and Georgetown University) and I were solicited by Ed to write a projected multi-part series of scientifically correct articles for *The Dinosaur Times* about the Mesozoic Era—the time when dinosaurs ruled this planet. The first installment would discuss the Mesozoic in general; the subsequent essays would give more details about the Mesozoic's three basic divisions, the Triassic, Jurassic and Cretaceous periods. The series was to be written in a basically simple and straightforward, yet non-condescending, language that young readers could understand, and which would impart to them a lot of real information.

Since Mike—or "Dinosaur Mikey" (formerly "Hadrosaur Mikey") as he is affectionately known by friends—was a professional scientist with whom I got along quite well, I decided to enter the collaboration. (Mike and I have since gone on to collaborate on other projects, including a long article about dinosaurs in popular culture for *The Complete Dinosaur*, a major book he edited with James O. Farlow, published in 1997 by Indiana University Press.)

Together we wrote the suite of articles, Mike doing most of the research and writing the first drafts, I doing the final drafts. The entire series, lamentably, was never published in its entirety due to the unfortunate premature demise of *The Dinosaur Times*. What was published in this series, "The Mesozoic Era," "The Triassic Period" and "The Jurassic Period," appeared in *The Dinosaur Times* numbers 1, 2 and 3, respectively, which all came out in 1993; the remaining two articles, "The Early Cretaceous" and "The Late Cretaceous," became casualties of that abrupt cause of a periodical's extinction—cancellation.

The following composite of all the articles we wrote for this projected series appears through the courtesy of Ed Summer and Mike Brett-Surman.

Our Earth has been in existence for a very long time. The history of this planet goes back some 4.5 billion years, with at least some kind of life existing here for most of that time. The first life appeared approximately 3.5 billion years ago. However, only a small part of history concerns the animals we call dinosaurs.

The dinosaurs—a very specific group of animals—lived during an expanse of time which geologists have named the Mesozoic (meaning "middle life") Era. This era began approximately 248 million years ago. No dinosaurs lived before or after the Mesozoic (unless we consider birds to be dinosaurs, as do some scientists). If we could time travel to those ancient, early Mesozoic days we would see that there were no warmblooded animals (no birds or mammals). In fact, no upright animals of any kind were alive. There were no flowers, not even grass!

Dinosaurs ruled most of the Mesozoic Era, occupying every continent. However, dinosaurs only made up about 10 percent of Mesozoic animals. The skies were the home of pterosaurs (flying reptiles) which were like "cousins" of dinosaurs, but not real dinosaurs. Water was the kingdom of such non-dinosaurian reptiles as icthyosaurus (the so-called "fish lizards," actually reptiles though they somewhat resembled dolphins), plesiosaurs (real-life sea serpents, reptiles with paddles instead of legs, and sometimes with very long necks), and giant turtles. There were also some of the same reptiles we have today (lizards, snakes, and crocodiles), even primitive mammals and the first birds.

The Mesozoic Era can be divided into three geologic periods which scientists call the Triassic (about 248–206 million years ago), Jurassic (206–144 million years ago), and Cretaceous (144–65 million years ago).

In the Triassic, all the Earth's continents were joined in a huge land mass called Pangaea. This "super-continent" was surrounded by a gigantic ocean called Panthalassa. Today, the Equator runs through Ecuador, but in the Triassic period it cut through what is now the state of Florida.

The Triassic world was warm and dry. The Appalachian Mountains, in the Eastern United States, were the tallest peaks. It was a time of change. Late in that period, true dinosaurs began to take over the niches (how an animal makes its living; food, habitat, territory) previously dominated by more primitive reptiles.

The earliest dinosaurs and mammals appeared in the Triassic. Among the dinosaurs that lived at this time were *Eoraptor* and *Herrerasaurus*, small, primitive meat-eaters (carnivores) that walked on their hind legs. There were also plant-eaters (herbivores) like the smaller and primitive *Pisanosaurus*, and very large plant-eaters like the long-necked *Plateosaurus*.

The dinosaurs really took over during the second Mesozoic period, the Jurassic. Pangaea split into two big continents, Laurasia in the Northern Hemisphere and Gondwana in the Southern. True seasons were yet to come. Instead of "summer" and "winter," Jurassic animals experienced "warm and wet" and "warm and not-so-wet." The sea level was higher and many large land areas were flooded. Seed-bearing gymnosperms (like pine trees) literally took over the plant kingdom.

The Jurassic period was a kind of "golden age" of dinosaurs. Some of the best known and largest land animals of all time, the long-necked sauropod dinosaurs, appeared and had their heyday—the big theropod (or carnivorous dinosaur) *Allosaurus*, herbivore *Camptosaurus*, armor-plated and spike-tailed *Stegosaurus* and the most famous dinosaur of all, the huge *Apatosaurus*.

The Cretaceous, the last period of the Mesozoic, was a time of dynamic change. Grass didn't exist, but angiosperm plants produced a new invention: the flower. The Rocky Mountains formed, creating changes in the environment. What is now the United States was divided in half by a great inland sea called the Niobrara. Kansas and Nebraska were under waters ruled by great sea reptiles like the snaky-necked plesiosaur *Elasmosaurus* and *Tylosaurus*, biggest and most dangerous of the mosasaurs (a group of marine lizards closely related to monitors). More modern types of birds were flying in skies currently ruled by the largest pterosaurs.

A greater variety of dinosaurs than ever before lived during the Cretaceous period. Ornithischians (a large, diverse group of herbivores) dominated the planet. Included in this group were the armored ankylosaurs (the "living tanks" of the dinosaur world), the duckbilled hadrosaurs such as *Edmontosaurus* and *Anatotinan*, the "bone-headed" pachycephalosaurs and the horned dinosaurs, or ceratopsians, like *Triceratops*.

The Cretaceous also saw a new kind of theropod, *Deinonychus*. Comparatively intelligent, quite active and agile, this hunter was equipped with a deadly "sickle-claw" toe that it probably used for disemboweling prey instead of walking. The largest meat-eaters of all times lived during this period. One was the famous *Tyrannosaurus*, a living killing machine 40 feet long.

The end of the Cretaceous marked both the end of the Mesozoic Era and that of the dinosaurs (unless, again, we categorize their apparent descendants the birds as feathered dinosaurs). No one knows why all the remaining dinosaurs died off at this time. Perhaps they couldn't adapt to the changing conditions of their world. Some paleontologists find spectacular causes, like the impact of a gigantic comet, to explain the dinosaurs' disappearance.

After the dinosaurs were gone, mammals (warm-blooded, hairy animals)—who first appeared while there were still dinosaurs—got their big chance. In the subsequent Cenozoic Era, mammals rapidly evolved, filling niches vacated by their reptilian predecessors. Mammals would rule this planet for the next 65 million years.

The famous Ice Age ended only about 12,000 years ago, just "yesterday" in geologic terms (and so, contrary to what many people incorrectly believe, it was not the coming of that colder age that wiped out the dinosaurs). During that time, in the Pleistocene Epoch (1.5 million–12,000 years ago), early human beings fought the woolly mammoth and sabretooth cat. But neither human nor mammoth nor sabretooth cat ever saw a living dinosaur.

The Triassic Period

The Triassic (248–206 million years ago) was the first of the three "periods" of the Mesozoic Era. The word Triassic means "triad" in Latin, so named for the three rock levels that make up this period.

During the Triassic period, the giant "super-continent" Pangaea was still a single body of land located mostly in the Southern Hemisphere.

The temperature at this time had risen by about ten degrees centigrade worldwide. Thanks to the warm climate and the fact that Pangaea hadn't broken up yet, a visitor to the Triassic might enjoy a pleasant walk from what is now London to New York in just a few days. The weather conditions were mostly dry. Unlike today, when we have four seasons, the Triassic only had two: wet and dry.

This period is noted for its wide stretches of open land. There was no grass, no flowers, no dense forests, although there were many different kinds of plants. The tallest trees were conifers (those bearing cones like evergreen trees). There were also ferns, cycads (woody plants, most of them having unbranched stems), and cycadeoids (plants resembling cycads, but not necessarily related to them).

The Early (or Lower) Triassic (248–242 million years ago) was still the domain of two animal groups that had thrived during the earlier Permian period (286–248 million years ago). The first group consisted of amphibians (animals adapted to live on both land and in the water, like frogs). The second were the therapsids, a group of "mammal-like" reptiles (*e.g.,* the carnivorous cynodont *Cynognathus* and herbivorous dicynodont *Kannemeyria*) that are thought to have been warm-blooded and which started off the evolutionary changes that led to true mammals (like *Morganucodon*).

By Middle Triassic times (242–227 million years ago), new kinds of animals—all diapsid reptiles (they have two openings on back of the skull, separated by a "temporal bar" of bone)—began to dominate the land previously ruled by amphibians and therapsids. The first "ruling reptiles" or archosaurs (a group that would soon include the dinosaurs) made their debut. Crocodiles, archosaurs that have survived to modern times, began to appear and diversify. Eventually they would become a major reptilian group. Also appearing were the rhynchosaurs, a group of relatively small reptiles that would enjoy a brief but successful life span during the Late Triassic.

Things really began to change during the Late (or Upper) Triassic (227–206 million years ago). It was during this time that animal groups never before seen on this planet first appeared. Among these new groups were the first modern amphibians, the first lepidosaurs (generally small, insect-eating reptiles like modern lizards and snakes), the first mammals (like *Megazostrodon*)—and the first dinosaurs.

The origins of dinosaurs are not entirely clear. In former years, paleontologists thought that dinosaurs evolved from a large and very diverse grouping of armored archosaurs collectively called "thecodonts" or "thecodontians." This term or classification is no longer considered valid. Today, however, it is believed that the earliest dinosaurs evolved from small two-legged carnivores like *Marasuchus* (formerly called *Lagosuchus*). Among the oldest known dinosaurs are *Staurikosaurus*, *Herrerasaurus*, and the recently discovered *Eoraptor*, all of which were found in South America. It was generally believed that these three animals were so-called "protodinosaurs" that lived before the split of the Dinosauria into two great groups, the Saurischia (the "lizard-hipped" dinosaurs) and Ornithischia (the "bird-hipped" dinosaurs). Now, however, thanks to work by paleontologist Paul C. Sereno, it seems that all three may indeed be among the first saurischians. They may also belong to the Theropoda, the vast group of meat-eating saurischians.

Among other early dinosaurs appearing about this time were *Pisanosaurus*, which is the earliest known ornithischian; *Coelophysis*, a somewhat more advanced theropod; and *Plateosaurus*, the first truly big dinosaur (up to 25 feet long).

By the end of the Triassic period, dinosaurs had become the dominant land animals. Their success can be attributed to various factors, including a change in the design of the thigh bone and shin bone that let them stand erect, their adaptation to dry conditions, superior eyesight, and ability to move fast.

However, the dinosaurs' true reign as monarchs of the Earth was yet to come.

The Jurassic Period

The Jurassic period (about 206–144 million years ago) was named for the Jura Mountains on the border of France and Switzerland. It is the second major division of the Mesozoic Era.

There was turmoil—great activity—in the Earth itself. Pangaea, the "super-continent," was starting to break apart. It broke into two new continents: Laurasia (made up of what today is North America, Greenland, and Eurasia) and Gondwana (South America, Africa, India, Australia, and Antarctica).

By the middle part of the Jurassic period, the world was flooded by epeiric seas. These were shallow, salt water seas that were found on the inside of continents. The climate was still very warm at this time. The dry conditions of the Triassic were giving way to wet environments. What is now North America wrenched itself away from Africa. Rocky palisades were forming. Laurasia was drifting northward.

Cycads, plants that first appeared during the Triassic period, dominated the land. The first gingkos—gymnosperm plants that are common even today—made their bow. Grass and flowers, however, would not appear for a long time to come.

The land masses of the Jurassic were dominated by dinosaurs. Many were of gigantic size.

Among the Saurischia, prosauropods became extinct during the early part of this period. They were replaced by the giant, long-necked sauropods—the prosauropods' apparent descendents. Among the sauropods were the well-known *Apatosaurus*, *Diplodocus*, and *Brachiosaurus* (the latter being the first dinosaur to be seen in full view in the movie *Jurassic Park*). Their long necks let them eat plants on the ground or leaves from tall trees. They required all the food they could get! Some of these creatures (like the recently discovered *Seismosaurus*) were well over 100 feet long!

Theropoda, the group of meat-eating dinosaurs, branched off into a number of different smaller groups during the Jurassic. Carnosauria is one of these groups. The biggest, deadliest known carnosaur of the Late Jurassic was *Allosaurus* (up to 40 feet long). Its major weapons were its powerful three-clawed hands. There are a great many specimens of this dinosaur, so we know it well.

Another theropod group is Ceratosauria. It evolved skull ornamentations like horns and crests. The largest known ceratosaur, about the same size as *Allosaurus*, was the dinosaur that gave this group its name, the nose-horned, four-fingered *Ceratosaurus*.

While other theropods were getting to be bigger land animals, another group did something different. They remained small, evolved long front limbs, and let their scales develop into … *feathers!* By the end of the Jurassic, these theropods took to the sky as birds. This vast, beautiful group of flying and feathered "theropod dinosaurs" (as many scientists classify birds) is still with us today.

At this time, the Ornithischia split into two major dinosaurian groups: 1) Thyreophora—armored types that walked on all fours (like the plated, spike-tailed dinosaur *Stegosaurus*), and 2) Ornithopoda, a large group of agile, bipedal or two-legged plant-eaters (such as the small *Dryosaurus* and larger *Camptosaurus*).

The most incredible remains of Late Jurassic dinosaurs were found in the Morrison Formation at Dinosaur National Monument in Utah and Colorado. There is a vast wall of fossils, including the bones of numerous dinosaurs, that can be viewed by visitors to the monument.

The Jurassic period was also the domain of other non-dinosaurian groups of reptiles. The skies were dominated by flying reptiles called pterosaurs (sometimes incorrectly called "flying dinosaurs" in popular books), whose wings consisted of a membrane of skin attached to an extended finger. Although primitive birds, like the famous *Archaeopteryx*, were already present, true birds would not rule the skies for many millions of years.

The waters were ruled by marine reptiles such as the sea serpent–like plesiosaurs and porpoise-like icthyosaurs.

On land, the mammals—still tiny and timid—had already split into about a dozen major groups.

But the dinosaurs still had a long, long time to rule the Earth.

The Cretaceous Period

Early Cretaceous

The world was a warm and wet place during the Early Cretaceous (144–121 million years ago), that beginning part of the third (and last) period of the Mesozoic Era. (The word Cretaceous comes from the Latin word for "chalk," and was so named because of the chalk deposits of Southeast England that are of Cretaceous age.)

The continents that had been unified into the "super-continent" called Pangaea were breaking apart. The Atlantic Ocean was already starting to form and North America was moving to the northwest. Toward the end of the Early Cretaceous much of this planet was covered by seas. In fact, most of North America was more sea than land.

By this time, there was a big change in the dinosaur world. The end of the Jurassic period was marked by a gap of several million years in the fossil record. In Lower Cretaceous rocks, where we find dinosaurs again, much is very different.

Among the Saurischia, sauropods, which had been the dominant plant-eaters worldwide, were now only a minor part of the fauna. Most of these large, long-necked dinosaurs lived on the Gondwana continents. Members of the sauropod family called the Titanosauridae replaced the more famous Late Jurassic sauropods around the world, while members of the Ornithischia became the main plant-eating dinosaurian group.

Ornithischian dinosaurs are characterized by having a true beak, which was partly made up by a bone (called a *predentary*) found at the tip of the lower jaw. All ornithischian dinosaurs had a greatly enlarged gut area. They also possessed teeth in more than one row. These features allowed the animals to chew plant food better and then keep it in the gut longer for better digestion.

There are only two major dinosaur faunas known from the Early Cretaceous of North America:

The Cloverly Formation fauna is known from Wyoming and Montana. In the Cloverly can be found the large plant-eater *Tenontosaurus* and its apparent major enemy (and one of the most famous of all dinosaurs), the sickle-clawed theropod *Deinonychus*. Other dinosaurs known from the Cloverly included the ankylosaur or armored dinosaur *Sauropelta*, a large megalosaurid theropod known only from teeth and a few limb bones, and the small theropod named *Microvenator*.

The other major fauna is from the Arundel Formation in what is now the Washington, D.C., area. Here there was the ankylosaur *Priconodon*, known only from fossil teeth. There was a large theropod of the group Dryptosauridae, mostly known from teeth and a small number of bones. There was also *Pleurocoelus*, a sauropod related to the Jurassic period's giant *Brachiosaurus*.

Although the Arundel Formation is famous for its rather scrappy dinosaur remains, it is better known for its plant fossils. Some of the earliest angiosperms (flowering plants, which now dominate our world) have been found in these beds. (Until the Early Cretaceous, herbivorous dinosaurs ate only gymnosperms, like conifers, ginkgos, and seed ferns.) After the angiosperms began to diversify, they really took over, becoming the most numerous kinds of plants by the end of the Cretaceous.

A few dinosaurs have been found in other Cretaceous localities, like the Trinity Formation in Texas, and the Wealden in Europe (best known for *Iguanodon*, one of the first dinosaurs discovered).

Several dinosaur trends were going on at this time that would determine their evolution until their extinction. The once major theropod group called Carnosauria was gradually dropping in diversity to be replaced by members of the Coelurosauria, a group famous for having skeletons similar to those of birds. This is not surprising, as one Late Jurassic coelurosaurian group, most paleontologists believe, seems to have evolved into birds!

Pterosaurs began their long decline into extinction during the Cretaceous. Gone were the long-tailed rhamphorynchoids which were common during the Jurassic. The surviving pterosaur group, the pterodactyloids, was losing its members in competition with a rapidly diversifying group, the birds.

Mammals were also changing. Gone were the famous Jurassic mammals like the docodonts and triconodonts. Two new mammalian groups, the marsupials and placentals, would appear during this time, eventually to dominate the earth. For now, however, these mammals just sat in the nighttime shadows, awaiting their turn to rule.

Late Cretaceous

The Late Cretaceous period (99–65 million years ago), the last part of the Mesozoic, dramatically opened with a withdrawal of the large inland seas.

The climate during the Late Cretaceous was more seasonal. There were dry spells. There were also dramatic geologic changes. Mountains began to build up in the western part of North America, as that continent continued to drift to the northwest.

In the plant world, angiosperms continued their rapid expansion into shrubs and flowering plants. Angiosperms became so important as a food source, in fact, that their success could explain why such dinosaurian groups as hadrosaurs (duck-bills) and ceratopsian (horned) dinosaurs also diversified during this time. The hadrosaurs specialized in eating plants of the soft fiber varieties. Ceratopsians preferred using their powerful jaws to chomp through hard fibers, horned dinosaurs like *Triceratops* having jaws strong enough to break through tree trunks. For these reasons, the duck-billed and horned dinosaurs became the most abundant plant-eating groups, achieving this success by eating different kinds of foods and, therefore, without competing against one another.

Pterosaurs, the flying reptiles, were declining in the Late Cretaceous. Only the larger pterosaur species were abundant at this time, especially in Laurasia. On that northern super-continent lived the huge crested *Pteranodon* and, even bigger, the ultimate flying vertebrate (backboned animal), *Quetzalcoatlus*, which was about the size of a small airplane.

Birds were expanding into many groups all over the world, with the first modern birds making their initial appearances. Some Late Cretaceous birds became so specialized that they lost the ability to fly, becoming the first ground birds. Also appearing during this time were the first birds that were entirely adapted to living in the sea, such as *Hesperornis*.

Mammals continued to increase during the Late Cretaceous. These included the very first primates—a group that would eventually lead to human beings—to appear in the fossil record.

The dinosaurs continued to multiply at this time, especially the two-legged ornithopods and the armored ankylosaurs. The stegosaurs or plated dinosaurs, most abundant during the Late Jurassic, were almost gone. The unusual "bone-headed" dinosaurs, the pachycephalosaurs, made their debut, but remained a small group that never became an important part of any fauna.

Among the theropod dinosaurs, the birdlike coelurosaurs diversified into many groups. The largest of these coelurosaurs was one of the most famous dinosaurs of all time, *Tyrannosaurus*. There were some Late Cretaceous dinosaurs and birds that were so similar in the structure of their skeletons that even the experts have been confused trying to identify them!

About 10–15 million years before the end of the Mesozoic Era, the dinosaurs were at their peak of diversity. During the last eight million years of their existence, from 73–65 million years ago, they started to decline for reasons that we still do not understand.

For now, the story of the extinction of the dinosaurs remains another subject altogether.

NATURAL
PREHISTORY

In 1993, dinosaurs enjoyed an all-time high in popularity, largely due to the overwhelming success of Steven Spielberg's mega-budgeted blockbuster movie *Jurassic Park*, which had been based on the best-selling novel of the same title by Michael Crichton. It seemed as if everything—from candy to shower curtains to pajamas—had a dinosaur on it.

To capitalize on this dinosaur-sized craze that was sweeping across the globe, Starlog Telecommunications, the company which produced the highly successful fantastic-film magazines *Starlog* and *Fangoria*, issued a one-shot magazine simply titled *Dinosaur*. The publication was offered in two versions, the more expensive—and collectible—edition having a stiff-paper, three-dimensional cover. As it turned out, the book would be quite successful in itself and be published in various reprint and foreign-language editions.

I was solicited by the magazine's editor Anthony Timpone to write the following article more or less summarizing and discussing dinosaurs in general and their early discoveries, but also noting some of the more recent finds and ideas about these great reptiles. For trivia buffs, the title of the article was simply "Real Dinosaurs" as listed in *Dinosaur*'s table of contents. This article, as well as its follow-up printed in section three of this book, is reprinted courtesy of Timpone and Starlog Telecommunications.

For more than a century and a half, the people of this world have had a love affair with dinosaurs. Ever since dinosaurs' fossil remains were

first discovered and recognized as such, scientists and laymen alike have
been intrigued by these fascinating creatures. Today, the names of these
animals—which seem as long as some of the dinosaurs themselves—can
be rattled off effortlessly by children just beginning to learn their ABCs.

Like the dragon and other fabulous monsters of myth and media,
dinosaurs appeal to us because they embody both fantasy and reality. On
one level, their appearance and sometimes great size give them an almost
alien feel; on another, the fact remains that these creatures were very real.
We can visit a museum and see their fossilized bones, skin, footprints,
and eggs as evidence of their existence. In a sense, dinosaurs were real-
life monsters, their remains a link to the history of our planet and to our
own history upon it. Because the last dinosaurs perished some 65 million
years ago, they are "safe" monsters that—despite their sometimes formidable appearances—can do us no harm.

The study of these animals (the science of vertebrate paleontology,
or the study of fossil animals having backbones) contributes to the piec-
ing together of the puzzling history of our Earth. The interpretation of
dinosaurian remains also stimulates the imagination, as paleontologists,
like scientific Sherlock Holmeses, attempt to determine what these beasts
were like when they were alive.

Just what, then, *is* a dinosaur?

When asked, most people probably think they know, although the
answers they would give are not always correct. That's understandable,
given that many dinosaur buffs can claim only movies and comic books
as their "reference sources" (instead of scientific journals). Also, many (if
not most) popular books about dinosaurs are replete with inaccuracies,
outmoded information or outright untruths. To many laymen, dinosaurs
are any "prehistoric reptiles"; their definition sometimes includes non-
reptiles such as amphibians, mammals and even invertebrates.

The Dinosauria (the large group to which all dinosaurs belong) con-
stitutes a very specific assemblage of reptiles, which—despite misinformation perpetuated by movies, comic books, merchandise and even some
non-fiction—does not include such familiar reptilian groups as the flying
pterosaurs, aquatic plesiosaurs, mosasaurs, and icthyosaurs. To be classified
as a dinosaur, the structure of the animal's bones must meet certain cri-
teria. Anything falling outside that set of parameters is, quite simply, *not*
a dinosaur. All dinosaurs were land-based animals that lived during the
Mesozoic Era (248–65 million years ago), which is divided into three
periods: the Triassic, Jurassic, and Cretaceous. The first dinosaurs seem
to have appeared in Late Triassic times, some 234 million years ago.

The dinosaurs were the most successful land vertebrate in this planet's history. They occupied every terrestrial niche, literally dominating our globe for some 140 million years. Their fossilized remains have been collected from every continent—including, in recent years, Antarctica.

The existence of dinosaur bones has been known for many centuries—probably even during human prehistory, although the origins attributed to them in those pre-paleontology days were usually fanciful. Such occasional finds were then believed to be the remains of dragons, human giants, and other impossible monsters, or even animals that "missed the boat" during the biblical Flood. In ancient China, fossilized vertebrate remains were believed to be "dragon bones" with medicinal powers.

One such incorrect interpretation involved the first illustration ever published of a dinosaur bone, printed in 1676. The Reverend Robert Plot published what appears to be the distal or far end of a femur (the upper hind leg bone) of the large carnivorous dinosaur *Megalosaurus* (a name meaning "big lizard," which wasn't applied until 1824). As dinosaurs were still unknown at that time, Plot believed that this specimen was part of some giant human being. Because of its shape, Plot originally dubbed the fragment *Scrotum humanum* (the first published dinosaur name).

An October 1787 publication reported the discovery of a very large thigh bone in New Jersey. This specimen may have belonged to the duck-billed dinosaur *Hadrosaurus* (named in 1858, meaning "bulky lizard"). If so, this bone would have been the first dinosaur fossil found and collected in North America. Unfortunately, the results of this discovery, if any, were never recorded.

It wasn't until the first half of the 19th century that dinosaur remains were identified as indicators of a new group of reptiles. *Megalosaurus*, the same creature that inspired Reverend Plot to envision giant people, was the first dinosaur to be officially named and described. The original remains which resulted in the naming of this dinosaur were scanty, consisting only of an incomplete lower jaw and some other parts, which were found in northern Oxfordshire, England.

In the wake of that historic find, the fossil remains of two other large and equally fantastic reptiles, both plant-eaters (the spike-thumbed *Iguanodon*, meaning "iguana tooth" because of its resemblance to teeth of the modern lizard, and the armored *Hylaeosaurus*, or "wood lizard"), were found in England. These, as well as other early British discoveries, prompted the future Sir Richard Owen (1802–1894), a leading comparative anatomist, to regard *Megalosaurus*, *Iguanodon*, and *Hylaeosaurus* as elephantine reptiles very much unlike modern lizards. On the historic day August 2, 1841, in an address to the British Association for the Advancement of Science, Owen proposed that all of these creatures be recognized as a dis-

tinct group of "saurian reptiles." For this group, Owen coined the new word
"Dinosauria," which combined the Greek words *deinos* (meaning "fear-
fully great," later interpreted as "terrible") and *sauros* (for "lizard," though
sometimes revised to mean "reptile"). The word "dinosaur," needless to
add, has remained in our lexicon ever since.

Following Owen's announcement, more dinosaur discoveries began
to be made in other countries. Before the dawn of the 20th century, a treasury of dinosaur remains had been recovered from North America, as well
as Europe and Canada.

Of course, in the days when dinosaur paleontology was still in its
infancy, the interpretation of these fossil bones was, more often than not,
rather incorrect. During the early 1850s, when sculptor Benjamin Waterhouse Hawkins was commissioned to make, under Owen's direction, a set
of life-sized prehistoric animal models for London's Crystal Palace
grounds, he fashioned *Megalosaurus* as a hump-backed, short-tailed monster with a crocodile-like head. Hawkins's *Iguanodon* resembled some oversized iguana lizard sporting a horn on its snout. Both animals were
depicted walking on all fours. Later discoveries would show that these
dinosaurs were actually quite different from Hawkins's imaginative though
fanciful portrayals. The supposed nose horn of *Iguanodon*, for instance,
proved really to be a spiked thumb; both this dinosaur and *Megalosaurus*
were also found to have walked on their hind legs.

Until relatively recently, most dinosaurs in movies and other popular media have been based on an outdated image—both in appearance
and behavior—that has persisted since the late 1800s. Dinosaurs were portrayed as pea-brained, stupid, tail-dragging saurians. Some were supposedly too heavy to walk on land, spending most of their time lounging
around in swamps, with the water buoyantly supporting their enormous
weights.

These images were perpetuated by an early group of artists, the best
of whom was inarguably Charles R. Knight (1874–1953). Reproductions
of Knight's fine drawings, paintings, and sculptures of extinct animals
and plants received very wide circulation. Though somewhat inaccurate
in various ways today, Knight's works had no serious competition in their
own time, and are difficult to equal—let alone surpass—even now, both
as art and as valid interpretations of ancient life forms. Knight worked
very closely with contemporary paleontologists, most notably Edward
Drinker Cope (1840–1897) and Henry Fairfield Osborn (1857–1935). The
artist based his restorations of extinct animals on the fossils themselves,
working up from the bones and utilizing his own vast knowledge of living
animals' anatomy and behavior. Artistic gaps filled by neither bones nor

scientists were supplied by Knight's own (usually correct) educated guesses.

It was Knight's classic depictions of dinosaurs and other extinct animals that have had the most profound influence on motion pictures and other forms of popular art. Sculptor Marcel Delgado, for example, working with animator Willis H. O'Brien, based all of his stop-motion models for the movies *The Lost World* (1925) and *King Kong* (1933) on Knight's works. Sharp-eyed dinosaur buffs can even point out which Knight piece inspired specific Delgado creations, as if the original paintings and sculptures had magically come to life.

Until more recently, perhaps, as with movies like *Jurassic Park*, there has never been a Hollywood movie that accurately portrayed dinosaurs based upon what scientists know about them today. Put in historical perspective, the dinosaurs in the original *Lost World* remain among the most accurate ever to appear in a movie, based as they were on the scientific information available about these animals back in the 1920s. The dinosaurs of most later motion pictures, right up to some of those made today, have been based upon the old Knight originals, or upon other films that had been inspired by Knight.

This creates a problem, at least as far as accuracy is concerned. A good number of movie special-effects artists and technicians who create dinosaurs were influenced, on evidence, not by Knight *per se* but by other movies inspired by Knight's work. What excites these creators may not be the paleontological data available today, but rather the Knight-inspired movies of O'Brien and his successor, Ray Harryhausen. That's why we still see such ubiquitous cinematic inaccuracies as the three-fingered, upright-posed, tail-dragging *Tyrannosaurus*—which in fact had only two fingers, and walked horizontally, tail off the ground.

Dinosaurs are also often perceived not as real animals subject to the many laws of science, but simply as *monsters*—and, as such, are portrayed any way the filmmaker desires. It is this attitude that has hatched such (sometimes beloved) mythical, impossibly huge movie saurians as Godzilla, Gorgo and Harryhausen's "Rhedosaurus" from *The Beast from 20,000 Fathoms*. Often dinosaurs are seen as simply "giant lizards," and are portrayed exactly as such when low budgets preclude more elaborate special effects.

Actually, what we know today about dinosaurs is far more interesting than the outdated image of dim-witted, lumbering behemoths that has continued to dominate the screen. By the 1960s, dinosaurs (despite the public's continued fascination with them) were generally considered to be evolutionary "dead ends" by the scientific community, creatures that left behind no descendants and thus were unworthy of much serious study. Like the Edsel, they had becomes symbols of obsolescence.

This attitude dramatically changed when, in 1969, Yale University paleontologist John H. Ostrom named and described the sickle-clawed *Deinonychus* (meaning "terrible claw"), one of the most important new dinosaur discoveries of the later 20th century. *Deinonychus* was a very birdlike carnivore that deviated a great deal from the older image of dinosaurs. Professor Ostrom presented evidence strongly suggesting that *Deinonychus* was an active and comparatively intelligent creature with a relatively large brain. Evidence suggested that this dinosaur, somewhat like the wolf, hunted much larger prey (including the herbivorous dinosaur *Tenontosaurus*, or "tendon lizard," which Ostrom also named and described) in groups akin to packs. The structure of its skeleton also indicated a very close relationship not with traditional reptiles, but with birds.

The discovery of *Deinonychus* inspired many modern paleontologists to regard dinosaurs as something far more important than dead-end curiosities of a bygone age. Again, scientists actively began to search for their remains, making some of the most important (and sometimes spectacular) dinosaur discoveries of the past couple of decades. Some of these findings led to new and often controversial ideas about dinosaur physiology, behavior, and intelligence.

One theory that arose from such discoveries was that dinosaurs—or at least some of them—were not ectothermic (cold-blooded and taking in heat from an outside source), but endothermic (warm-blooded and generating heat from within, like mammals and birds). The chief advocate of dinosaur endothermy has been paleontologist Robert T. Bakker, a former student of Ostrom. The author of many scientific and popular articles on this intriguing possibility, as well as a familiar media personality, Bakker has presented various arguments supporting this theory. Other paleontologists, however, have made their own cases that some, and perhaps most, dinosaurs were not warm-blooded in the strict sense.

Among the more recent dinosaur discoveries offering evidence that these animals may have been warm-blooded, as well as smarter than formerly thought, was that of the duckbilled *Maiasaura* ("good mother lizard," the name appropriately coined in the feminine gender), whose bones were discovered in Montana in 1978. Thanks mainly to the work of paleontologist John R. Horner, we believe that this kind of dinosaur, at least, was quite unlike the old concept perpetuated by many books and movies.

Until then, dinosaurs were believed to have abandoned their eggs, as do most modern reptiles, to hatch in the warmth and light of the sun,

During the 1970s, dinosaurs began to be portrayed as active and possibly warm-blooded animals, as exemplified in this illustration by paleontologist Robert T. Bakker of two *Leptoceratops gracilis* individuals. Reproduced with permission of Canadian Museum of Nature, Ottawa, Canada (neg. #71-4432).

leaving their infants to fend for themselves in their hostile environment. That, however, would probably have resulted in a very high infant mortality rate, especially in a world also inhabited by hungry carnivorous dinosaurs.

Found at the original *Maiasaura* dig site were the tiny bones of 11 *Maiasaura* babies, as well as numerous pieces of fossilized eggshell. The later discovery of an egg containing a *Maiasaura* embryo constituted the first such dinosaur find in the United States. This evidence led Horner and his colleague and friend, the late Robert Makela, to suggest that—at least in the case of *Maiasaura*—the babies stayed together in the nest, where their parents fed them for an extended period. Such complex social behavior was not suspected in dinosaurs, which were still largely being viewed as brainless, lumbering brutes. Horner further speculated that the babies, 13 inches long at hatching time, grew to 10 feet in length by the end of their first year. Such rapid growth, as fast as that of many birds, required a high metabolism—the kind sustained by warm-blooded animals.

Other recent dinosaur discoveries have expanded our interpretation of these wondrous animals, with occasionally surprising developments. For example, sauropods (a dinosaurian group typified by the well-known *Apatosaurus* and *Diplodocus*) were thought to more or less fit the same mold: very large bodies, small heads, long necks, and pillar-like legs. But two dinosaurs whose remains were discovered in Argentina disputed that all of them were very much alike. *Saltasaurus* ("Salta lizard," named for Salta, the province where it was discovered) was armor-plated, while *Amargasaurus* ("Amarga lizard," named for the formation where it was found) sported two parallel rows of neck and back spikes, some 21 inches tall. The Chinese *Shunosaurus* ("Szechuan lizard"), like some armored dinosaurs, had a tail ending in a large, bony club.

The recently discovered *Seismosaurus* ("earth-shaker lizard"), from New Mexico, presently holds the title of longest dinosaur, with a possible length of between 150 and 180 feet. Another relatively recent surprise was the Argentinean theropod (carnivorous dinosaur) *Carnotaurus* ("flesh-eating bull"), whose head was equipped with a pair of large, bull-like horns, one above each eye.

Strangely enough, the area that seems to fascinate most non-scientists about dinosaurs is the fact of their extinction. Many reasons have been offered for the death of all the dinosaurs, from such low-key explanations as their being unable to adapt to changing environments, to more spectacular scenarios like crashing comets and exploding supernovas. But to many paleontologists, including Horner, dinosaur extinction is scarcely as important or interesting as the animals' success.

Today, most (though not all) paleontologists agree that one line of small theropod dinosaurs evolved into birds. In fact, birds are now often officially classified as feathered theropods. The implications of this are profound and also quite wonderful. Looking to the skies, we can see that what could be the *real* dinosaurs—not the clumsy, obsolete *reel* monsters we may have grown up with, but a diverse, beautiful and thriving group of animals, their numbers comprising more than 9,000 species—are still with us.

Dinosaurs no longer rule the Earth, but they may have soared off into a new domain.

TRACKING *"TRACHODON"*

I have a "problem" with people not using correct names for things, particularly and not surprisingly, the names of dinosaurs.

A great number of persons on this planet—from laymen to scientists—love dinosaurs. However, many dinosaur "buffs" have little or no knowledge of the actual science of dinosaurs, and, therefore, derive more satisfaction from viewing dinosaur movies, collecting dinosaur toys, or assembling dinosaur model kits than visiting a museum or reading a technical article published in a journal. Numerous dinosaur "fans" tend to regard dinosaurs as subjects of nostalgia, their current interpretations of these animals based upon some toy or comic-book illustration fondly remembered since childhood. As such, these fans often prefer keeping their perceptions of dinosaurs *as they were* when those old toys and kits and comics—some of them dating back decades—were true items of inspiration.

It became increasingly annoying to the author that so many fans persisted in using old and out-dated names for dinosaurs simply because a certain name had appeared in an old and fondly recalled children's book, or was stamped on some plastic Miller or Marx toy manufactured during the 1950s.

Among the most commonly misused dinosaur names has always been *Trachodon*, usually designating the classic "duckbilled dinosaur." One day, in a burst of frustration, I wrote the following article and sent it off to *Prehistoric Times*, a popular fanzine produced by Mike Fredericks, hoping that, at least in its pages, the readers—most of whom seemed to be chiefly interested in assembling model dinosaur kits or collecting dinosaur memorabilia— would finally understand why this name is incorrect. I even (naively, it seems) dared hope that *Edmontosaurus*, the correct name for this dinosaur, would soon, and perhaps forevermore, be

used by *"PT"* readers. Alas, *Trachodon* popped up (even mis-
spelled) in a subsequent article published in that very same issue!
    Oh, well—here goes another attempt in hopes that this piece
will succeed in its original intent.

To many of us who grew up in the 1950s and '60s, the name *Trachodon*—identifying the classic "duckbilled dinosaur" of the Late Cretaceous period—is that of an old familiar friend, and one, though officially
abandoned more than a half century ago, still cherished by those nostalgic for the treasures of youth.

    Dinosaur enthusiasts interested enough in these animals to go beyond
the names printed in popular (usually children's) books, or stamped on
plastic toys, have discovered that many names—including *Trachodon*—
have been, over the decades, assigned to this dinosaur favorite. When
examining these names, one finds that a *Trachodon* is an *Anatosaurus* is an
Edmontosaurus is (perhaps) a *Shantungasaurus* is a ... well, the list continues.

    So, what happened?

    Why have there been so many different names and why has there
been so much taxonomic confusion over this one hadrosaurid (a member
of the Hadrosauridae, or the family of duckbilled dinosaurs)? Why, in fact,
should a correct name for an extinct creature be used at all, when an incorrect name, like *Trachodon*, is known and beloved by so many? And why,
if that name was already obsolete during World War II, has it been perpetuated in popular books and on merchandise for so many years following this change?

    Indeed, the name *Trachodon* has been a source of confusion, frustra-
tion, even anger to many of us interested in dinosaurs (enthusiasts and
collectors as well as scientists). Contributing to this muddle, no popular
publication has ever dealt completely with the *Trachodon* issue, nor have
most popular writers even been aware that this name, or its "successor"
Anatosaurus, are incorrect.

    Traditionally, information about extinct life has been disseminated
through two basic outlets: "the literature," that is, peer-reviewed articles,
written by scientists based on their *original* work and published in credited professional journals; and "the media," including popular adult and
children's publications, news and information programs, motion pictures,
and merchandise.

Popular books are often the product of staff writers who have no real interest in or knowledge of dinosaurs (and who next month could be assigned to write a text about ships, farming, football or any other subject), or other authors whose primary reference sources are already existing popular books. Dinosaur-related merchandise is generally designed using popular books as references. Mistakes corrected or information updated in "the literature" can take decades (if ever) to filter into the popular books. Only in recent years, thanks to organizations like The Dinosaur Society, has there been a concerted effort among paleontologists to ensure that information about dinosaurs given to the public is accurate and up to date. (The influx of excellent and paleontologically correct dinosaur sculptures and model kits during the 1990s and beyond is a direct result of this interaction between science and popular art.)

Trachodon was a classic victim of the long existing gap between "the literature" and "the media"; the confusion regarding its name and what it represents has origins dating back to the earliest days of North American dinosaur discoveries, before anyone even knew what a hadrosaur really was.

The odyssey of *Trachodon* begins with paleontologist Joseph Leidy of the Academy of Natural Sciences in Philadelphia who, in 1856, gave the new genus and species combination *Trachodon mirabilis* to seven worn, unassociated mandibular teeth collected by Ferdinand Vandiveer Hayden from the Judith River Formation in Montana. Among these cotype specimens, one tooth possessed a single root, while another was double-rooted (a feature later found to be a feature identifying a ceratopsian or horned dinosaur).

That same year, Leidy described the new species *Thespesius occidentalis*, founded upon several cotype specimens including vertebrae and a toe bone, also collected by Hayden, from the Lance Formation, Grand River, South Dakota. In later years, this species would sometimes be regarded as the same as *Edmontosaurus annectens* (see later), but is, according to hadrosaur expert Michael K. Brett-Surman, too poor for positive identification.

Two years after *Trachodon* and *Thespesius*, Leidy also named and described the more completely known *Hadrosaurus foulkii*, founded on a partial skeleton, missing the skull but including some well-preserved mandibular teeth, which had been found some 20 years earlier by William Parker Foulke in Haddonfield, New Jersey. Eventually, Leidy recognized similarities in some of his *Trachodon* teeth to those of *Hadrosaurus*. In 1868, realizing that the double-rooted (=ceratopsian) tooth differed from the others, he proposed that the name *Trachodon* be reserved exclusively for that one specimen, referring the remaining teeth to *Hadrosaurus*.

Full-scale model of the classic "duckbilled dinosaur" popularly called *"Trachodon"* (actually *Edmontosaurus annectens*) made by Louis Paul Jonas Studios for the 1964 New York World's Fair. Courtesy Sinclair Oil Corporation.

Over the years, other paleontologists, apparently unaware of Leidy's abandonment of the name for the single-rooted teeth, would continue to refer hadrosaurid remains, mostly based on scrappy fragments, to *Trachodon*. An impressive list of additional species was subsequently assigned to this problematic genus, each one of them later declared invalid or referred to other genera. Finally, in 1988, paleontologist Walter P. Coombs, Jr., of Western New England College recommended that *T. mirabilis* be designated a *nomen dubium* (a doubtful name) and used only in historical discussions.

Adding to this early confusion was pioneer paleontologist Edward Drinker Cope's 1876 genus *Diclonius*, to which Cope referred three individual species based upon fragmentary detached teeth from the Judith River Formation of Montana, all of which were later referred to *Trachodon*. In 1988, Coombs would demonstrate that these teeth cannot be identified below the hadrosaurid level.

New, more complete dinosaur-fossil discoveries were being made in North America by the latter 19th century. In 1871, Cope's professional rival Othniel Charles Marsh of Yale University collected an incomplete skeleton, lacking most of the skull and a good portion of the tail, from the Niobrara Formation of Kansas. Professor Marsh believed that these remains belonged to a new species of Leidy's "headless wonder" (as fossil skeletons lacking skulls are frequently dubbed) *Hadrosaurus*, which he originally called *H. agilis*; in 1890, after the subsequent collection of more hadrosaurid material, Marsh recognized this skeleton as generically distinct and named it *Claosaurus agilis*.

In 1882, a complete hadrosaurid skeleton was collected by Jacob L. Wortman and R. S. Hill from the Lance Formation in South Dakota. A second, nearly complete skeleton of the same kind of animal was found by Oscar Hunter in 1904 in the Lance Formation of Montana. Fortunately, these specimens included skulls, and the heads superficially resembled the heads of ducks. The skeletons were mounted at the American Museum of Natural History, the first in a quadrupedal pose, the other standing tall on its hind legs, inspiring the famous life restoration painted by artist Charles R. Knight in 1909.

Cope initially thought the first of these skeletons belonged to Joseph Leidy's *T. mirabilis*; in 1883, believing Leidy had entirely abandoned the name *Trachodon*, Cope referred it to *Diclonius mirabilis*, the name it retained for many years.

Hadrosaurid discoveries continued to be made, prompted in part by the rivalry between Cope and Marsh to name and describe new species. In 1891, the prolific fossil collector John Bell Hatcher recovered two hadrosaurid skeletons from the Lance Formation of Niobrara County,

Wyoming. The next year, Marsh referred both of them to his *Claosaurus* as the new species *C. annectens*.

A similar species from Canada, *Edmontosaurus regalis*, was introduced in 1917 by Canadian paleontologist Lawrence M. Lambe, established on a complete skull and most of the skeleton found five years earlier by Levi Sternberg (one of the famous Sternberg family of fossil collectors) in the Horseshoe Canyon (then lower Edmonton) Formation, Red Deer River, Alberta.

For decades no one really bothered to sort out the Mesozoic mess that hadrosaurid taxonomy had become. It was not until 1942, in their classic monograph on North American duckbilled dinosaurs, that paleontologists Richard Swann Lull and Nelda E. Wright attempted to make a critical evaluation of these very similar animals, pointing out that some species had been based on only meager remains. Starting afresh, Lull and Wright proposed the new (and appropriate) name *Anatosaurus* (meaning "duck lizard") for the two excellent specimens referred to *Claosaurus annectens*, the new combination becoming *A. annectens*. According to Lull and Wright, other hadrosaurid material described over the years could also be referred to this species. At the same time, Lull and Wright referred the two American Museum mounted skeletons to this genus as a second species, *A. copei*. They also recognized a Canadian species *A. saskatchewanensis*, based on a skull and skeleton collected by Charles M. Sternberg in 1921 (originally described by him in 1926 as a new species of *Thespesius*) from the Frenchman Formation, Saskatchewan.

Lull and Wright accepted both *Edmontosaurus* and *Anatosaurus* as valid dinosaurian genera, distinguishing *Edmontosaurus* by its larger size, more robust muzzle and lower jaws, greater number of teeth, and also by other cranial features.

More than 30 years after Lull and Wright's monograph, yet another addition was made to the hadrosaurid bestiary. *Shantungosaurus giganteus*, a giant form closely resembling *Edmontosaurus* and founded on an incomplete skeleton from Shandong, People's Republic of China, was named and described in 1973 by Hu Cheng-Chin.

In 1975, Michael Brett-Surman examined material referred to both *Edmontosaurus* and *Anatosaurus* and found that the differences between them observed by Lull and Wright actually had to do with age and growth, with no taxonomic significance. In other words, both *Edmontosaurus* and *Anatosaurus* were separate names given to the same animal (the same situation as with *Apatosaurus* and *Brontosaurus*). According to the rules established by the International Commission of Zoological Nomenclature (or ICZN), the older name (*Edmontosaurus*) takes priority and is therefore valid. At the same time, Brett-Surman found the so-called *A. copei*, with its very long, low head, to be distinct enough to separate from the genus *Edmontosaurus*.

In 1989, Brett-Surman recognized two possibly valid species of *Edmontosaurus*, the rarer and more robust *E. regalis* and more common and gracile *E. annectens*, differences that might constitute sexual dimorphism. At the same time, Brett-Surman concluded that, with the exception of size-related features, *Shantungosaurus* cannot be distinguished from *Edmontosaurus*. Is *Shantungosaurus* simply a bigger *Edmontosaurus*? Quite possibly, although, according to Brett-Surman, a synonymy between these two cannot now be demonstrated, as only one specimen of *Shantungosaurus* has yet been published for comparison.

The following year, Michael Brett-Surman referred *A. copei* to its own genus and species, *Anatotitan copei*.

Thus, after a century and a half of naming and renaming (and, consequently, confusion), we are left with *Edmontosaurus* and *Anatotitan*, valid names for two similar yet generically distinct animals that many of us grew up knowing as one (named *Trachodon*). We are also left with a double-rooted tooth still bearing that venerable old name, but probably referable to the contemporaneous horned dinosaurs *Triceratops* or *Torosaurus*.

Why should we use correct names when the old ones are so ingrained and even revered?

Paleontology, unlike some other fields of science, is not a static discipline. New dinosaurian genera and species, new ideas and interpretations about dinosaurs and their world, are introduced by scientists all the time. We have learned to accept much of the new and reject what is outmoded or incorrect, this fact clearly reflected in recent dinosaur art.

Besides that, science in general, like any other area of study, has its rules. For scientists to communicate, both to each other and to laymen, and to best accomplish their work, they must speak a common language, one in which the terms are consistent for all. In these so-called "modern" times, when science is often a target of mistrust, even disdain and fear by the public, it is important, though opinions among scientists can vehemently differ, that certain basics, including its language, remain consistent. Petty arguments (*e.g.*, the bickering over the use of obsolete names) can fuel more anti-science sentiment, "evidence" that scientists cannot agree on anything and are therefore not to be trusted. (The long exposed "Piltdown Man" forgery is still regularly dredged up as an example of scientists misleading the public.)

All right, then, the name *Trachodon* is as extinct as any of the animals, duckbilled or horned, it has represented; still, in the hearts and memories of many of us, it may always occupy a special niche.

REMEMBERING THE FIELD MUSEUM'S HALL 38

A very special "home away from home" for me for more than 40 years was Hall 38—commonly called "the dinosaur hall" by visitors, although most of the fossil treasures it offered were non-dinosaurian—at what is now The Field Museum in Chicago.

When the hall of this, among the greatest of natural history museums, was finally closed down and its contents were moved to the other side of the building for a new and more modern display, I wanted to get my thoughts, memories and feelings about the original hall down on paper. About the time I got the idea to write an article about it, the husband-wife team of Allen A. and Diane E. Debus had recently begun publishing their own fan magazine *Dinosaur World*, inspired somewhat by *Prehistoric Times*, and for which I served as a consulting editor. The article, then simply titled "Remembering Hall 38," appeared in the fanzine's second issue in 1997.

On June 11, 1994, The Field Museum in Chicago's Grant Park area opened its new "DNA to Dinosaurs" exhibit to the general public. Like a number of other major natural history museums, The Field Museum, whose fossil displays had remained virtually unchanged since the museum first opened its doors in 1921 (an outgrowth of the old Field Columbian Museum in Jackson Park, a physically deteriorating institution that was later rebuilt to become what is today the Museum of Science and Industry), had entered the "modern" age of paleontology. This new exhibit, though featuring many specimens, displays, and art pieces that had become "old friends," now presented them in new and often dynamic ways to reflect modern paleontological knowledge and ideas.

I made sure that I was present that historic summer morning up on the museum's second floor, to be among the first non-staff visitors to walk through the newly renovated Halls 25, 26, and 29 which, in earlier years, had displayed both plant and various special exhibits. (The rather dark east wing of the second floor, facing Lake Michigan and Lakeshore Drive, had been mostly devoted to botany; indeed, this was one of the museum's least visited areas.)

Staff workers in The Field Museum's geology and exhibits departments had done an impressive job on the new display. Most of the old and familiar skeletons and other fossils were part of the new exhibit, as were some new ones. Most (unfortunately, not all) of the Charles R. Knight classic murals, painted from 1926–31, were there, albeit not in the artist's originally intended sequence, while some of them were showing signs of age and a lack of care. And yet, despite the gain in knowledge that the new exhibit offered, I could not escape the sense of loss of what had for me truly become a "home away from home."

In past years—while the institution went through such name variations as Field Museum of Natural History, Chicago Natural History Museum, back again to Field Museum of Natural History and, most recently, simply The Field Museum—most exhibits relating to geology and paleontology were displayed in the west wing of the museum's second floor, which was easily accessible via staircases at both the main (Roosevelt Road) and rear entrances.

In a way, the climb itself previewed what was to come, many of the stone steps (as well as the floors) visibly containing tiny invertebrate fossils. Both staircases were connected by the west gallery, Hall 32, which featured exhibits of Tibet and China. Three geology-based exhibit halls—Hall 34 ("physical geology"), 36 ("useful minerals"), and 37 ("fossil plants & invertebrates," including George Marchand's famous underwater dioramas)—intersected Hall 32. All of these rooms led directly to a longer one spanning the full length of the museum's west wing, Hall 38 (also known as Ernest R. Graham Hall, named after one of the museum's early Board of Trustees members), the "Hall of Fossil Vertebrates."

Memories of my first visit to Hall 38—a place I would eventually come to know and love and eventually feel I owned—are small yet significant. The monumental event occurred in 1949 or early 1950, while I was in kindergarten and not yet interested in dinosaurs. I'd been only slightly aware of dinosaurs at the time, through such media as movies and comic books. My main science-related interests back then were modern skeletons and astronomy. Many of my hours, in fact, were spent meticulously copying from books pictures of animal and human skeletons and drawing what I believed to be accurate depictions of the cosmos. When, one Sunday morning, my mother announced that our family and some friends were going to visit the (then in lower case) Field Museum, it was mainly the contemporary bones, but also the promise to see mummies (I *really* thought my mom had said "mommies"), that were the lure.

I only remember one thing about that first visit to Hall 38—looking through a glass window at a skeleton I couldn't quite figure out. The skeleton was displayed lying on a big section of earth. The bones were a brownish color, not the typical white I'd seen in the skeletons of modern day animals and people on exhibit downstairs. Furthermore, they were embedded in the ground itself and it was difficult to determine where bones ended and earth started.

My mother explained that this was the skeleton of an animal so old that its bones had "turned to stone." Somewhere about that time I was given one of those small "rock collections" that kids often receive from adults, with a piece of "petrified wood" among its separated specimens, but the concept of a "fossil" was still mostly foreign to me. During that initial visit to the hall, my mother's words made a profound impression on me, though it would not be until years later that I understood them, and later still that I would learn that the bones were those of a South American ground sloth named *Scelidodotherium*.

That first Field Museum experience was truly inspiring, and return visits, usually in the company of friends and their parents or with my Cub Scout pack, filled up many a Saturday or Sunday morning and afternoon. Numerous memories of those subsequent trips to the museum and its exhibits are vivid. Oddly, however, at least several years would pass, even as my scientific interests shifted toward fossils and prehistoric animals, before I would again enter Hall 38. Stranger still, during those years I had somehow, at least temporarily, managed to *forget* my original experience with that enigmatic brownish skeleton. For a while, then, the museum mostly meant to me such more recent displays as the skeletons of elephants, whales and apes, Egyptian mummies, stuffed animals, and shrunken heads.

The only logical explanation I can offer is that it was the very location of Hall 38 that was the culprit in keeping me separated from it for so long. The vertebrate fossil hall was on the second floor and, quite probably, my mother, Julia Glut, and the mothers of my friends did not particularly relish climbing that long flight of stairs. It was, I suppose, a very long journey that offered exhibits in which, among our group, only I may have found fascination. I vaguely remember once asking my mother what was up on the second floor and her reply being something like "nothing we'd be interested in seeing."

By 1953, my mother had shown me pictures of dinosaurs (reproductions of three Charles R. Knight murals done in the late 1920s to early '30s) in our home's *American Standard Encyclopedia*; my favorite comic book was Joe Kubert's *1,000,000 Years Ago* (which would soon change its name to *Tor*); favorite film, Ray Harryhausen's new movie *The Beast from 20,000 Fathoms*; and I was just starting to seek out books about prehistoric animals at the public library.

Around that time, with my childhood interest in extinct animals soaring, I boldly rejected the explanation that there was nothing of interest on the Field Museum's second floor and insisted we go to that mysterious world of "upstairs." I distinctly remember taking that long walk down Hall 36, passing geology exhibits of little interest to me, and, getting closer to the adjoining Hall 38, spotting the hindquarters of some gigantic animal, its darkened bones even darker in that room's dim light. Rushing ahead, I found myself gawking up at the mounted partial skeleton (only the latter half) of the dinosaur *Apatosaurus* (a specimen described by then Columbian Museum paleontologist Elmer S. Riggs in 1903, who at the same time and in the same Museum-published paper synonymized the better known *Brontosaurus* with this genus). Above and to the left of the skeleton was a very large, familiar Knight mural showing the animal as it appeared in life, lumbering toward a lake past a couple of sleeping crocodiles—one of the three pictures I had seen at home in our encyclopedia.

Looking around, seeing more darkened skeletons and also a series of similar murals (two of which, one featuring *Stegosaurus*, the other *Tyrannosaurus* charging toward *Triceratops*, which I'd also seen in that encyclopedia) filling all the upper wall space, the import finally struck me: I was standing in a room filled with the *real* bones of *real* dinosaurs, animals which, up until that time, I had only seen pictures of or read about. In that moment my life would be forever changed.

Some of my impressions of that second visit to Hall 38 will remain with me until I, like the creatures displayed in it, become extinct. I remember seeing a mounted skeleton of the giant ground sloth *Megatherium*, its massive front limbs propping the skeleton up behind a tree. Because the skeleton was big and standing up on its hind legs (suggesting the *Tyrannosaurus* depicted in my *1,000,000 Years Ago* comic book), I somewhat logically assumed it to be that of the dinosaur *Tyrannosaurus*, which, back then, I was still calling "Trynoceros" (rhyming with "rhinoceros").

Skeleton of the giant ground sloth *Megatherium americanum*, collected in Argentina in 1927 under the supervision of Elmer S. Riggs, as originally mounted in Hall 38. Courtesy The Field Museum (neg. #GEO79522).

Near the *Apatosaurus* skeleton were several mounted leg bones (belonging to *Brachiosaurus* and *Camarasaurus*, the latter then called *Morosaurus*, these specimens all having been described long ago by Riggs). One glass case displayed a set of the famous dinosaur models sculpted around 1915 by Smithsonian Institution paleontologist Charles Whitney Gilmore. And yes, I was reunited with my old forgotten, "turned to stone" friend *Seclidotherium*.

From that moment on, Hall 38 was always the first place we'd go when we visited the museum, sometimes on a weekly basis. Of course, the mummies, "cavemen," stuffed animals (especially Bushman the gorilla, whom I'd seen many times while he was still alive and ruling Chicago's Lincoln Park Zoo) and other exhibits also continued to hold my interest, but Hall 38 was now the main reason for going.

Hall 38 was succinctly described in the museum's *General Guide* book (1955 edition, published "in house") thusly:

The fossil fishes, amphibians, reptiles, birds, and mammals exhibited in this hall are arranged, in general, according to their biological relationships and illustrate how the various vertebrate forms had developed. The entire geological sequence of life is indicated in a series of mural paintings of the processes of earth formation and of animals and plants in their natural surroundings. At one end of the hall is a life-size reproduction of a forest of the Coal (Carboniferous) period. At the other end of the hall are three restoration groups: extinct three-toed horses, extinct mammals known as Titanotheres, and a Neanderthal caveman family of Europe. Introductory exhibits illustrate how bones are buried, preserved, and found.

Among the hall's petrified treasures were skeletons of various primitive reptiles, pelycosaurs (such as three-dimensional skeletons of the sail-backed *Dimetrodon* and *Edaphosaurus*), a number of dinosaur specimens (including a nice skull of the ceratopsian *Triceratops* collected by Riggs, skulls of the hadrosaur *Edmontosaurus* and ceratopsian *Anchiceratops*, and a skeleton of the primitive ceratopsian *Protoceratops* with eggs collected during the American Museum of Natural History's expeditions to the Gobi Desert led by Roy Chapman Andrews in the 1920s), marine reptiles, pterosaurs, birds, and mammals (including ground sloths and glyptodont collected by Riggs in Argentina). The hall's woolly mammoth skeleton, which had originally resided at the nearby Chicago Academy of Sciences, was distinguished as the first mammoth specimen to be mounted in North America.

At one end of the hall, a full-scale diorama of a "Coal Age" forest, complete with animal life, had been recreated so realistically that looking at it from behind its glass barrier was almost like gazing through a window to the past. At the opposite end of the hall were other life-sized displays, including three different kinds of families: Tiny primitive three-toed horses called *Mesohippus*, the giant rhino-like "titanotheres" of the genus *Brontops*, and a group of Neandertals.

There were also, of course, those great Charles R. Knight murals, numbering 28 in all, which the artist would always regard as his greatest body of work. Knight had designed these murals so that, while each stood alone as both a superb piece of art and a realistic re-creation of a scene from Earth's prehistory, they also, taken together, constituted one colossal masterpiece, with one picture complementing another. At either end of the hall were scenes done in the triptyc format—three individual paintings which, when viewed together in the intended sequence, made yet another scene. (Many of the cases also displayed small, more recently done paintings by museum staff artist John Conrad Hansen.)

For those visitors desiring to take home something of Hall 38 besides memories, including Knight's artwork, the museum provided a few souvenirs, most notably picture postcards. For a while, from about 1930 through the later 1950s, a set of 14 black-and-white postcard reproductions ("printed by the photo-gravure process") of Knight's murals could be purchased, complete with an envelope to hold them all, for the dinosaurian price of 30 cents.

Over the years, other postcards, some in black and white, others in color, could be purchased in the museum's book and gift shops, reproducing a few of the more popular Knight murals (*Apatosaurus, Stegosaurus,* Irish "Elk" [actually deer], Rancho La Brea Tar scene, *Protoceratops,* and *Tyrannosaurus/Triceratops*), as well as such full-sized dioramas as the Coal Age swamp, ancient horses, *Brontops* group and the Neandert al mother. (During the Fifties, the museum also made available a large library of 35mm slides, mostly reproducing both the Knight and Hansen paintings.)

Though postcard subjects, formats, and sizes changed over the years, Hall 38 itself would undergo relatively minor alterations during the years following my early visits. Those sauropod limb bones, as well as a series of *Brachiosaurus* vertebrae exhibited in a nearby case, would be removed by the early 1950s and put into the museum's "oversized bone room" for storage (the *Brachiosaurus* remains brought back for public display in the museum's spacious Stanley Field Hall during the 1990s). Doomed to storage-room limbo would be the suite of Gilmore sculptures. Some of Knight's murals would grow darker after years of dust accumulation or would otherwise show signs of wear and damage. Museum staff artist Maidi Wiebe would add some new small paintings to the exhibit cases, including a *Protoceratops* standing bipedally over a nest of eggs.

In 1956, two "new" dinosaur skeletons—a theropod *Gorgosaurus* (which would later be re-labeled *Albertosaurus,* but which could turn out to be *Daspletosaurus*) and hadrosaur *Lambeosaurus*—would be displayed at the museum (then going under the Chicago Natural History Museum name). However, these skeletons, the meat-eater posed looming over the downed duckbill, would never grace Hall 38; instead, they were given a more prestigious home in Stanley Field Hall. A diorama, with figures sculpted by Maidi Wiebe, reflected the scene as portrayed by the posed skeletons. In later years, this miniature scene would find its way into Hall 38.

One of the most significant improvements in Hall 38 was made in the later 1950s, reportedly as a result of a chance meeting in the gallery between a little boy and none other than museum president Stanley Field himself. Field had been adamant about having an honest relationship with the public, displaying only *real* fossil remains, not casts, and avoiding composite skeletons. Therefore, he had insisted that the museum's *Apatosaurus* skeleton, though only about half complete, be displayed as is (although the hind limbs were not part of the original specimen). As the story goes, Field noticed that this child appeared to be puzzled by the skeleton. When Field asked the child what was the matter, the boy replied with something like, "Gee, mister, is this the front end or the back?"

Almost immediately, Stanley Field was putting into operation his plan to display the complete *Apatosaurus* skeleton, with elements from other specimens, as well as casts, filling in for the missing parts. As the skull of *Apatosaurus* was not yet known, a cast from an original Carnegie Museum of Natural History specimen of a *Camarasaurus* skull, previously displayed in a nearby case, completed the mount. One April day in 1958, the reconstructed *Apatosaurus* skeleton was "unveiled" to the public, its name on the exhibit's label changed to the more popular though incorrect *Brontosaurus*. (Some two decades later, the mount would finally possess the correct skull, courtesy of another Carnegie cast.)

I cannot overemphasize how significant Hall 38 was in my life. In a way, I felt that the hall and everything in it belonged to me, so strongly, in fact, that I resented when things got moved, removed, or replaced. Needless to add, it was devastating to hear, sometime in the early 1990s, that Hall 38 was going to be dismantled forever and its contents moved to new accommodations on the other side of the building.

It seems as if the decision to bring Hall 38 to its extinction was made without a great deal of fanfare. One day, upon a visit to The Field Museum's Geology Department, several of the staff members told me that the new halls were already in the development stages. Shortly after that announcement, Field Museum paleontologist John J. Flynn took me on a tour through what would soon be the new halls. Bones were lying on the floor and a new Coal Age forest—a walk-through display, this time—was already recognizable in its early stages of construction. The tour over, I took a nostalgic stroll back to Hall 38. Part of it had already been partitioned off, while behind that barrier the *Apatosaurus* skeleton was already undergoing dismantling. In a way, it was to me as if someone had begun swinging a demolition ball at my own home.

The change-over took place efficiently and rather rapidly. Subsequent visits would reveal fewer and fewer of the old hall's occupants still in the room. Before long Hall 38 would be storing things having nothing to do with fossils or paleontology.

As the new exhibit would be displayed in a number of halls rather than just one, the museum's fossil treasures could be grouped together according to their age or classification. For example, all the specimens from the Mesozoic Era occupied a single hall. The fossil mammals, including the ground sloths (Riggs's *Megatherium* now remounted in a vertical pose that showed off its truly awesome height), mammoth, and the full-scale *Brontops* models, no longer had to share their space with dinosaurs and mosasaurs. Particularly effective was the museum's grouping together of the skeletons of a number of Permian period reptiles and amphibians — like the fin-backed *Dimetrodon* and *Edaphosaurus*, and squatty *Eryops* — each of which, in Hall 38, had formerly occupied its own glass case.

The new fossil halls on the museum's east side are very successful, as well they should be. They have been expertly designed and offer to the public up-to-date information about the extinct animals and plants which are represented by the fossils displayed. My old colossal friend, the composite *Apatosaurus* skeleton, newly mounted in a more dynamic pose, now looks at a window toward the lake (not unlike its fleshed-out counterpart in the Charles Knight mural). The dinosaur's majestic, lighted form can be glimpsed from cars passing The Field Museum at night along Lakeshore Drive.

Yet, if I close my eyes, it takes no effort to remember what it was like gazing up at those darkened, stone-like bones for the first time one day in Hall 38 so many decades ago.

In Search
of *Spinosaurus*

The giant long-spined, meat-eating dinosaur *Spinosaurus* has
long been a popular one among people interested in extinct animals—despite the fact that, for almost a century, no one has really
known what this intriguing creature looked like, and that the original fossil specimens upon which the genus was based have long
since "vanished."

The following article—in its original, only slightly shorter form,
and titled "The Search for *Spinosaurus*"—originally appeared in
the fifth issue (1998) of *Dinosaur World*. It was printed therein as a
"lead in" essay to a lengthy interview conducted with invertebrate
and vertebrate paleontologist Jack Bowman Bailey, who had
recently published his findings regarding *Spinosaurus* and other
dinosaurs possessing long dorsal spines. I was invited to write the
piece while enjoying a telephone conversation with *Dinosaur World*
editor and publisher Allen A. Debus, during which I'd mentioned
to him a few ideas about long-spined dinosaurs that coincidentally
happened to be similar to Dr. Bailey's.

Although this article is essentially a popular one, it follows the
practices used in technical journals regarding references; that is,
dates appearing in parentheses and following a person's name cite
specific references listed in the bibliography following the essay.

The first time I ever encountered *Spinosaurus*—the generic name
given to a possibly 50-foot long theropod dinosaur, apparently bigger

than the famous *Tyrannosaurus rex*, and distinguished by long neural spines—was approximately in 1956.

I was attending my sixth grade of grammar school in Chicago, and for several years had long been intensely interested in things prehistoric. Much of my time was spent haunting the local public library (the original Hild branch on Lincoln Avenue on Chicago's North Side, long since relocated to across the street), scouring its rarely changing collection of books in the "science" and "animals" sections, desperately trying to find some text I hadn't seen before, or already checked out many times over. By that time, I was beginning to outgrow the standard inventory of volumes about extinct animals available in the second-floor children's section of the library, but was still too young to own the adult card required to take out books from the general readership sections on the main floor. Fortunately, my mother was of the correct age and possessed the necessary library card, and through her I was able to take home—for two full weeks at a time (plus two additional "renewal" weeks)—all the "adult" books I could hunt down and mentally devour.

It was during one of my expeditions through the first-floor "adult" stacks that I discovered *Vertebrate Paleontology*, by Alfred Sherwood Romer (1945). Of course, I was not then aware that this book was a classic "benchmark" text on the subject. My main interest was in the "Classification of Vertebrates" section in the back of the book, primarily because of its listings of all known (at the time, anyway) dinosaur genera. One tantalizing name, listed among the Theropoda (the major grouping of carnivorous dinosaurs) was *Spinosaurus*.

Even more intriguing was the brief description of this "critter" (a word Romer sometimes used in correspondence when informally discussing dinosaurs and other extinct animals) the author gave of *Spinosaurus*, which he noted lived in Egypt during the Cretaceous period, the last of three divisions of the Mesozoic Era: "This large flesh-eater is poorly known but was remarkable in that the neural spines were greatly elongated, rather after the fashion of some of the Permian pelycosaurs ... some spines had a length of about 6 feet." Unfortunately, Romer did not accompany his short description with an illustration of the beast, either as a life restoration or skeleton.

I read Romer's words several times over: "...large flesh-eater ... neural spines ... greatly elongated ... pelycosaurs..." Immediately my youthful imagination conjured up the fantastic image of some huge bipedal *Tyrannosaurus*-like reptile sporting a large dorsal sail—in effect, a creature resembling the much smaller Permian-age pelycosaur *Dimetrodon*, only walking on its hind legs.

Remember that this was the middle 1950s, a time yet decades away from the discovery of most of the many unusual and sometimes bizarre theropod dinosaurs that are so well known to us today. It would be many years before theropod names like *Diplophosaurus, Carnotaurus,* and *Deinonychus* would be common ones in the dinosaurian lexicon, familiar "household" words even among young children. Cranial crests, bull-like horns, sickle claws, and other such often spectacular features were still unsuspected in these animals. Indeed, excluding such rare exceptions as the nose-horned *Ceratosaurus,* large theropods like *Allosaurus, Megalosaurus,* and *Tyrannosaurus* (such features as size, arm length, and number of fingers notwithstanding) tended to look—at least superficially to us young readers of dinosaur books—generally somewhat alike. To suddenly discover a big carnivorous dinosaur having a body possibly adorned with something as spectacular as a large *Dimetrodon*-like dorsal sail was truly special.

Speaking for myself (and also recalling the attitudes and opinions of some fellow young dinosaur enthusiasts of the era—that is the Fifties, not the Mesozoic), dinosaurs and other kinds of prehistoric animals (*e.g.,* giant ground sloths and cave bears), for that matter, seemed to be particularly appealing, or "sexy" using today's jargon, if they walked upright on two legs rather than down on all fours. For some reason unknown to me, perhaps because modern reptiles (excluding snakes) and most mammals are quadrupeds, a prehistoric reptile seemed to be "more prehistoric" if stomping around or reared up on its hind feet.

Perhaps this notion has some long-term, and most likely forgotten, connection going back more than a century, when Joseph Leidy (1858), curator of the Academy of Natural Sciences of Philadelphia, originally interpreted the duckbilled *Hadrosaurus,* the first dinosaur known in North America from substantial fossil remains and the second to be named on that continent, as a bipedal kangaroo-like rather than quadrupedal rhinoceros-like animal, as earlier but similar forms like *Iguanodon* had been incorrectly envisioned.

How exciting it was to see, in the occasional children's book (*e.g., The Book of Prehistoric Animals,* by Raymond L. Ditmars and Helene Carter, 1935), the sauropod *"Helopus"* (later renamed *Euhelopus*) standing tall on its hind legs, its very long neck proudly raised high. It was "neat" or "cool" to see, in some fanciful comic strip or book, animated cartoon, coloring book, or science-fiction movie, an otherwise quadrupedal prehistoric reptile—a plated stegosaur, horned ceratopsian, or long-necked sauropod, for example—surprisingly walking upright like a *Tyrannosaurus* or *Allosaurus.*

For example, stop-motion effects artist Ray Harryhausen's (1972) imaginary "Rhedosaurus," in the science-fiction movie *The Beast from 20,000 Fathoms* (Warner Bros., 1953), was a wonderfully designed quadrupedal creature, with its theropod-like head and spiked neck, back, and tail. Through Harryhausen's animation artistry, the enormous prehistoric reptile made its relentless way—walking on four legs—through the panic-stricken streets of New York City. Yet, one of the "Beast's" most memorable bits of destructive business in the film, for me and also some of my friends, was the scene in which the animal reared up on its hind legs and smashed through a downtown Manhattan building. In fact, this image was so powerful, when the film was first released, that more than one of my friends left the theater insisting that the "Beast" had walked on its two hind legs throughout the entire movie. Oddly enough, some kids I knew at the time were certain that the "Beast" was not the tuatara-like giant reptile that spent almost all of its screen time on all fours, but an actual *Tyrannosaurus* adorned with large and pointy dorsal spines.

As a child I made my own contributions to getting graviportal creatures, that should have stayed down on all fours, raised up on their hind legs. In those 1950s days, when dinosaur toys and models were rarer than real dinosaur bones in most museum collections, I sometimes supplemented my desire to see bipedal reptiles by propping up some toy lizard or alligator, or by posing a crudely sculpted clay model of a *Triceratops* or other four-footed creature, to stand up like a theropod.

By the time I first read about *Spinosaurus* in Professor Romer's book, I had become quite familiar with pelycosaurs like the meat-eating *Dimetrodon*. The latter—as well as its herbivorous contemporary, the fin-backed pelycosaur *Edaphosaurus*—provided ubiquitous images gracing just about every children's book about prehistoric animals published during the 1940s through 1950s (*e.g.*, the popular *Animals of Yesterday* by Bertha Morris Parker, 1954). Certainly, *Dimetrodon* was an appealing creature with that prominent sail adorning its back. But remove that sail and, at least in my uneducated mind, what remained was something looking mostly like a lizard or crocodile. (Proving this observation, lizards and alligators, since the silent days of motion pictures and for many years through the sound era, have been outfitted with rubber fins, horns, crests, and other exotic appendages in order to pass them off as prehistoric reptiles; see Glut, 1980.)

No doubt, there were desires in my unenlightened mind, as well as in those of other young enthusiasts of prehistoric animals of the era, to see our tyrannosaurs and other giant theropods with strange ornamentations like horns and dorsal spikes—like the sometimes more spectacular, though inaccurate, prehistoric monsters of the movies—and also more lizard-like animals such as *Dimetrodon* parading about on two legs. *Spinosaurus*, as least via the image conveyed by Romer's short but intriguing text description, seemed to satisfy both of these yearnings.

By 1957 (since 1953), I had already written and illustrated my own share of crude but passionate amateur "books" about prehistoric animals, the latest of which was titled simply *The Dinosauria*. The text, produced by a manual typewriter, included a paraphrased version of Romer's description of *Spinosaurus*. Like Romer, I did not include an illustration of the animal, my unstated excuse being that I still had no idea of how *Spinosaurus* really looked.

One eventful afternoon of that year the mystery of *Spinosaurus* at last seemed to be solved. About a year previously I had begun to visit, sometimes on a weekly basis, the third-floor Geology Department of the Chicago Natural History Museum (now renamed The Field Museum), almost always on Thursdays (when admission was free) upon getting out of school. While up there, I spent most of my time bedeviling the staff scientists and preparators with my questions about dinosaurs, fossils, and extinct life in general. During one such Thursday of 1957, to help satisfy my naïve desire to acquire a picture (*i.e.*, life restoration) of every known dinosaur (a quest inspired by a scene in *The Beast from 20,000 Fathoms* in which an attempt is made to identify the titled creature by going through batches of illustrations), Dr. Rainer Zangerl, the museum's curator of fossil reptiles, sat me down in his office amid a stack of paleontology books, most of them, as I recall, printed in foreign languages.

Among these prized publications was the fifth volume of Jean Piveteau's (1955) now-classic series of tomes grouped under the overall title *Traité de Paléontologie*. The book was written in French, a language I could neither speak nor read; but, to my delight, it contained hundreds of pictures. One of these illustrations—in the section titled "Dinosauriens," coauthored by Albert F. de Lapparent and René Lavocat—popped out at me as if I had just stumbled upon some prehistoric Holy Grail. It depicted an upright, *Tyrannosaurus*-like skeleton possessing very long back spines, not unlike those of the mounted *Dimetrodon* skeleton on display in this same museum's Hall 38, the "Hall of Fossil Vertebrates," down on the second floor. Among the French writing in the picture's caption was the identifying name *Spinosaurus aegyptiacus*. Although I wasn't aware of it then, the illustration was Lapparent's and Lavocat's largely hypothetical skeletal reconstruction of this dinosaur, which German Professor Ernst Stromer had named and described back in 1915. Nor was I cognizant, at the time, of how little original skeletal material was actually known of this animal—mostly part of the lower jaw, some neck and tail vertebrae, and a number of those characteristic elongated neural spines—and consequently incorporated into this first full-skeleton reconstruction, and that the actual fossil remains had unfortunately been destroyed during air strikes made by Allied bombers during World War II. (In later years, Lapparent's and Lavocat's *Spinosaurus* skeletal reconstruction was reprinted in various publications—*e.g.*, Glut 1972, 1982—and would be the basis of inspiration for a number of life restorations now believed to be incorrect.)

Nevertheless, the quest to unmask this enigmatic dinosaur seemed truly to be over, and only after about a year or so of searching.

Foolishly believing that I, at last, knew precisely what *Spinosaurus* looked like, I eventually made a stop-motion clay model of the creature and, adding a Godzilla-like fiery breath, starred it in a science-fantasy sequence of a 1960 amateur movie (ostensibly made as a high-school science fair biology project) titled *The Age of Reptiles*. Except for the dorsal sail, my *Spinosaurus* resembled Godzilla more than it did the actual dinosaur it purported to be, or even a *Tyrannosaurus* for that matter.

Not until the mid–1970s, while working on my book *The New Dinosaur Dictionary* (1982), did I discover that *Spinosaurus* was not yet well known enough from the fossil evidence to attempt any reasonably accurate life restoration. Thanks to vertebrate paleontologist Robert A. Long, I was able to see a rather faded photograph of the now lost-forever holotype spines. Through Rob, I learned that *Spinosaurus*, unlike the vast majority of known theropods, might have been a quadrupedal animal, its forelimbs perhaps relatively long, and that its hands were three-fingered. There were, as I would later see, some superficial resemblances between what was known of the snout and jaws, with an atypically greater number of teeth, with those of crocodilians. I also began to hear unofficial rumors from a few paleontologists that *Spinosaurus* might not even be a dinosaur, but instead some kind of huge crocodile-like reptile. If that were true, dashed would be all of my childhood desires to see either that cool, fin-backed tyrannosaur-type dinosaur, a bipedal *Dimetrodon*, or some weird hybrid of both.

When I asked artist friend William Stout to do a good number of life restorations for *The New Dinosaur Dictionary*, I requested that he include among them, though it was only poorly known from fossil material, *Spinosaurus*. Marrying his best educated guesses with what was actually known of the animal, somewhat based on Lapparent's and Lavocat's reconstruction, Bill produced a fine and dramatic life restoration—with a sail-back—that went on to become a kind of standard for this dinosaur.

Still, there seemed to be something not quite right with the *Dimetrodon*-like fin-back approach. It was easily noticeable that the long neural spines of *Spinosaurus* were quite different from those of the non-dinosaurian reptile *Dimetrodon*. According to Lapparent's and Lavocat's 1934 drawing (and from what I'd remembered of the photograph of the holotype spines), the spines of *Spinosaurus* seemed to be rather robust and flat looking in side view, becoming significantly wider distally. Contrarily, those of *Dimetrodon* were more rounded and relatively much longer, becoming increasingly more narrow toward their summits.

In 1976, French paleontologist Phillipe Taquet named and described a new dinosaur from Niger, a large ornithopod (one of a group of mostly bipedal plant-eaters) named *Ouranosaurus*. There was plenty of time for Bill Stout to do a life restoration of this interesting creature. Unlike *Spinosaurus*, this herbivore was known from a well-preserved, nearly complete skeleton. Like *Spinosaurus*, the new dinosaur had long neural spines, which were robust and expanded distally, therefore quite different from the long, narrow spines of *Dimetrodon*. After agreeing to do the picture of *Ouranosaurus*, Bill told me that, through the paleontological grapevine, he had heard comments from a number of workers that the long spines of this dinosaur might have supported withers or a kind of hump, as in some long-spined mammals, rather than a sail or fin. By inference, then, might not this idea very well also apply to *Spinosaurus*?

As *The New Dinosaur Dictionary* was my book, Bill graciously asked me how I would prefer having *Ouranosaurus* restored—as having a fin-back or a hump. Recalling some of the mounted skeletons of certain long-spined mammals I had seen in various museums, I told Bill it might be interesting to portray *Ouranosaurus* both ways, assuming that at least one of them would be correct. A subsequent examination of a mounted skeleton of *Bison antiquus*, a large Pleistocene mammal with exceptionally long neural spines resembling those of *Ouranosaurus*, displayed at the George C. Page Museum of La Brea Discoveries in Los Angeles, indicated to me that Bill's "humpbacked" version was more likely the correct one, as I could hardly imagine a sail-backed buffalo.

Now, paleontologist Jack Bowman Bailey, of the Museum of Geology, Western Illinois University, has published a study of various dinosaurs possessing elongated neural spines (*e.g.*, *Spinosaurus*, *Ouranosaurus*, the hadrosaur *Hypacrosaurus*, the giant theropod *Acrocanthosaurus*, etc.), comparing them with other long-spined animals, including certain pelycosaurs and mammals. Dr. Bailey has stated that he was inspired by various sources, including Bill Stout's original *Ouranosaurus* restoration in *The New Dinosaur Dictionary*. It was Bailey's conclusion that these dinosaurs were not fin-backed, but had humps, the spines supporting muscles and ligaments employed in efficient long-distance locomotion.

As *Spinosaurus* is now believed to be related to *Baryonyx*, an English theropod described by Alan J. Charig and Angela C. Milner (1986, 1990, 1997) as having relatively long forelimbs and possibly having been capable of at least sometimes assuming a quadrupedal pose, earlier ideas that *Spinosaurus* was able to walk on all fours may not be incorrect. Furthermore, *Baryonyx* possesses a skull with snout and jaws resembling both those of *Spinosaurus* and crocodilians, and with approximately twice the number of teeth of most typical carnivorous dinosaurs. *Baryonyx* also has a relatively long neck; this, along with the other above-mentioned features, suggested that this dinosaur may have been a fish-eater, spending much of its time on river banks, coming down on all fours to catch its watery prey.

During these many years since Professor Stromer first named and described this rare and somewhat mysterious dinosaur, *Spinosaurus* has intrigued both scientists, artists, and lay persons alike. Even toys and sculptures of this dinosaur have been offered for sale, although these, like the illustrations of *Spinosaurus* made in the past, have been largely hypothetical.

However, more information has resurfaced in recent years concerning *Spinosaurus* than had accumulated ever before. Dale A. Russell (1996), a paleontologist formerly with the Canadian Museum of Nature, Ottawa, and currently at the North Carolina State Museum of Natural Sciences, in Raleigh, recently described a second species of *Spinosaurus*, which he named *S. maroccanus*, its distinguishing features including a relatively longer and more slender neck than previously suspected in the genus. Perhaps *Spinosaurus* was—like *Baryonyx* may have been—primarily a fish-eater that fed while in a quadrupedal pose.

Furthermore, in early 1998, University of Chicago paleontologist Paul C. Sereno returned from Niger with a vast treasury of dinosaur fossils weighing in the tons, much of this material reportedly belonging to spinosaurids, such as the new genus *Suchomimus*.

Perhaps in the near future, following more than 80 years of imagining and guessing, paleoartists will be able to show with reasonable accuracy how *Spinosaurus*—among the most unusual and largest of all known carnivorous dinosaurs—appeared during life. No doubt the result will not be the sail-backed *Tyrannosaurus* or bipedal *Dimetrodon* many of us conjured up in the fantasies of our youth, indeed, perhaps not the animal some of us wanted it to be, but it will be *Spinosaurus* nonetheless—this time, for real.

References

Charig, Alan J., and Angela C. Milner, 1986, *Baryonyx*, a remarkable new thero-pod dinosaur: *Nature* 324: 359–361.

_____, 1990, "The systematic position of *Baryonyx walkeri*, in the light of Gau-thier's reclassification of the Theropoda in: Kenneth Carpenter and Philip J. Currie, editors, *Dinosaur Systematics: Approaches and Perspectives*. Cambridge, New York and Melbourne: Cambridge University Press, 127–140.

_____, 1997, *Baryonyx walkeri*, a fish-eating dinosaur from the Wealden of Sur-rey: *Bulletin of The Natural History Museum, London* (Geology) 53 (1): 11–70.

Ditmars, Raymond L., and Helene Carter, 1935. *The Book of Prehistoric Animals*. Philadelphia: J. B. Lippincott Company, 64 pages.

Glut, Donald F., 1972, *The Dinosaur Dictionary*. Secaucus, New Jersey: Citadel Press, 218 pages.

_____, 1980, *The Dinosaur Scrapbook*. Secaucus, New Jersey: Citadel Press, 320 pages.

_____, 1982, *The New Dinosaur Dictionary*. Secaucus, New Jersey: Citadel Press, 288 pages.

Harryhausen, Ray, 1972, *Film Fantasy Scrapbook*. Cranbury, New Jersey: A. S. Barnes and Company, 118 pages.

Lapparent, Albert F. de, and René Lavocat, 1955, Dinosauriens, in: Jean Piveteau, editor, *Traité de Paléontologie*. Paris: Masson and Cie, 785–962.

Leidy, Joseph, 1858, Remarks concerning *Hadrosaurus: Proceedings of the Academy of Natural Sciences of Philadelphia*, pp. 215–218.

Parker, Berta Morris, 1954, *Animals of Yesterday*. Evanston, Illinois: Row, Peterson and Company, 36 pages.

Romer, Alfred Sherwood, 1945, *Vertebrate Paleontology*. Chicago; University of Chicago Press, 722 pages (2nd edition).

Russell, Dale A., 1996, Isolated dinosaur bones from the Middle Cretaceous of the Tafilalt, Morocco. *Bulletin du Museum national d'Histoire naturelle, Paris*, ser. 4 (18), Section C, nos. 2–3, pp. 309–402.

Stromer, Ernst, 1915, Ergebnisse der Forschungsreisen Prof. E. Stromer in den Wüsten Ägyptens. II. Wirbeltierreste der Baharije-Stufe (unterstes Ceno-man). III. Das Original des Theropoden *Spinosaurus aegyptiacus* n. g. n. sp.: *Abhandlungen der Bayerischen Akademie der Wissenschaften*, 18 (3), pp. 1–32.

_____, 1934, Ergebnisse der Forschungsreisen Prof. E. Stromer in den Wüsten Ägyptens. II: Wirbeltierreste der Baharije-Stufe (unterstes Cenoman). 13. Dinosauria: *Ibid.*, 22, pp. 1–79.

Taquet, Phillipe, 1976, Géologie et Paléontologie du Gisement de Gadoufaoua (Aptien du Niger): *Cahiers de Paléontologie*. Paris: Editions du Centre National de la Recherche Scientifique, 191 pages.

FOSSIL FOOLERY

Strangely enough, this piece began as an April Fool's Day prank posted over the Internet, subsequently evolving into a text piece. In a way the whole matter reflected my own admittedly old-fashioned, yes, even "dinosaurian" reaction to so many people's dependence on computers and their addiction to the Internet, specifically to dinosaur-related websites and chatrooms.

Like the previous article in this collection, the hoax involved *Spinosaurus*, but also another giant long-spined dinosaur, the recently named and described spinosaurid *Suchomimus*, and ... no, that would be giving it away prematurely.

The joke was launched over the Internet the morning of April 1st, 1999, precisely one minute after midnight. For the sake of credibility, the text was posted by Diane E. Debus, wife and cohort of Allen A. Debus, one of the publishers of the fan journal *Dinosaur World*. It was presented as if it were a real item submitted to Al by an anonymous dinosaur fan (or "dinophile"). The plan was to let the joke play itself out. To maintain its integrity, all pre-requested responses were also to be posted on April 1. The gag would then be finally revealed, with all of its hidden secrets exposed, in a future article by Al or me, to be published in one of the dinosaur fanzines.

The text of the joke was posted by Al, who, upon my suggestion, accepted no responsibility for it. "Hi, folks. What do you think of this puzzle?" Al wrote:

> Someone named the "Masked Dinologist" mailed this note to me anonymously, thinking perhaps we would print it in the letters column of a dino-fanzine I'm involved with. Personally I don't believe a word of it, but you can all ponder his ideas about "this Stromerosuchus." Has anyone else heard about this discovery? According to him, seems like some of you may have. The

Masked Dinologist's note is quoted verbatim below. Anyone know who this could be? Take care, enjoy, and in case you're wondering, no, I am not the "Masked Dinologist."

Al then graciously agreed to write up this exposé—actually, making it part of a more inclusive survey of fossil-related hoaxes in general that have bedeviled scientists and laymen alike for more than a century—including in it the actual text that was leaked into cyberspace, but also my confess-all response explaining all the hows and whys of the joke (the latter constituting the second part of the text that follows below). Al's piece was eventually published as "Fossil Foolers," a take-off on his *Dinosaur World* column "Fossil Fillers," in the 37th issue (1999) of the fan magazine *Prehistoric Times*.

The first part of the piece that follows is the actual word-for-word text of the article that I wrote for the Internet screens, its awkward fan-writer's style, misspellings, and incorrect grammar left intact. The second part is a somewhat revised and expanded version of my personal response, the original of which was included as a sidebar to Al Debus's article.

As it turned out, while "Fossil Foolers" was being proof-read by paleontologist Kenneth Carpenter, Ken graciously pointed out to Al Debus that "Stromerosuchus" is actually what is known in scientific nomenclature as a *preoccupied* name, having been long ago assigned to a Late Cretaceous crocodile from North Africa. That being the case, my generic name "Stromerosuchus" should properly be renamed ... perhaps "Eustromerosuchus," translated as "true Stromerosuchus," or better yet "Dinomimus," meaning "Dino[saur] mimic." To my knowledge, neither of these replacement names has yet been given to any prehistoric creature, dinosaurian, crocodilian, or otherwise. The specific name "ornatus," of course, would remain the same.

At the 1998 meeting of The Society of Vertebrate Paleontology in Salt Lake City, I overheard some really cool discussions among some very famous paleontologists (in the lobby, at social events, the auction, *etc.*) regarding Spinosaurids. The discussions were sparked by some recently published articles about Spinosaurids (like Suchomimus), but mainly by a revelation made at the meeting (see below). Everything was supposed to be "top secret" until all the work was written up and published in a journal at some future date (while we true dino-lovers have to wait, as usual). But luckily I'd brought along a small cassette recorder!

Paleontologists from Germany told some really amazed American and Canadian theropod experts this: Prof. Ernest Stromer, who named Spinosaurus in 1915, really collected more of this unusual animal than shown in all the old pictures. But he never found time to work on this additional material. For years these fossil bones stayed jacketed up in Munich, even as Germany found itself in a second world war. In 1940, anticipating a possible air strike of Munich, Stromer wisely sent these unopened jackets to a Herr C. Nagle, an anthropologist friend at the University of Ingolstadt. So, when Allied planes bombed Munich, not all of the Spino type specimen got destroyed. In 1960, these long-forgotten jackets were "rediscovered." Only recently were the jackets finally opened and their contents prepared and studied.

Remarkably, there were enough "new" bones to fill in gaps, so for the first time ever, a SCIENTIFICALLY ACCURATE reconstruction of the skeleton of Spinosaurus could be made. Even more exciting, some jackets contained fossils of a NEW KIND of animal, which Stromer had identified on the jackets only as "Spinosaurus C."

I know, Spino and all the other Spinosaurids are supposed to be theropods with crocodile type features (long snout, more teeth, *etc.*) or, as someone recently put it, "dinosaurs trying to be crocodiles." These "new" fossils, though, reveal quite the opposite to be true! In an upcoming article (which probably won't be out for at least a year!), a combined group of theropod and fossil croc experts are going to prove that Spinosaurus and all other Spinosaurids are NOT DINOS at all, but a group of derived "crocs trying to be dinos." In other words, all the old ideas about these animals are wrong! The authors will say that dino-synapamorphies previously seen in Spinosaurids are either 1) plesiamorphs also found in primitive archosaurs, or 2) wishful thinking, as Spinosaurids have always been ASSUMED to be dinos.

Looking back at the old pictures, the new skeletal reconstruction of Spinosaurus is a letdown. (I managed to glimpse a rough sketch made by one of the German scientists.) Turns out that all Spinosaurids (including Spinosaurus, Baryonyx & Suchomimus) walked on all fours. And Spinosaurus's skeleton really looks mostly like a giant alligator with long back spines. (By the way, the paleontologists I tape-recorded agreed that Spino's spines supported a cool Dimetrodon-like sail, not that ugly "hump" recently imagined by that newcomer Bailey.)

Far more interesting, especially for paleo-artists and sculptors, is the so-called "Spinosaurus C." It's a big Spinosaurid to be named (and frankly, I don't see the harm in giving out names before they're "official"; I mean, let's lighten up already!) ... Stromerosuchus ornatus, meaning "Stromer's ornate crocodile." It'll be so named because of its two forward-directed horns, one over each eye, and the single rows of sharp spines that run along the body on either side of the back sail. The Stromero sail, by the way, is about twice as high as Sucho's and half that of Spino. (This critter should make a great toy or model kit!)

Originally, of course, Spinosaurids were classified as dinos. Now we're to be told they're actually a group of prehistoric crocs linking up the primitive Protosuchus (check out the old Burian painting) with the huge Phobosuchus (which some stuffy paleontologists now insist on calling Deinosuchus; will this "renaming" never end?) of Upper Cretaceous times. (And let's be honest, how many of us non-pros hadn't already noticed the similarities in the snouts of Phobo, Spino, Bary and now Sucho?)

OK, I know this kind of info is supposed to stay confidential until all the research is done and the article comes out. To be honest, I did hold back for months. I was afraid I might get into trouble, as I was seen hanging around those discussions and we all wore name tags (and my name frequently turns up in dino-zine lettercols). But then I thought, hey, ever hear of Free Speech? And the Freedom of Information Act? Last time I looked, this was still the USA. Does Free Speech apply to everything but dino-info? I DON'T think so!! It's about time the high & mighty "real" scientists stop sitting on and, yes, hording their precious data, sometimes for years, while those of us who TRULY LOVE dinos must wait and wonder about what's scientifically accurate or not. Besides, this is ONLY about fossil crocs, NOT dinos—and in a year or so, it'll all be old news anyway.

Listen up, dino-lovers! I've been real careful not to name names (hint: the paleo-artist illustrating the article isn't from the USA). And I haven't given away the (let's face it, boring) "details" (the apamorphies, *etc.*). Just the more interesting stuff like the name Stromerosuchus, how Spinosaurids really looked and the fact that these animals AREN'T dinos. We're almost into the New Millennium and today people "want to know." That explains the high ratings of those recent TV shows where masked magicians and wrestlers tell all. In that same spirit, I've brought this dino-scoop to countless dino-lovers who resent having to wait to know the truth, usually in some article we'll probably never see or fully understand anyway. The "Dinosaur Renaissance"? Call this the "Dinosaur Revolution." See you at the next SVP, where I promise to again follow my own motto...

"Dig out news! Good luck until then..."
"The Masked Dinologist"

Why did I do it?

Oh, maybe just for the Hell Creek of it.

Maybe I was just in one of those crazy moods that dull Chicago afternoon of January 1999 when I conceived this master plan. Perhaps I'd already seen too many friends become addicted to computer screens, websites, and dinosaur chatrooms. Grown tired of "dino-fans" continually prodding me for some not-yet-published information that had been told to me in confidence by a paleontologist friend, just for the sake of making another drawing or sculpture or model kit of yet another "new dinosaur." Maybe I'd become weary of fan writers who refuse to use correct names for prehistoric animals, their proper spellings, or the correct grammar and punctuation. Or tired of seeing a new name for a prehistoric creature, coined by some hard-working paleontologist only to have it leaked to some popular publication before that taxon had a chance to appear officially in a peer-reviewed journal.

To be honest, I've always loved to pull April Fool's Day jokes.

However, what probably *really* spurred this joke into motion on that otherwise boring day was a friend telling me that, while surfing the Internet, he'd come across a gossipy exchange between two people—one a stranger, the other a long-time friend—concerning a project of more than 30 years ago, my original *Dinosaur Dictionary*. The former person was complaining about omissions (*e.g.*, *Deinonychus*) that were entirely out of my control. (I had finished writing that book before *Deinonychus* and some other more recent dinosaurs were published. About four years lagged between the book's completion and its eventual publication in 1972.) The latter person was apparently trying to defend his old friend, albeit in a subtly condescending way.

Anyway, my start button was activated!

I decided right then and there to launch an April Fool's Day gag that would send dino-cyber-addicts on a hopefully enthusiastic wild goose chase (appropriately, geese are birds, and birds are now regarded by many paleontologists as feathered dinosaurs). The gag, of course, would be a good-natured one that we could all laugh about afterwards.

At the joke's inception, I'd envisioned a grand scam of Berringer Stones or "Piltdown Man" proportions, though I doubted anyone would really search the dusty University of Ingolstadt collections looking for Professor Stromer's allegedly forgotten fossil specimens. A number of paleontologist friends, including theropod (*i.e.*, carnivorous dinosaur) expert Thomas R. Holtz, Jr., were alerted of the joke well in advance of post time and invited to participate; at least one (Tom) did; a few agreed to sit back and watch the action and maybe participate somewhere down the line. The idea was to launch the prank on April 1st, as near to midnight as possible, and then let the thing run its course, with no commenting on the responses, if there were any. People agreeing to come "in" on the gag were told not to post their responses after April 1st. Everyone privy to the fact that the joke was "in the works" as asked to keep it all secret; apparently, they all complied.

Was the joke worth the preparation and several months' wait, and was it a success?

I believe it was, though not on the grand dinosaurian scale that I'd originally envisioned. But the people who responded generally did so in various predicted ways: 1) either going along with the joke entirely, pretending it was for real and expressing their outrage over this unethical leak of information; 2) actually believing it, and commenting accordingly; or 3) (and most surprisingly) figuring out that it was a gag, given its date of posting, but actually taking the time to warn the rest of the cyberworld that this was, after all, probably just an April 1st prank.

One of my hopes was that someone would actually go ahead and, without waiting to see if the alleged jointly authored paper ever got published, boldly forge ahead and draw, paint, or sculpt a "scientifically accurate" and "museum quality" (by now almost clichéd terms used to described dinosaur illustrations, sculptures, and model assembly kits) life restoration of the "true" *Spinosaurus* or the new "Stromerosuchus." Did anyone go to all that trouble? If the answer is "Yes," they might have been in for a surprise (see below).

From the outset, I'd intended to make the whole thing an *obvious* gag to anyone reading the text having a basic knowledge of vertebrate paleontology. The piece was composed in a rather awkwardly written style to suggest it was authored by someone doing his or her best to transcribe what was heard on a tape recording, but not always knowing how a word should be spelled or what it meant. For example, words like "spinosaurid"—indicating a member of a family-level group—are never capitalized (although the family names, such as Spinosauridae, always are). *Suchomimus, Spinosaurus, Baryonyx,* and all other generic names are always spelled in italics. It's "Ernst," not "Ernest" Stromer. Dinosaur fan writers tend to perpetuate the annoying (to me, at least) practice of shortening the formal names to such "cutesy" abbreviations as "Spino" and "Sucho," not to mention the ubiquitous "dino." And too many of them seem to feel that, among all the creatures in the paleo-bestiary, only dinosaurs—and not such "mundane" animals as, for Godzilla's sake, crocodiles—have any real importance.

In other words, the text was supposed to give the impression of having been written by a "dinophile," someone having more of a "goshwow!" fascination with dinosaurs than any serious scientific interest in or knowledge of them.

In addition to the intended "errors," the text was peppered with actual clues—the kind that the Riddler might impulsively slip to Batman before committing a crime—to give away the whole affair as bogus to anyone bothering to hunt for them. For the record (Cro-Magnon drum roll, please), the most significant clues in the piece are:

1. "1940" was the year the motion picture *One Million B.C.* was released (see below).

2. "C. Nagle" refers to actor Conrad Nagle, who played the anthropologist who appears at the beginning of *One Million B.C.* and provides some explanatory narration.

3. "Ingolstadt" is the town in Mary Shelley's novel *Frankenstein* wherein Victor Frankenstein creates his Monster. (My friends know that the "Frankenstein" topic is one of my passions, aside from dinosaurs.)

4. "1960" was the year *The Lost World* movie remake debuted in theaters (again, see below).

5. "Synapamorphies" should be spelled "synapomorphies," "plesiamorphs" should be "plesiomorphies," and "apamorphies" is really "apomorphies."

6. Anyone with any real understanding of spinosaurids would know that their skeletons exhibit more than enough theropod synapomorphies—or shared derived characters that define a class or real grouping of taxa—to classify these animals as dinosaurs, despite the superficial similarities of these dinosaurs to crocodilians.

7. According to the description, the "real" *Spinosaurus* should have looked exactly like the finned alligator (see photograph, section three of this book) that appeared in *One Million B.C.* (and, as stock footage, countless movies and TV shows thereafter), which should have been obvious to film buffs. (This would have been a classic example of reality imitating art; that is, science apparently discovering a real fossil animal that coincidentally matched a creature from the movies. This claim had already been made, though somewhat erroneously, for the movie *Jurassic Park*, when, during filming, a dinosaur named *Utahraptor*, similar in size and form to the film's "raptors," was discovered in Utah.)

8. And "Stromerosuchus" would be identical to the similar sailbacked 'gator—although this time horned and armored—appearing in *The Lost World* (1960) and subsequently seen stock footage.

9. The bit about *Deinosuchus/Phobosuchus* was a personal dig at the many dinosaur fans who persist in using the "old names" (*e.g.*, "*Trachodon*" for *Edmontosaurus* or *Anatotitan*, and "*Brontosaurus*" for *Apatosaurus*), even though those names are outdated and incorrect, sometimes by nearly a century.

10. "Dinologist," if that even were a real word, should more correctly be spelled "dino-ologist"—meaning one who studies "dinos," not "dins" as "dinologist" implies—or better still, "dinosaurologist."

And finally...

11. Did anyone think of arranging the first letters of each paragraph, and the first letters of each word of the closing slogan, to see what they spelled out?

April Fool, from Don Glut
"The (now) Unmasked Dinologist"

Two

PERSONAL PETROGLYPHS

AMATEUR ANIMATION: DINOSAURS AND ANCIENT APES

From circa 1954 to 1969, my main hobby was making amateur science-fiction, horror, and fantasy movies. During that decade and a half I made about 40 of these mini-productions, most of them shot in Chicago, where I lived until 1964's move to Southern California. While I made them, I began to entertain ambitions of someday working as a professional make-up artist, special-effects man, actor, stuntman, or producer; ironically, I thought little about becoming a writer or director, two areas in which I would inevitably make my career.

Although I'd always enjoyed writing, I did not really begin to think of writing seriously (let alone professionally) until the early 1960s. My grades for creative writing in grammar and high school (and later college) had never been very good and my English and writing teachers never really encouraged me to improve. Around 1961, I had started corresponding with the first professional writer I ever knew personally, Los Angeles–based (and former Chicagoan) Ron Haydock, then a freelancer for *Famous Monsters of Filmland* magazine. The growing friendship that resulted between us largely inspired me to pursue my own writing career.

Dinosaurs were the main attraction in a good number of my amateur films. Some of my movies got written up, with accompanying photos from them, in various monster-movie magazines and specialty fan-produced publications, so-called fanzines, some of them written by Ron Haydock. Indeed, I seem to have been among the first fans to become known for making such films. And while many of my friends were wasting their extra money on cigarettes and pop, I was perpetually saving up mine to purchase, and then have processed, hundreds of feet of 16mm movie film.

Oddly enough, perhaps, I'd also never actually set out to become a movie-maker. Rather, I wanted to *show* movies featuring dinosaurs and other fantastic creatures on our home screen. In those early-Fifties days, monster movies were generally not available for home distribution, as they later would be either on 16mm, 8mm or super-8 film, videotape, laser disc, and DVD. Luckily, we always had a 16mm silent movie camera and projector in our family for recording various family events.

In 1953 I saw, for the first of many, many times, the movie *The Beast from 20,000 Fathoms* featuring Ray Harryhausen's wonderful "Rhedosaurus," a gigantic amphibious Mesozoic reptile invented for the film. I wanted to show a movie like that at home at my leisure. Naturally that was an impossible dream back then, so I decided to make my own "home movie" version of the film. The result was a very short and crude black and white effort shot in my backyard titled *Diplodocus at Large*, featuring myself and two slightly younger friends, with my diligent mother working the camera.

This was decades before popular magazines, books and television shows began to reveal how special effects for the movies were created, so kids like myself had to figure out "how to do them" on our own. Having had no idea how the "Rhedosaurus" was made to move (I believed for years it was some kind of robot), I improvised using an "Ollie the Dragon" sock puppet, actually "shaking" it to simulate the strobe-effect of the stop-motion model I'd seen in *Beast*.

It wouldn't be until 1959's *Dinosaur Destroyer* that I discovered or invented stop-motion—quite literally. Still thinking that the "Rhedosaurus" and other such creatures were mechanized models, I set off to find another, more practical, and less expensive method to accomplish the same result. It seemed reasonable to me that if cartoon drawings could be brought to life through a series of still frames, shot in sequence and then projected, the same result could be had by moving a model one frame at a time. I experimented with some "pixillated" eating utensils and it worked. At that moment I had, in effect, invented the stop-motion process all over again.

The following piece is made up of two short articles that I wrote for fanzines that featured articles about amateur movies.

The first article, originally entitled "Tor the Torrible"—about the 1962 film *Tor, King of Beasts*, my own version of *King Kong*, with the ape's name inspired by that of Joe Kubert's 1950s comic-book caveman hero—is, to me, historically important, since it was the first article I ever wrote with a prehistoric theme (and consequently the one in this collection requiring the most extensive polishing). It was published in the mimeographed debut issue of *Shazam!*, a fanzine edited and published, on a borrowed mimeograph machine in Chicago, by Dick Andersen and me in 1962.

The second piece, "Amateur Animation" (which required considerably less revising, proving how one's writing style can improve in just a few years), appeared in the first issue (November 1965) of Leonard Minter's photo-offset fanzine *Ready for Showing*. Interestingly, the latter book also presented articles by Paul Davids and Mark McGee, both of whom would someday have professional careers in the motion-picture business, and another by future critic and TV personality Leonard Maltin; it would cover-feature a photo of Taurus, a Kong-like monster sculpted and animated by still-to-be-professional David Allen for the movie *Equinox*.

Of all the many home-made science-fiction and horror films I have produced over the years, among the most rewarding and enjoyable for me to make was *Tor, King of Beasts*, my own version of *King Kong*, which I shot, on 16mm black and white film, in 1962.

First, the plot: Members of the Adventurers' Club, led by one Carl Denham (named after the original character in *King Kong*), attempt to reach the red planet Mars in a rocket ship of Denham's design. Among the ammo on board is a box of powerful gas bombs. The take-off is successful; but upon leaving the Earth's atmosphere, the craft encounters a meteor shower, is hit and directed back to Earth, where it crashes atop an isolated plateau. Running from the rocket, which explodes to nothingness, the crew find themselves in a "prehistoric graveyard" filled with non-fossilized skeletons and bodies of giant animals. Then Tor makes his appearance, ripping up trees. One crew member is crushed in the grip of the mighty gorilla. Tor growls in defiance and disappears into the thick jungle.

Denham, always on the lookout to make an easy buck, leads the crew after the brute, hoping to capture it. Making their way through the foliage, the crew discover a giant, reptilian footprint. The monster that made the print, a huge *Stegosaurus*, sees them, charges, but is stopped, after a round of gunfire, by one of Denham's gas bombs. Still after Tor, the crewmen track him to a river which they must cross. The water, however, is already occupied by an enormous *Apatosaurus*, which overturns the boat and kills two of the explorers, chasing the others onto the shore. The co-pilot of the space ship seeks safety in a tree, but the dinosaur's darting head gets him. Now only two crew members are left! Meanwhile, Tor encounters a *Tyrannosaurus* and battles the monster to the death. Denham and the only other crewman track the ape to its cave, where it battles a slithering plesiosaur. Tor drops the sea serpent, leaves the cave and stands near the edge of the cliff, meeting and destroying yet another adversary, the batlike flying reptile *Pteranodon*. Deciding this to be an excellent opportunity, Denham throws a couple of gas bombs. Tor staggers, rubs his eyes, and falls off the cliff into a mudbank below. Climbing down the cliffside with a rope, the two explorers reach the base of the plateau and, sighting a ship, flag down their transportation back to civilization.

In Chicago, Tor is placed on exhibition at $20 per ticket. But fearing the flashes from the newspaper photographers' cameras, the monstrous ape breaks loose and escapes from the theater. First stop: Denham's surviving crew member. Tor looks through his window. A titanic hairy hand crashes into the building but is met by a butcher's knife. Then, in the tradition of another giant ape, Tor wrecks an L-train, after which he destroys an armored truck. Finally Tor climbs the Prudential Building from which this creature from the dawn of time is shot down by jets.

Admittedly, this "ape-pic"—with its prehistoric world inhabited by dinosaurs and dominated by a giant gorilla—bears an intentional resemblance to my favorite giant-monster movie, *King Kong*, although my version of the story was modernized. Making this movie also involved various special effects (mostly stop-motion animation) and other challenges:

Animated models—not only those used in this movie, but also those seen in professional movies like *King Kong*, *The Son of Kong* and *The Beast from 20,000 Fathoms*—are difficult to photograph so that they look larger than life and appear to be really alive. For one thing, no matter how many individual frames of film are exposed to create an animated sequence, the models animated still retain that "jerky" or "shaking" movement that is so typical of such figures. This is due to the fact that each successive frame of movie film in a single scene is actually a separate photograph. If you were to hold a strip of film up to the light showing a man waving his hand, you would see that the image of that moving hand is really preserved as a blur. An animated hand, however, would not be shown as a blur but rather a series of still photographs, one on each frame, each image in perfect focus. Thus, a strip of film featuring animated models, shot one frame at a time with each frame in perfect focus, appears to "jerk" when projected. (The smooth shots of the dinosaur running in *The Beast of Hollow*

Mountain, a movie of 1956, were reportedly accomplished by blurring the film image.)

Miniatures must also be photographed at just the right angle. If high (or downward) angles are used, the models will look small, as they really are. In order to be most effective, miniatures should be shot with the camera aimed at them at table-level; a trick to make the models appear bigger than they really are is to shoot them from a low (upward) angle.

An interesting effect, which can, in a way, serve as something like a poor man's traveling matte, is the so-called perspective or depth of field shot. This can easily be accomplished with the use of a wide-angle lens, if the sun is shining brightly and your depth of field is appropriate. Set the camera on its tripod with some distant scene, such as a city skyline or forest, as your background. Then set the model to be animated fairly close to the lens. With both model and background in focus, the result can be a wonderful and quite easy way to achieve a gigantic-monster effect. A particular scene in *Tor, King of Beasts*—in which an *Apatosaurus* chases a crew member into a tree—turned out to be one of the best effects scenes in the movie.

In fact, during an August 1962 showing of this film at the Hollywood home of Forrest J Ackerman, editor of *Famous Monsters of Filmland* magazine, Bert I. Gordon, producer of *The Magic Sword* and many other special-effects fantasy films, was much impressed by this scene and asked how I did it. Both Ackerman and Ray Craig, a former student filmmaker at USC whose special-effects work was far superior to that in many professional science-fiction movies (he had a stop-motion robot in his film *On the Bench*), asked to view the scene twice. About that same time, in a movie-projection room at the CBS television studios in Hollywood, film editor Bob Burns, with authors and *Fantastic Monsters of the Films* editors Ron Haydock and Jim Harmon, also asked to see the scene twice. (The first time I had attempted this kind of perspective shot was in 1959 for an amateur color film entitled *The Fire Monsters,* based on Japan's *Gigantis, the Fire Monster.*)

In *Tor, King of Beasts,* a group of explorers discovers the ape-monster Tor's prehistoric plateau via rocket ship. My set—our home's basement—had to be decorated with various items to give it the intended appearance of a space vehicle. A miniature spaceship (an old plastic toy bought at a five and dime store) was utilized for exterior shots of the craft. When "invisible" (actually black) threads were not used, panning across the model, which had been set on a stationary black or blue background, gave the illusion of flight.

Scenes involving meteors proposed more interesting challenges. One scene required the ship's "telescreen" (a cardboard prop with a white sheet of paper for the screen) to reveal the huge chunks of rock zooming through space toward the camera. I set the camera atop its tripod, raising it to its full height. The lens was focused upon a black piece of cloth (actually the Dracula cape I used in earlier non-dinosaur movies). Then, with the camera set for slow motion (64 frames per second), I dropped the rocks from behind and close to the lens in such a way that they converged at a point on the cloth. Upon being processed, I spliced the film into its sequence upside-down so that the slow-motion stones moved in reverse when projected. The desired effect had been accomplished: Meteors, zooming through the black void, diverged and continued out of frame as they shot into the foreground. This sequence was then projected onto the prop "telescreen" and rephotographed, the end result being that the zooming meteors were seen on the monitor screen. To give the illusion that the "telescreen" was "warming up," I also projected onto it, just before the meteor footage, an image shot off a real TV screen.

All explosions in *Tor* were created by igniting a 50–50 mixture of sulphur and powdered zinc purchased from a local scientific supplies distributor. Superimpositions and dissolves (all done in the camera), movies projected onto projections of 35mm slides and then reshot, and rear-screen projection were all used in various parts of the movie.

The models of the giant ape Tor and his prehistoric friends were made to scale from plasticine modeling clay that I sculpted over wooden frames, and then painted. In the case of Tor himself, crepe hair (usually used for my amateur werewolf movies) was also attached using plastic-model glue.

Flood lamps can and do have a terrible effect upon clay models. Within seconds the tremendous heat would cause them to melt, distorting their features, often in the middle of a "big scene." For this reason, just as there were many Kong models, so were there many Tors. In fact, there were no less than eight Tor models, each one a different size, depending upon the requirements of the scene.

For the live-action jungle scenes, my cast and I went to the Chicago's Garfield Park Conservatory, which, on the inside, looks sufficiently like a prehistoric environment complete with ferns, moss, palm trees, shrubs, and so forth. Here there were new headaches to experience. The Conservatory is a public place and naturally visitors were walking about. Often we had to wait small eternities to expose only short lengths of celluloid. Other "jungle" scenes were taken at a nearby forest preserve.

Even though it was a lot of work, I must admit that making *Tor, King of Beasts* was also a lot of fun.

Yes, Tor was dead after his plunge from the skyscraper in downtown Chicago. But who could tell? There was *The Son of Kong*. Perhaps, atop Tor's plateau, it was possible that...

My animating of dinosaurs and giant apes did not begin with *Tor, King of Beasts*.

I had been interested in animation, I suppose, ever since I began frequenting the motion-picture theaters. As a very small boy, I would often sleep through the main feature attraction. My mother would awaken me in time to see the cartoon shorts, which were sometimes the only things of interest to me in that darkened auditorium.

Learning, while very young, the basic functions behind the phenomenon of animation (much of it by watching the then new *Disneyland* television series), I began to turn out literally stacks of two-drawing "flip book" cartoons, mostly executed in pencil or ballpoint pen. In time I grew more ambitious and began to draw entire scenarios on those popular "Big 5" tablets. By the time I had reached the sixth grade or so of elementary school in the middle 1950s, I had accumulated a veritable storehouse of now multi-pictured flip books on all manner of fantasy subjects—walking and fighting dinosaurs, scenes re-created from "Flash Gordon" movie serials, invisible men performing their antics, Frankensteins versus Wolf Men, and my favorite of all, Dracula to bat (and vice versa) transformations, the latter constituting the bulk of this output.

In 1953, I had been greatly impressed by a Warner Bros.–released prehistoric-monster film, *The Beast from 20,000 Fathoms*. Since I had, up to this time, not seen the greatest such movie of all time, *King Kong*, I considered *Beast* to be about the most fantastic display of special effects ever screened. It was the summer before my entering the fourth grade, and my most vivid previous encounters with filmed prehistory were in *One Million B.C.* and some of its stock-footage cousins.

I realized that I could not actually *own* or project *at home*—anytime I wished to—a print of *The Beast from 20,000 Fathoms*. The next best thing, then, was to *film my own* version of the picture, which to my friends and relatives (young and old alike) really seemed to be a harebrained idea. But despite all their sneers, that same summer saw the filming of my first amateur production, *Diplodocus at Large*, a nonsensical flick involving a hand-puppet monster that attacked a "Plasticville" town until an unexplained flying saucer from outer space happened by and killed the snaky-necked dinosaur.

One learns by making mistakes, and this film consisted mostly of mistakes. Among other things, *Diplodocus at Large* taught me quite a lot about miniature work, since in this film I unknowingly violated every applicable rule. The angles were shot downward, which made the models look that much smaller. I "shook" the puppet to give it an "animated" look (at that time I did not know that *The Beast from 20,000 Fathoms*–type monsters were animated rather than being mechanically operated). I did not own a tripod, so all of the scenes were shot hand-held. And the broken camera I used did not help matters, resulting in a "fluttery" image.

Discouragement after that original film forced me into a very early retirement until 1957, when I shot *The Earth Before Man* on a miniature sun-lit stage set up on chairs in my backyard. The angles mostly improved, as did the photography in general (no longer using the broken camera), yet still no tripod. But, now beginning to guess at how models could be made to move one frame at a time, I was still not willing to risk 100 feet of expensive (about $3.50) 16mm color film, since I had never tried animating anything before. The safe-but-sorry result was a combination of live pet lizards (anols, popularly mislabeled as "chameleons," and a horned lizard, or "horny toad") and thread-pulled models of dinosaurs and prehistoric mammals—waxy-plastic toys made by the J. H. Miller Manufacturing Corporation and sold in five and dime stores—all of which, in this film, conveniently lived at the same time and in the same place. As *King Kong* (which I had recently seen for the first time during a theatrical reissue in 1956) was already one of my favorite movies, I also threw in a giant gorilla, which, after encountering dinosaurs, challenged and promptly got killed by a woolly rhinoceros. The climax for the film was a quite unspectacular volcanic eruption.

Dinosaur Destroyer was my first film to feature real animation (I had employed it to a small extent in a few scenes in some of my previous horror films, like the crude bat/human changes in *Return of the Wolfman* in 1957, *etc.*), and the first to be shot using a tripod (a major breakthrough in my filmmaking hobby). The movie featured a horned and spike-backed *Beast from 20,000 Fathoms*–inspired prehistoric reptile of extraterrestrial origin, which hatched on Earth from an alien egg (inspired by the movie *20,000 Miles to Earth*, 1956). The monster grew to giant-size fast and this time invaded an 027-scaled electric-train layout in 1959, dying at the end of the movie of radiation burns. Most of the angles on the miniatures were directed upwards, so the made-up dinosaur looked fairly large.

This film was followed that same year by *The Time Monsters* and *The Fire Monsters*, both made in color. *The Time Monsters*, shot outside in the yard again, was the story of a group of very young scientists who invented a television that can look into the past. What they saw (mostly dinosaurs, but also some cavemen courtesy of a Marx "Playset"), needless to say, constituted the majority of footage. The animation had been considerably improved since the last film. As in *The Earth Before Man*, a Kong-sized gorilla was part of the stop-motion cast, battling the usual dinosaurs including a *Ceratosaurus*, and a volcano's action ended the prehistoric sequence.

The Fire Monsters was my own version of the Japanese *Gigantis, the Fire Monster*. In this one, Angurus and the second Godzilla (called Gigantis in the United States) battle each other in Chicago. This was my first film to feature "depth of field" photography. With adequate light and a wide angle or fixed-focus lens, it was possible to place the two models very close to the camera while using a real background. The result: The creatures seemed to be standing, or in this case also fighting, right in front of real, full-size downtown Chicago buildings, bridges and other familiar structures. This kind of effect can work quite well and make an audience wonder just how it was done.

The Age of Reptiles was shot in 1959–60, mostly over Christmas vacation from high school, and also featured a tape-recorded soundtrack with narration, music, and sound effects. Filmed as a biology-class science project, it showed a chronological "history" of the Mesozoic Era, with all three of its periods—the Triassic, Jurassic and Cretaceous—represented. This time there were no giant apes in the non-scripted storyline and the recreation of that age was fairly straightforward. And yes, there was another volcanic eruption which seemed to end the Mesozoic (much as I'd seen one do in the 1956 movie *The Animal World*). This was my first animated dinosaur movie shot *inside* the house, on a tabletop set in my basement (and was, consequently, the first in which the lighting did not subtly change from one frame to the next due to clouds and the passage of time).

In addition to the animation scenes, I included a lot of live-animal footage in *The Age of Reptiles*. As I lived in Chicago, it was a simple matter to phone the nearby Lincoln Park Zoo and ask to speak with its director Marlin Perkins, known to TV watchers as the host of the popular animal series *Zoo Parade*. When I told him I was doing a high-school science project, Mr. Perkins graciously invited me down to the zoo's reptile house, where an employee let me film from outside and behind the various displays.

This movie ended with a theoretical situation: What would happen if dinosaurs were alive today? More depth of field effects were used to show a very unscientifically correct fire-breathing, 400-feet-tall *Spinosaurus* (a fin-backed carnivorous dinosaur) smashing, once again, through Chicago's Loop, only to be killed by army weaponry. (The science fair judges awarded the film one of their lesser prizes, but were *not* impressed by its fanciful, Godzilla-inspired finale.)

Next year's science fair inspired me to do another film, this one about the possibilities of time travel, and also with tape-recorded music, sound effects, and narration: *Time Is Just a Place* (the title borrowed from an unrelated episode of the TV series *Science Fiction Theater*). The animation in this was quite poor (mainly due to a camera fault that created light flares at the beginning of each shot, requiring longer "takes" for each increment of movement) in the scenes where a time traveler journeys back to the age of the dinosaurs, as well as other time periods.

I finally decided to go the entire length with a movie about a giant prehistoric ape. *Tor, King of Beasts*, my own version of *King Kong*, was rushed out in 1962 in order to complete it before my high school graduation. (I wanted to utilize the school auditorium as a set, to fill it with some of my classmates, and also to screen the film before summer vacation began.) I tried some mildly successful rear-projection, accomplished some better stop-motion animation, and improved the depth of field shots.

My animation had usually involved three frames of film to every movement of a model, mostly because of the limitations of the cameras which I had to use. Consequently, the animated figures would move extremely jerkily. I later found that even a large movement will appear smoother if single-framed. After some more experiments along this line, I shot my best and most elaborate dinosaur movie, six months in the filming during 1964, *Son of Tor*.

Obviously, *Son of Kong* was my homemade version of the original 1933 giant-ape sequel *The Son of Kong*. The story involved Carl Denham's return to Tor's plateau. There Denham rescues Torro, the first ape's albino (and smaller) offspring, from a quicksand pool. Denham and his co-pilot encounter various prehistoric reptiles and other monsters, after which the volcano erupts. Torro returns Denham's favor by saving him from a river of flowing lava at the cost of his own life in the molten matter. Denham and his co-pilot escape in their plane as the plateau is destroyed.

Besides the stop-motion effects, I included more scenes with live reptiles in *Son of Tor*. The rhino iguanas (perhaps the same ones that made their screen debut in *The Age of Reptiles*) at the Lincoln Park Zoo came back, this time in black and white. But the most elaborate scenes were those staged on my tabletop miniature, featuring a young caiman with a *Dimetrodon*-like sail airplane-glued to its back, shot in slow motion in the fashion of *One Million B.C.*

In addition to Tor's son and the better-sculpted authentic Mesozoic animals in this film (including a flying *Pteranodon* and the spike-frilled horned dinosaur *Styracosaurus*), such familiar but imaginary movie creatures as the monster stars of *The Beast from 20,000 Fathoms, Gorgo, 20*

Some of the stop-motion performers modeled by the author for *Son of Tor* (1964), including *(left to right) Pteranodon*, "Ymir," *Styracosaurus*, "Rhedosaurus," Godzilla and giant ape Torro. Photograph by Charles F. Glut, ©D. F. Glut.

Million Miles to Earth (the "Ymir"), Godzilla, King of the Monsters!, The Giant Behemoth, and *Gorgo* made stop-motion "guest appearances."

Son of Tor went in for the old (and by now) reliable depth of field effects (as when Godzilla stalks one of the explorers, or when an aggressive, land-bound *Kronosaurus* gets dynamite rammed into its jaws) and the other kinds of camera trickery, but also employed such advances as improved model work and better backgrounds. I also stumbled upon a method of placing the model and live actors into the same scene without using the old depth of field trick. A painted bit of scenery with two holes, each opening covered by a makeshift rear-projection screen (a piece of translucent glass), coupled with the use of two movie projectors, was the secret. Onto one screen was projected a movie of the actor; on the other, a scene featuring the animated model. Re-shooting allowed the capture of the scenery, actor and model, all together as one composite frame. This overall effect really can bewilder an audience not trained in special effects, and that amazement can indeed make all the time and effort put into creating such a scene worthwhile.

Son of Tor was my last "home movie" to animate dinosaurs and other ancient creatures; this film, like all those that preceded it, was indeed an enjoyable and satisfying experience. It was completed about a half year prior to my moving from Chicago to Los Angeles to attend cinema classes at the University of Southern California, the latter constituting a turning point in my life. From that point on, my interest in making dinosaur movies would be on a professional rather than amateur level. Never again would I—atop a tabletop set in my backyard or basement—move clay figures of prehistoric creatures and shoot them one frame at a time.

MAN-LIZARD,
STONE-AGE AVENGER

As stated in other parts of this book, I have always loved the comics, especially the comic books published during the 1950s and 1960s having prehistoric themes. It was only natural, then, that my first real attempt at creating—and, I hoped, someday selling—a professional comic book or strip series would be set in a prehistoric environment.

Traditionally, comic-book superheroes have origin stories, both on the fictional page (a tale showing how the character became what he or she is) as well as in reality (how the writer or artist created the concept). The true origin of my creation *Man-Lizard, Stone-Age Avenger* dates back to about 1963. The title character—originally named "Lizard Man"—was inspired directly by two classic comic-book series drawn by the great artist and writer Joe Kubert, *Tor* (St. John Publishing Corp.), a 1950s periodical about a noble caveman hero (covered elsewhere in this volume), and *Hawkman* (National Periodical Publications, now DC Comics), a 1961-revived superhero concept with roots back to the early 1940s. The Hawkman, in his '60s incarnation, was really an extraterrestrial policeman who, upon coming to Earth, donned an identity-concealing hawk-like uniform. The outfit included a helmet that resembled a hawk's head and exposed only this superhero's lower face.

Innumerable costumed and usually super-powered heroes had existed over the years, all of them basically inspired by the original Superman, their usual battle turf generally set anywhere from the late 1930s through the distant future. None of them, however—to my knowledge, at least—had adventures regularly set in what is popularly referred to as "prehistoric times."

The original concept for "Lizard Man" was simple and, I thought, commercial: He was "Earth's First Superhero," a caveman named Boran wearing a costume crudely tailored from the skins of prehistoric animals, and possessing powers and abilities far beyond those of any mortal caveman. Like *Tor*, this series—and various others I would eventually script professionally over the years— would be set in some time-lost "neverland," where dinosaurs and humans somehow managed to coexist. Furthermore, superheroes had recently entered a new "Silver Age" of popularity, and dinosaurs were always well received in the comics.

Since my earliest years, I'd loved to draw, but my work would never attain professional standards. I began to make drawings of the character, even sketching out simple comic-book pages featuring the "Lizard Man," his costume based on both Superman's (primitive versions of the form-hugging shirt, tights, trunks and boots) and, more directly, that of the Hawkman.

Inevitably, during the Christmas season of 1964–65, it was the wise suggestion of comic-book fan Roy Thomas—who would go on to become one of the most important professional comic-book writers and editors in the late 1960s and beyond—and possibly also of comic-book historian and college professor Jerry G. Bails, that I changed the rather silly sounding name of "Lizard Man" to the better (and somehow less silly) "Man-Lizard."

Realizing that the strip needed a professional artist, I stopped trying to draw it and, as writer only, began to submit my *Man-Lizard, Stone-Age Avenger* idea to the various comic-book companies, always without success.

Years later, around 1969, I was able to spend one glorious afternoon discussing the *Man-Lizard* concept with legendary comic-book artist and writer Jack "King" Kirby, the creator of *Captain America* and countless other strips, who would later create the *Devil Dinosaur* comic book at Marvel Comics. For at least a few months, influenced by Jack's incredibly imaginative suggestions, the *Man-Lizard* concept would remain mutated into something more resembling his own complex *New Gods* series at DC, rather than my own much simpler original version. Kirby kept telling me, "You can't have Tarzan just running around bare-assed through the jungle anymore." And so, during that memorable day, the *Man-Lizard* concept evolved from a simple magnetism-based superhero who fights prehistoric menaces, to an entire world of bizarre and colorful characters. Included in this revamped concept was a secret race of reptilian humanoids that had devolved from a line of dinosaurs. Their civilization was approximately on a par with that of humans during the first World War, their technology including crude guns, tanks, and even biplanes!

In the early 1970s, Gerry Conway, a friend who then happened to be an editor at DC, seemed mildly interested in doing a *Man-Lizard* "tryout" book. By now, although still slightly influenced by Kirby's more radical suggestions, Man-Lizard and his world had reverted mostly to their original and much simpler conceptions, although the hero's super-abilities were now more reptilian in origin. No longer magnetically-powered as he was originally, Man-Lizard was now able to mimic the powers of certain reptiles—*e.g.*, run at incredible speed, change color, scale sheer cliffs, lift tremendous weights, even shed his skin. But I did not pursue the DC possibility, since it was that company's (and most other's) policy to own all rights to the characters they published, and I wasn't prepared to give up *Man-Lizard* for a quick sale.

There was also a time, around 1966–67, that I tried selling a full-length screenplay based on the strip. I wrote it as an assignment for Professor Irwin Blacker's script-writing class at the University of Southern California film school, which I was attending at the time. The screenplay introduced the new character Gigan, a *Triceratops* that Man-Lizard befriends and eventually rides like a trained elephant. At the time, Blacker personally knew the King Brothers, who had made the prehistoric-reptile movie *Gorgo*, and thought he might be able to help sell my property to them. The hoped-for sale never happened.

Shortly after, I also wrote a chapter or two for a novel based on the character, and, if memory serves correctly, submitted the concept to at least one Hollywood animation studio for a possible Saturday morning cartoon show.

Although Man-Lizard himself never officially saw print in an illustrated story, some elements from his storyline would later be recycled for other comic-book tales I wrote. These included *Tragg and the Sky Gods*, a series I created for Western Publishing Company in the 1970s, and which was, in some ways, an unofficial "spin-off" from "Scaly Death," an illustrated (by Billy Graham) story I wrote for the fifth (June 1970) issue of Warren Publishing Company's *Vampirella* magazine. "Devil Woman," written by me and drawn by Alfredo Alcala, was another pseudo offshoot of *Man-Lizard*. This story, which appeared in the 90th issue (September 1980) of *Vampirella*, was about a beautiful cavewoman who is banished from her male-dominated tribe because she is, perish the notion, self-reliant and resourceful. Her name was Lona, which happened to be that of Man-Lizard's once-intended mate. I always believed that both "Lonas" were one and the same character, with "Devil Woman" set somewhat after she and Boran had parted company and he continued his super-heroic adventure.

Although a number of future "Devil Woman" episodes were plotted, Lona's solo adventures never continued beyond her first.

The closest that Man-Lizard ever came to appearing in a professional publication was during the late 1960s for an "almost was" magazine called *Ka-Pow!* In 1969, just a couple of years after the project was put together and then prematurely killed, brothers Rob and Jeff Gluckson asked me to write an article about *Man-Lizard* and *Ka-Pow!* for their fanzine *Guts* "...the magazine of intestinal fortitude." The original version of the piece, titled "*Ka-Pow! Comics*, the Magazine That Never Was!," offered much additional information—not covered herein—about the other weird superheroes of *Ka-Pow!*

A tidal wave of monster-movie magazines were spawned during the 1960s. Some of these short-lived publications were *Monster Mania, Modern Monsters* and the British *Shriek*. James Warren's *Screen Thrills Illustrated* (a nostalgic magazine devoted to serials, "B" movies, Western movies, *etc.*) had already gone extinct, while Warren's black-and-white, comic-format magazines (*e.g.*, the horror titles *Creepy* and *Eerie*) had already toppled from their peaks and were beginning to slip in quality toward mediocrity.

January of 1966 brought *Batman* to television as a network series. This event hatched a craze that almost totally snuffed out the waning movie-monster and secret agent fads of just a few years earlier. James Bond was rapidly becoming, to many fans, familiar, routine, and less exciting and original than he seemed back during the less complicated days of *Dr. No.* Fantastic powers and abilities, as well as flashy costumes, were steadily replacing the suaveness and gimmicks of the "superspy." The unabashed, all-frills costumed superhero was definitely "in."

The publishing market seemed right for two new quality magazine projects, both conceived by the present writer, exploiting the current popularity of costumed superheroes.

The first project was patterned after the before-mentioned *Screen Thrills Illustrated*, but done in the way I personally had wished the Warren magazine would have been done. Originally titled *Movie Marvels*, this film magazine was to be completely devoted to superheroes, serials and related topics.

The second project—and the main subject of this article—would have been distinguished as the first comic-book magazine to feature a costumed superhero who lived during the "Stone Age." This was to be a black-and-white magazine, as were Warren's, but offering superheroes instead of the usual horror anthologies. Because this publication would technically be a *magazine* rather than a *comic book*, it would not—like Warren's—be restricted or censored by the Comics Code Authority.

Therefore, we could present superheroes so "way out," so out-of-the-ordinary, that they would probably not get Code approval for a regular color comic book. Not that our costumed heroes would be portrayed in bad taste, be gory for "gore's sake," or be pornographic; but they would have some grounding in reality, despite the fantastic premises behind their origins, special abilities, and reasons for combatting evil, and as such, would sometimes act outside the law (or, more practically, beyond the limitations imposed by the CCA). In other words, the intent in this magazine was to give the readers super-heroic tales offering things that could not be found within the color pages of the standard comic books.

Spearheading this collection of adventures would be the one starring a prehistoric, costumed superhero of my own creation, *Man-Lizard, Stone-Age Avenger*.

I was to edit both magazines, and my artist friend Larry M. Byrd—a familiar name in many quality monster-movie magazines—was to be art director. One morning in 1966, Larry and I presented the two projects to Jim Matthews, whose Prestige Publications company was responsible for *Modern Monsters* magazine. Matthews liked our ideas and tried to convince his distributor, Kable, that the projects constituted a couple of potential hits. Larry and I were asked to show the Kable folks something real upon which they could base their judgments whether to give the projects a "go" or reject them.

Movie Marvels would actually reach the stage of my writing a number of articles, and Larry doing a full layout of the first issue, including photostats of all the pictures to be featured. Unfortunately, that was as far as the first project went. The magazine, by now retitled *Ka-Pow!* (a familiar comic-book "sound effect" made even more famous on the *Batman* TV show), was finally turned down—the popularity of *Batman* and superheroes, and the current revived interest in the old movie serials notwithstanding—because of the failure of another Kable publication that came out, perhaps, a few years too soon—*Screen Thrills Illustrated*.

The second magazine—called *Ka-Pow! Comics*, now that the movie-oriented publication was defunct—was another matter altogether. But in some ways, though theoretically a good idea, this magazine, its title returning to *Ka-Pow!* (the "*Comics*" deleted by a Kable representative to avoid any possible friction from the Comics Code Authority), may have been doomed from the outset. As conceived, the magazine was to star various oddball superheroes that, for one reason or another, might not be appropriate for mainstream comic books or be found entirely acceptable by the CCA.

A first issue was envisioned, some of it actually going into the early stages of production: The cover, which would probably reproduce a color painting by Larry Byrd, would feature all of the book's strange heroes, most prominent of the group being Man-Lizard. Like *Creepy* and *Eerie* (the magazines it would probably have shared newsstand space with), with their Uncle Creepy and Cousin Eerie, *Ka-Pow!* had its own "host character." Ours was Kaptain Ka-Pow, drawn by Larry. The good Kaptain would lend his wisdom and wit to the editorial page.

The following heroic-adventure strips were scheduled to appear in the premiere issue: *Man-Lizard, Stone-Age Avenger.* This ten-page strip, influenced both by Joe Kubert's *Tor* and also the 1940 movie *One Million B.C.*, was to appear in serialized format in every issue of *Ka-Pow!* This first installment, mostly related in flashback, would tell the origin of the prehistoric superhero and take him through his first adventure.

Boran, a handsome and noble Cro-Magnon caveman, is in love with Lona, the beautiful daughter of their tribe's aged chief. Unfortunately, someone else, the evil Graggu, has decided to take Lona for his mate. Despite his formidable appearance and gruff attitude, Graggu is basically a coward, and, therefore, has to win Lona by less than honorable means. One night, the evil caveman brutally kills the chief, planting evidence that implicates Boran as the murderer.

In the morning, Graggu's plan is realized, as Boran, given no opportunity to prove his innocence, is immediately branded a murderer. According to tribal law, Boran must be executed where he stands. A mob of angry cavemen forms, moving in to slay their tribesman and former friend. With no other way to save himself, the otherwise guiltless caveman swings his heavy stone-headed ax, plowing through the mob of attackers. Then he dives off a towering cliff, presumably perishing in the turbulent waters below. Lona watches this scenario in disbelief, not knowing if Boran is really innocent or guilty of killing her father, but realizing he must now be lost to her forever.

Unseen by the others, Boran manages to survive, battling his way through violent waters that hurl him against rocks and into the midst of hungry prehistoric sea reptiles. Filled with longing for Lona, hatred for his tribesmen, and being half-drowned, he finally reaches land. There, he vows never again to have anything to do with humanity, for if those he loved and respected have so rejected him, to whom can he turn as a friend?

Suddenly, Boran hears a loud rumbling, heralding a stampede of gigantic prehistoric animals, some of the creatures dying as they trample over one another in an effort to flee. Overhead, the caveman sees the reason for all the commotion—a glowing meteorite streaking overhead, finally crashing into the ground. After the confusion has settled, Boran looks at the weird rock from the sky, still not entirely burned up, smoking ... sizzling. Furthermore, the rock—composed of some alien "lodestone" type mineral—is magnetic, attracting objects on one side, repelling objects on the other.

Naturally curious, Boran gingerly reaches out and touches the giant stone. At that moment, the meteorite explodes, bathing the caveman in its strange radiation. Boran has inexplicably survived the explosion. Soon, he realizes that he has absorbed into his own body the mysterious magnetic powers once contained within that celestial rock. Furthermore, by utilizing various combinations of his new abilities to attract or repel objects, Boran can simulate "flight" (repelling the ground, maneuvering by both repelling and attracting) and perform acts of "superhuman strength" (gripping something with magnetic force, lifting the same object with repulsion).

Finding the bodies of a green-skinned *Ceratosaurus*, a nose-horned meat-eating dinosaur, and a reddish-brown shaggy mammoth killed during the stampede, Boran fashions a disguise for himself, thereby making the world's first superhero "costume." Donning the scaly skin-tight dinosaur skin, offset by cuffs, "trunks" and boots of mammoth hide, his face mostly concealed beneath a "helmet" made from the ceratosaur's head, Boran the caveman ceases to exist. In his place, and now possessing the power to avenge himself against his former tribesmen, stands Man-Lizard.

Although Man-Lizard sets out on a mission of vengeance, he soon finds himself thrust by fate into a significantly different role. Although he kills Graggu, Man-Lizard also performs acts of heroism for which he is hailed as a hero by the rest of the tribe. Unfortunately, with Graggu dead, there is no one alive who might testify to Boran's innocence in the murder of the chief.

Not really wanting to be a hero and still bearing mostly resentment for his former tribesmen, Man-Lizard reluctantly performs heroic acts on their behalf. Most of these noble acts are because of his love for Lona, but they also stem from his own instincts to do what is right. His main problem, of course, will always be that he can never unmask, for once he does he becomes exposed as that hated "killer" Boran. The caveman is, therefore, continually plagued with trying to adjust to this new and unasked-for role in his violent primitive environment.

In future episodes, Man-Lizard would have to pit his might, powers, and wit against such prehistoric menaces as hungry dinosaurs, evil cave people, and possibly even a primitive "super villain" or two.

The first page of that first installment of *Man-Lizard, Stone-Age Avenger*, with its big splash panel (the usually large opening panel of a comics story), would depict the costumed caveman in the sky, battling for his life against an enormous *Pteranodon*, this scene introduced by the following stage-setting caption:

"He was a loner—an outcast in a world one million years ago! An isolated tropical world where titanic monsters from the Age of Reptiles overlapped the dawning years of Man. He despised his fellow men. While forever threatened in the shadow of the dreaded dinosaur! Pitting his awesome powers against the terrors of his world, he was Earth's *first* superhero—He was ... MAN-LIZARD! STONE-AGE AVENGER."

The other *Ka-Pow!* superhero features:

Sky Altitude. This one-page strip starred a character created years before by its writer Ron Haydock and appearing in various fanzines, a Captain Midnight–type air-ace hero who flew around in an old, dilapidated biplane, and even had his own fan club.

Legendary Super-Heroes. A single-page strip written and illustrated by George Barr, featuring such mythical characters as Samson and Hercules.

Commander Birdman. Created and written by Larry Byrd and drawn by Charlie Scarborough, the Commander—a familiar character already seen in monster magazines and a few low-budget movies—was "almost" a humorous take-off on Hawkman.

Rat Pfink and Boo Boo. Spoofing Batman and Robin and based on a movie by Ray Dennis Steckler, in which Ron Haydock portrayed the rock 'n' roll-singer/superhero.

Steelmask. Created and written by best-selling author Jim Harmon, who had already featured the character in published prose, featuring a slouch-hatted, pulp magazine-style hero who wears a mask to conceal the fact that his face has been destroyed by acid.

Count Noctilio. The world's first vampire superhero, using his supernatural powers to combat evil, written by me.

Nin-Jitsu. Probably the first Ninja comics hero, created by artist Jiro Tomiyama.

Finally, *Jawbreaker*, written by me and illustrated by Landon Chesney, about a bored movie stuntman who dons a mask and fights crime just for the excitement.

No doubt, with me at the editorial helm, one or possibly all of the above characters would, like Man-Lizard, have been fighting dinosaurs or some other ancient menace during their future careers, had the magazine ever been published.

The decision-makers at Kable were extremely interested in *Ka-Pow!* and its characters, and fully realized the newsstand and subscription potential in a magazine featuring superheroes not restricted by the Comics Code Authority. Our main problem, though, involved the sample package we were required to send to Kable's New York office where the magazine's inevitable fate would be decided. This package was to include a *substantial* amount of finished (that is, penciled and inked, plus lettering) artwork. However, attempting to get professional artists, or even professional-quality fan artists, to work "on spec" and to meet deadlines was a task almost as super-heroic as some of the stunts performed by the likes of Man-Lizard.

Artist Jeff Jones agreed to illustrate *Man-Lizard, Stone-Age Avenger*. Jones was then still basically a very good fan artist who had not yet seen his work in any professional publication, but who would go on to become one of the most respected pro artists in the field of fantasy illustration. He penciled and inked a simple splash page. What particularly impressed me was that the submitted page seemed to be entirely original, that is, there were no "swipes" from other artists. Furthermore, Jeff respected my demand that the *Pteranodon* not be copied from any previously published illustrations, such as those done by artists like Charles R. Knight (I having long been against copying other artist's illustrations, especially those of prehistoric creatures, in comics and textbooks).

In a letter from Jeff Jones to Larry Byrd, the artist stated, "I think it is original enough not to resemble any other artists' work. The poses are mine. Hope it is suitable." It was; more so, it remains this writer's personal favorite among all of Jeff's fine body of work.

Alas, only some of the artists solicited came through with their samples, either on time or at all, and so were able to meet Kable's imposed deadline only in part. There was simply not enough time for us to get enough sample material to impress the Kable Powers That Be. By the time that I had written most of the scripts for the first issue, and Larry had broken them down, letterer Bill Spicer had set down their text over the flats, and some of the artists had sent in their sample pages, it was too late. The superhero fad—or so, Kable informed us, despite the rising sales of the mainstream comic books—was basically all over, and there was no room for a magazine inspired by that phenomenon.

Man-Lizard, Stone-Age Avenger would go through many and sometimes quite different stages of evolution. There would be a number of completed comic-book scripts written, in various styles depending upon to which publisher it was submitted subsequent to *Ka-Pow!* Each of these would employ its own standards concerning the amount of violence, blood, and sex shown. The motion-picture script, wherein the lead character takes on his *Triceratops* mount and gets a secret cave of operations, would be written by the author, as well as the first chapter of a proposed Man-Lizard novel. They, too, would remain unrealized.

Man-Lizard was conceived as what I believed to be an original concept for a hero, a prehistoric, costumed super-doer; soon, however, other similar characters would subsequently make their media appearances, both in the comics (*e.g.,* Pete Von Sholly and Mike Van Cleeve's *Tyranostar*) and on television (*e.g.,* Hanna-Barbera's *Mighty Mightor*).

Ka-Pow! and its various characters have remained, for the most part, in limbo, at least insofar as comic books or strips are concerned. However, it is not impossible that Man-Lizard and some of the other original characters may someday materialize in some medium. Perhaps there is still a place for a hero who likes to swing a stone-headed ax, crush an evil caveman or two, or vanquish a menacing dinosaur—a hero like Man-Lizard.

THE TRIALS OF DAGAR,
PREHISTORIC WARRIOR

Most of my professional writing output of the 1970s consisted of scripts written for various comic-book companies. As a long-time comic-book fan, actually working in the industry was, for many years, a real dream come true.

Of course it was only natural that dinosaurs, cavemen and other things prehistoric would frequently be featured into these scripts. I worked for most of the major comic-book companies during those years—Warren, Marvel, DC, Archie, Charlton, and others—with a good percentage of my writing done on assignment for Gold Key, the comics line of Western Publishing Company.

Dagar, the mercenary-warrior hero I created for Gold Key's *Dagar the Invincible*, was not a prehistoric hero *per se*—at least not in the same sense as was Joe Kubert's Tor the Hunter. Dagar was not an ax-carrying caveman like Tor, but a relatively civilized sword-carrying hero of the descriptively named "sword and sorcery" genre, which had arisen basically in the pulp magazines of earlier decades and was currently enjoying a new life in numerous comic books featuring burly warriors, particularly Marvel Comics' highly successful *Conan the Barbarian*.

But Dagar certainly lived in a prehistoric time period, albeit a mythical one that was never discovered by archaeologists or pale-ontologists, in which early civilizations were based upon and governed by magic and sorcery rather than science and industry. In this very ancient realm that never was, Dagar would encounter and often have to fight creatures that had survived from the previous age of clubs and stone-headed axes, including sabretooth cats, mammoths, giant ground sloths, dinosaur-like dragons and reptiles, even enormous serpents.

119

Dagar the Invincible enjoyed a healthy run, being published for most of the decade in a series spanning 18 issues, two of which were reprints of the first issue. In addition to this "official" series, Dagar also appeared in *Gold Key Spotlight* and made brief guest appearances in *Tragg* and *The Occult Files of Dr. Spektor*.

This article about *Dagar the Invincible*, originally titled simply "The Trials of Dagar," was written for the fifth (July-August 1973) special sword and sorcery issue of *Comixscene*, a tabloid periodical published and edited by innovative comic-book writer and illustrator, and former musician and escape artist, Jim Steranko.

Dagar, a young mercenary warrior living during a mythical prehistoric era of monsters and magic just following the Stone Age, had already battled his way through a number of issues of Gold Key's sword and sorcery comic book *Dagar the Invincible*. He continued to fight evil forces despite the often poor distribution of Gold Key titles in some major cities. And although there may be relatively few comic-book collectors who had even heard of (let alone actually *seen* and *read*) an issue of *Dagar the Invincible* (cover dated October 1972), his first issue outsold every other Gold Key title for that month, with further adventures having been scripted up to a full year in advance. Somebody must have been buying the magazine, which made this author, the creator and writer of Dagar, quite happy.

Dagar's comic-book origin was that of a young, blond-haired orphan boy, living at a time when many creatures—mostly strange mammals, but also an occasional monstrous reptile like the giant spike-backed lizard that Dagar slays in his second-issue adventure (January 1972), and the likewise slain, corpse-eating "earth-lizard" in the eighth issue (July 1974)—from the Stone Age still lived. Dagar witnesses the genocide of his entire nation of Tulgonia (an "in-joke" name that the publishers never seemed to catch, as when I first began this book the stories were published without a byline) by the hordes of Scorpio, a powerful evil sorcerer. The boy's grandfather, once a great warrior, saves young Dagar from the massacre so that he might be trained in all manner of combat and someday avenge his people. Later standing by his grandfather's deathbed, the adult (and by now quite cynical) Dagar, representing his nation personified, vows to become a mercenary warrior, bearing as he does no love for his fellow men, and to destroy the fiend Scorpio.

That was Dagar's *official* origin.

Dagar's *real* beginnings go back nearly six months before his "birth"

at Gold Key. During the spring of 1971, I had written a sword and sorcery comic-book script entitled "Castle of the Skull," featuring a one-
shot barbarian hero named Shaark. The story had been first submitted by
my agent Forrest J Ackerman to the line of black and white horror-comics
magazines issued by the Warren Publishing Company to which I had sold
many scripts before. It was promptly rejected by then story editor J. R.
Cochran. The story immediately got recycled to Skywald, another publisher of black and white comics magazines, which returned it with a note
that the story was acceptable, but that the backlog of scripts flooding their
offices had necessitated that it be resubmitted the following winter. That
was too long for me to wait.

About that time (the early 1970s) I had begun writing horror and
science fiction scripts for *Mystery Comics Digest*, a new publication from
Gold Key (a division of the very large Western Publishing Company).
One of my early submissions to the *Digest* was a story titled "Lizard
Sword," which featured Daggar, yet another one-shot barbarian hero I'd
named. The Gold Key editors were surprised and a bit confused by the
story and its hero, the "sword and sorcery" genre being an entirely alien
concept to them. Wisely they bought the script but, perhaps just as wisely,
requested a new and better title, which I changed to "Wizard of the Crimson Castle." The story then went into a stack of scripts waiting to be
drawn by the company's new artist "discovery," Jesse Santos.

Jesse had been one of the top artists in his native Philippines, working as a staff illustrator for the *Halawak* comic magazine and chief artist
on *Paraluman* magazine. In 1967 he had been elected vice-president of
the Society of Philippine Illustrators and Cartoonists (SPIC), and in 1970
he became a member of the Society of Western Artists. Jesse worked in
pen and ink, water color, oil paints, tempera, pastel, and acrylic, and had
already earned an enviable reputation as a fine and much in demand portrait artist. Seven of the comic books he drew in the Philippines had been
made into motion pictures, some of these in the popular "James Bond"
spy genre.

In 1971, just before I became a freelancer for Gold Key, Jesse Santos began getting art assignments at that company, handling both pen-
cils and inks. Jesse started drawing the *Brothers of the Spear* feature when
that strip was awarded its own magazine. Because of his rugged style,
Santos was the artist chosen to illustrate "Wizard of the Crimson Castle."

However, before "Wizard" was shipped out to Jesse at his studio
in San Jose, California, I submitted a second sword and sorcery tale to
Gold Key. It was entitled "Demon of the Temple," and again starred the

character Daggar. At first the editors, Del Connell and Chase Craig, frowned on the idea of using the same character again in a new story, disliking any kind of heavy continuity in their books, arguing that no reader would see both stories. After much effort, I finally managed to convince the editors that it didn't matter, really, since each story stood up as an individual tale, neither relating directly to the other. With both scripts in their hands, however, Connell and Craig began to see this new (to them) kind of story as a possible series. I made a presentation, complete with an origin, and submitted it as "Daggar the Invincible." Soon afterward, Western's New York office made the final decision to proceed with the new book. We were in business.

Getting the old "Castle of the Skull" script back from Forry Ackerman, I set out revamping it, altering the hero from Shaark to Daggar, at the same time giving the character more of a personality and altering him to fit within the more severe restrictions of Gold Key's self-imposed and quite rigid censorship policies. The script was approved with the exception of the name—Daggar, the editors contended, was too much of a pun on the word "dagger." Indeed, I had purposely given the hero a dagger to use in the premier story, when he slays an attacking prehistoric sabretooth cat (who leaps upon him on the second page of the initial story) to tie-in with the weapon. Although I wanted to title the magazine with the hero's name as is the custom, Del Connell preferred the less dynamic, in my opinion, *Tales of Sword and Sorcery*. Perhaps both "swords" and "daggars" spelled out on the same cover were simply too much deadly weaponry for a usually rather tame company like Gold Key!

What followed was perhaps one of the most difficult phases of comic-book writing—creating a new name. "Dragar" was suggested; but I argued against this to avoid future jokes about our new hero wearing a dress. Del made up a dummy cover with the name "Zagar"; but that was abandoned when I showed them a Skywald Publishing Corporation comic book featuring the jungle hero Zangar. I knew that if Gold Key didn't like Daggar they certainly wouldn't care for my original Shaark.

Eventually everyone settled on "Dagar." I was pleased, still pronouncing it with the short "a" as in "dagger." But most of the Gold Key staff and, as it turned out, the buyers too, pronounced it "Day-gar," with the long "a," which I for a long time did not like, perhaps fearing it might offend our Italian readers. (Not until after our third issue was published did I learn of an old comic book called *Dagar*, published by Fox during the 1940s, about a desert sheik hero.)

Tales of Sword and Sorcery, number one, was shipped out to the printers, with art by Santos and with a two-part story bearing the separate titles

"The Sword of Dagar" and "Castle of the Skull." In this story Dagar is pitted against Scorpio's inhuman minion Ostellon, a villain with mystical control over bones. Among the supernormal threats Dagar must face is Ostellon's resurrection and animation of the entire articulated skeleton of a giant woolly mammoth, which he sets upon the sword-carrying hero. Swinging a primitive mace and chain, Dagar reduces the skeletal prehistoric threat to a pile of inanimate bone fragments.

When this first issue was released featuring a non–Santos painting re-creating the mammoth-skeleton sequence on its cover, I was happy to see that the title had been changed to the more dynamic (and commercial) *Dagar the Invincible*, almost my original choice. The cover, not surprisingly, featured the attacking mammoth skeleton.

Coincidentally, this first *Dagar* issue was scheduled to be published the same month as the issue of *Mystery Comics Digest* featuring "Wizard of the Crimson Castle." Both stories had rather similar surprise endings, so Del Connell changed the hero of "Wizard" to "Duroc." Now, inadvertently, we had *two* sword and sorcery heroes.

I promptly envisioned an eventually separate Duroc series, but knew that he would have to be somehow different from Dagar. The funny thing about Dagar was that although he appeared to be just another barbarian hero, whose type appeared in numerous comic books published by other companies, he was *not* really a barbarian. Yes, he looked like a barbarian and fought monsters and bad sorcerers with a broadsword. But Dagar came from a civilized nation and possessed a nobility which prevented him from stealing or wantonly killing. Duroc, I decided, should be a *true* barbarian in the strictest definition of the term. And while Dagar would brood much of the time over his lost people, the jovial Duroc would seek out danger and adventure just for the thrill of it. To compliment his new characterization (and to make him look less like Dagar, since both his and Dagar's stories were being drawn by the same artist, Jesse Santos), Duroc was given longer (and brown) hair, a mustache and goatee in all of his subsequent stories.

Duroc made a very brief guest appearance in "Death Between Floors," the second story in the fourth issue (October 1973) of *The Occult Files of Dr. Spektor*. When the inked artwork for this story was purchased by the New York office of Gold Key, the powers-that-be decided that the name Duroc sounded too much like the hero of *Turok, Son of Stone,* that company's long-running series about two American Indians stranded in Lost Valley, a vast "lost world" populated by dinosaurs, cavemen and other prehistoric creatures. There were already two more Duroc stories, penciled by Jesse and awaiting lettering by Bill Spicer, for *Mystery Comics*

Digest. By the time those tales went to press, Duroc's name was altered to "Durak." Durak (the original character who had starred in the original "Daggar" story, "Wizard of the Crimson Castle") would eventually fight alongside Dagar in the latter's seventh issue (April 1974) in the story "Two Swords Against Zora-Zal."

What was the future of Dagar once he avenged himself on his people in the fourth (July 1973) issue? In that story, Dagar faces a number of challenges, including facing a gigantic sabretooth cat in an arena of death. The monster has been created by Scorpio himself by magically melding together three normal-sized animals. But despite his slaying of Scorpio in this issue, which did at least satisfy Dagar's reasons for living the life he does, the magazine continued. In the fifth (October 1973) issue's story "Another World ... Another Time," Dagar ventures into an eerie cave whose mystical energies zap him back through time to a yet more prehistoric environment than his own—a world in which, through yet more strange forces, dinosaurs and other ancient animal forms have somehow survived into the early age of man. There he meets Jarn, a caveman, sharing with him an adventure involving dinosaurs, pterosaurs and, of course, magic. Making a one-panel appearance in this story was Tragg— not spotted, I believe, by my editor, who frowned upon such "guest shots"—a Cro-Magnon caveman hero who had already appeared in a couple of stories recently published in *Mystery Comics Digest.*

The original script for this story featured Tragg himself; but the editor changed the name and appearance of Dagar's caveman partner in battle, making him more of a standard Neandertal. The editor feared that, as both Tragg's and Dagar's stories were both being illustrated by the same artist, the two heroes would appear in the same story looking too much alike. As it turned out, Tragg would eventually get his own comic book, *Tragg and the Sky Gods,* the first issue dated June 1975, which brought into the caveman's continuity alien invaders, based upon the "ancient astronauts" concept introduced by Erich Von Däniken in his books that were very popular at the time. Jesse Santos, who also drew the Dagar tales, illustrated the first two *Tragg* issues, after which the book was taken over by Dan Spiegle in order to ease Jesse's workload. Santos continued, however, to provide *Tragg*'s painted covers. Jarn, it would later be revealed, was actually Tragg's brother, while Tragg himself was a direct ancestor of Dagar, thus offering another explanation for their resemblance. Tragg's more modern appearance was shown to be the result of evolutionary tinkering on the part of the alien Sky Gods, thereby explaining the lack of family resemblance between him and sibling Jarn.

Dagar would also venture underneath the Earth's surface and to various exotic lands, sometimes accompanied by his beautiful companion Graylin. There would also be a multi-title storyline that thematically tied together the heroes Dagar, Tragg, and occult investigator Dr. Spektor, all of them sharing a common ancestry.

Editorial policy at Gold Key dictated a prescribed number of panels per page and a minimum amount of wordage, which often cut down on the characterization level that could be achieved by the competition. At Gold Key story was more important than characterization and, generally, any personality nuances not contributing directly to the story itself were edited out. There were also restrictions on how sexy the women characters could be portrayed and on the continued use of magic and monsters. And so, of necessity, *Dagar the Invincible* was different in many ways from the sword and sorcery features published by other companies.

Since Gold Key had not, for some years, run letter columns in their comic books, the editors got almost no feedback from the readers of *Dagar the Invincible*. That was indeed unfortunate. This writer, for one, would have liked to know how we were doing.

A LOVE AFFAIR
WITH DINOSAURS

Kyoryugaku Saizensen (or *Dino Frontline*) was a unique and unusual, relatively short-lived magazine produced during the 1990s by the prestigious Gakken Mook publishing company in Japan. This periodical, its text published entirely in Japanese, was unusual in that it was lavishly produced and, consequently, boasted a quite high cover price. Each issue contained serious articles written about dinosaurs illustrated with numerous photographs and drawings, many of them in color. Although most English-language popular magazines devoted to extinct animals have been largely geared toward a very young readership, this title was aimed at adults, including quite technical pieces written by professional and often high-profile paleontologists. Strangely, the vast majority of the magazine's audience seemed to consist not of scientists or the usual dinosaur buffs, but young Japanese housewives. Unfortunately the magazine was published only in Japan; there never was an English-language edition.

Among the articles published regularly in *Kyoryugaku Saizensen* were profiles of people whose names were known among dinosaur enthusiasts—including scientists, writers, artists, and collectors of dinosaur-related memorabilia.

The magazine's editor requested that I write the following article about myself, recording, as well as I could remember, the events of my childhood that led to my own early fascination with dinosaurs and other extinct animals, and how that evolved over the years into a serious interest (read: "obsession"). The article, first published in the fourth (1993) issue of *Kyoryugaku Saizensen*, appears here, somewhat edited, for the first time in English.

A large part of my life, professional and otherwise, has been associated with dinosaurs and other prehistoric creatures.

This association—a kind of "love affair" with these fabulous animals—began, quite typically, as a simple childhood fascination, an interest that is not uncommon to many children. My own interest evolved into a hobby and eventually erupted into a veritable career, spilling, like molten lava from some Mesozoic volcano, into the many fissures of my professional life.

Much of my professional career has been that of the freelance writer. My writing credits run the gamut of nonfiction books, novels, motion-picture and television scripts (both live action and cartoon animation), short stories, comic-book stories, articles, and even music. A good percentage of these works has involved dinosaurs and other forms of extinct life.

In fact, I find myself quite fortunate. Not only do I make most of my living in a profession that I love (*i.e.*, writing), but I'm able to write about subjects that are, to me, so fascinating and endearing—dinosaurs. For that, I am forever grateful. It is, I believe, what mythologist Joseph Campbell refers to as "following your bliss."

My professional life can be split into two basic categories—first, the entertainment business, and then, also, the more down-to-earth world of vertebrate paleontology. My work in the entertainment industry also includes a beginning new career as a producer and director of motion-picture and videotape projects, and also as a musician and singer (for the *Dinosaur Tracks®* music albums). In this latter category I write books and articles about the science of dinosaurs (including my "magnum opus" *Dinosaurs: The Encyclopedia* and its supplements), lecture at museums, universities, and dinosaur-related events, work as a consultant for film and television projects, and so forth.

Perhaps my real niche, as one might call it, is bringing the worlds of entertainment and science together on some kind of "happy meeting ground"—trying to introduce accuracy into popular dinosaur projects, and also making vertebrate paleontology (and real dinosaurs) more accessible and appealing to the general public.

Where and *how* did this "love affair" begin?

Well, its origins can be traced back to my childhood in Chicago, Illinois. However, it's difficult—perhaps impossible—to pinpoint an exact beginning.

I can, though, recall some vivid memories of my earliest exposures to these wondrous animals, including the following:

1. A 1948 issue (I was born in 1944) of the *Tarzan* comic book featuring dinosaurs, this story constituting the Apeman's discovery of and first visit to "The Valley of Monsters" (as the Jesse Marsh–drawn story was titled), which he would visit often during the succeeding years;

2. The original *One Million B.C.* (1940) movie seen on a neighbor's television around 1950, leaving me with stark mental images, particularly of the cave people fleeing for their lives during a combination volcanic eruption and earthquake, one of them losing a sandal in the mud just moments before getting enveloped by flowing molten lava;

3. Color pictures of dinosaurs, particularly one depicting a *Stegosaurus* being confronted by two hungry *Allosaurus* individuals, shown to me at a Cub Scout (circa 1951) meeting by a fellow den member in the book *The Golden Treasury of Natural History*;

4. A black-and-white postcard, flashed to me by a grammar school friend, reproducing a color mural of *Stegosaurus* as painted for Chicago's Field Museum of Natural History by that great artist of extinct life, Charles R. Knight; and finally

5. Seeing alien dinosaurs, actually no more than stationary models produced by Messmore and Damon to promote their "World a Million Years Ago" attraction (which featured the world's first mechanical prehistoric creatures), in 1951 episodes of the television science-fiction series *Tom Corbett, Space Cadet.*

None of these early experiences, however, really excited me enough to spur my transformation from a kid somewhat aware of dinosaurs into an authentic "dinosaur lover." However, after some very serious thinking and trying to sort out specific events and dates, I believe I've managed to trace this real "change over"—very soon to come—to three significant events:

First, my father died when I was less than one year old; also, I had no brothers or sisters. Since this family situation sometimes made me a rather lonely child, I often found escape in the colorful realms of both science and fantasy. As a very young child I was especially interested in astronomy (the Adler Planetarium in Chicago being a favorite place to visit on a weekend afternoon), modern-day skeletons (human and otherwise), and also science fiction. Having had somewhat of an artistic ability, at least on an amateur level, I'd sometimes spend hours drawing planets, skeletons, robots, and other related subjects, some copied from books or from memory, others out of sheer imagination.

One day, around 1949 or 1950, my mother Julia Glut took me to my first visit to the Field Museum (within convenient walking distance of

Ancient skeleton of the ground sloth *Scelidotherium*, a fossil treasure brought back from Argentina by Elmer S. Riggs, as exhibited in the former Chicago Natural History Museum's Hall 38. Courtesy The Field Museum (neg. #GEO78072).

the Planetarium) to see such wonders as Egyptian mummies. There I became especially amazed by some of the skeletons in the museum's hall of fossil vertebrates—including a towering mounted partial skeleton of an *Apatosaurus* and the holotype giant limb bones of *Brachiosaurus*, and also an articulated skeleton of the large ground sloth *Scelidotherium*. What particularly amazed me about the latter was that the bones were embedded in rock matrix, and it was difficult (for my young eyes, anyway) to tell where the bone ended and the rock began. The bones on display in this hall were also darkly colored, not "whitish" like those of the modern animals exhibited in other halls. My mother explained to me that these bones were so old that they had "turned to stone."

Second, in 1953, the St. John company published the first issue of its *1,000,000 Years Ago* comic book (which would later be renamed *Tor* after its caveman hero of that name). The comic book, expertly written and illustrated by Joe Kubert, one of the best artists in the field, was populated by some of the medium's most dramatic-appearing prehistoric creatures. Tor, his monkey- or lemur-like sidekick Chee-Chee, and the numerous denizens of their world, had a profound effect on my youthful imagination, offering me many illustrations to peruse and copy.

Finally, also in 1953, Warner Bros. studios released the science-fiction movie *The Beast from 20,000 Fathoms*. This spectacular black and white film featured a mythical prehistoric reptile, named a "Rhedosaurus" by Ray Harryhausen, the young stop-motion effects artist who brought the spike-backed animal to life. For about a week, local Chicago television stations ran preview trailers for the film, showing how this impossibly huge monster was revived from suspended animation after an atomic-bomb test, and how the animal then proceeded to smash its way through New York city. Particularly jarring (and attracting) to my young eyes was a scene in which this reptilian monster picked up a New York policeman in its colossal jaws and gobbled him up whole!

As a child of about nine years old, I was absolutely enthralled by such scenes. Soon afterward, on the drive back home from a vacation to an Illinois tourist spot called Starved Rock State Park, I coaxed my mother and other people we were with to stop at a drive-in theater that was running *The Beast from 20,000 Fathoms*. (Sitting through the co-feature, a seemingly unending costume drama called *Young Bess*, was positively excruciating!) Seeing *The Beast*, however, was sheer ecstasy; it was as if the movie had been made especially for me, catering to my own still blooming interest in extinct animals. To this day, more than four decades later, the motion picture remains one of my favorites.

It was a combination of the above three experiences that, almost overnight, made that big change in my life, influencing me profoundly. I was, to put it bluntly, forever hooked!

In the early to middle 1950s, the first dinosaur books that I owned and read were some that would later be considered classic titles, some of them geared specifically toward young readers. They included (in this order) *Animals of Yesterday* and *Life Through the Ages*, both by Bertha Morris Parker; *All About Dinosaurs*, by Roy Chapman Andrews who, in Mongolia, had found the first fossil eggs positively identified as those of dinosaurs; and, a year or so later, *The Dinosaur Book*, written for an older readership by my mentor (and eventual friend) Dr. Edwin H. Colbert, then of New York's American Museum of Natural History.

By this time I was already actively taking stacks of both children's and adult dinosaur books—the latter utilizing my mother's library card—out of the public libraries (always seeking out some new branch in the hopes that it housed some books I hadn't yet seen); making almost weekly visits to the Field Museum (usually on Thursday, when admission was free instead of the usual 25 cents) and its fossil exhibits that were rapidly becoming like familiar friends; and spending many hours at home drawing my own dinosaur comic strips, writing and illustrating my own dinosaur nonfiction books and fantasy stories, making dinosaur models out of plasticine modeling clay, even shooting my own amateur 16mm dinosaur movies. Dinosaurs, fantastic looking creatures that they were, made great subjects upon which to vent my youthful artistic urges.

My reputation—by the sixth grade at Chicago's St. Andrew Grammar

School—had earned me the nickname that remains with me today, "Dinosaur Don."

You might say that today, as an adult living in Burbank, California, I am basically doing the same things I did as a child back in Chicago—except that now I am getting *paid* for indulging in this long-time fascination. My house has been described by some old friends as an extension of my childhood "room"—a veritable museum literally cluttered with fossil casts, models, mechanical figures, toys, paintings, pennants, posters, and many other kinds of items, most of them pertaining to dinosaurs.

Just what is this appeal in dinosaurs?

For myself (and probably for many others), I believe the attraction is related to the fact that these animals, fantastic though they certainly were both in their appearance and behavior, *actually lived*. They were, in a way, "real monsters," as strange and wonderful as the creatures of our myths and legends. Some of them have left behind skeletons that, when mounted in museums for us to behold, often tower above us. Some dinosaurs may even, to some of us, appear to be scary. Still, formidable though some of them undoubtedly were, these "monsters" are really "safe"—unable to cause us any harm, separated as they are from us by many millions of years.

Perhaps the most amazing thing to me regarding my own interests in dinosaurs in particular and prehistoric life in general is that those interests—as did the dinosaurs during their lifetimes—continue to grow. The more one learns about these great animals the less, one realizes, is actually known ... and how much yet remains to be learned, as new fossil discoveries continue to be made and new theories are proposed.

To me, then, my "love affair" with these wonderful animals seems to be just beginning.

ACCORDING TO
THE FOSSIL RECORDS

Dinosaurs and rock 'n' roll—yes, they can relate to one another.

Before I ever made a professional movie, saw an article published either in a professional magazine or fanzine, or was paid for an acting job, I was a musician. Music was a talent that ran through my family, especially on my father's side. He, his two brothers and I were all able to play just about any kind of musical instrument—and song—"by ear." I took that ability with me all through my days as a rock 'n' roll musician, from my prehistoric "debut" in 1957, and onward. No one would have guessed that this music phase of my life would become deeply and permanently melded with the world of dinosaurs.

The following article about Fossil Records—the appropriately named company I share ownership of with artist, writer, and all-around dinosaur lover Pete Von Sholly, and which was founded many years later—and its prehistoric products, mostly the *Dinosaur Tracks* series of music albums, fairly growls for itself. It was culled, assembled, and edited down from most of the text of a number of individual articles that were run in the first—and, alas, only—issue of our company's *Dinosaur Tracks Newsletter*, which I edited and wrote in 1994. (The titles for these separate articles appear below as sub-headings.)

Although the audio cassettes sold well and continue to sell, hardly anyone bought the newsletter, perhaps because it wasn't promoted properly and they didn't really know it existed, after which I lost interest in continuing its publication.

As a couple of footnotes, part of our song "Earth Shaker" was also heard in the science-fiction comedy movie *Attack of the 60-Foot Centerfold* (1996), directed by Fred Olen Ray. All of our Fossil

Records audio tapes were also officially approved by the now defunct Dinosaur Society, an important group that, among other activities, rated commercially sold products involving dinosaurs for their paleontological accuracy and other qualities.

All Fossil Records audio tapes can be acquired from the company at 2805 North Keystone Street, Burbank, California 91504-1604. "Dinosaur Tracks" is a registered trademark ® of Fossil Records.

Welcome, Trackers!

Ever since the release of the original *Dinosaur Tracks* cassette album, we at Fossil Records have been asked by you "Trackers" (or, if you prefer, "Trackies") enough questions about the company and our Mesozoic music to fill the empty stomach of a *Brachiosaurus*. We would like to answer all of those questions individually. But, of course, that would be impossible.

This, then, will allow us to speak to everyone at once—answering questions, offering insights and giving "behind-the-scenes" information.

Backtrackin' Into "Recorded Prehistory"

"Prehistoric" Pete Von Sholly and I, both having been dinosaur buffs since we were kids, met at a professional artists and writers party held at the 1977 San Diego Comic Book Convention. Artist Pete and I were then working in those capacities in the comic-book industry and had both done our share of comics stories featuring prehistoric creatures. At the party Pete approached me about his possibly doing some new illustrations for my then upcoming book, *The New Dinosaur Dictionary*. Yes, Pete got the gig, and he and I have been good friends ever since.

What neither Pete nor I knew at that time was that both of us had previously enjoyed similar backgrounds as rock musicians and singers. Pete had played lead electric guitar in various upstate New York–based rock bands during the 1970s, most notably one called Mixed Company. I, a rock musician since that prehistoric year of 1957, had played in various bands in Chicago and Los Angeles. In the late 1960s, I was bass guitar/organ player for the Penny Arkade (later renamed the Armadillo), a rock group produced by Michael Nesmith, then one of the Monkees. (While in this group, I spent a lot of my time in the recording studio, playing in Hollywood nightclubs, doing interviews for the teen magazines and, mostly, rehearsing.)

A decade later in 1987, I co-produced and hosted a Los Angeles cable-TV talk show which had the working title of *The Dino Show*. Pete was scheduled to be one of the guests on the third (and final) show of the series, with frequent drawing partner Mike Van Cleave to discuss their *Tyranostar* comic book and proposed animated-TV series, featuring the titled superhero who had fantastic exploits on a strange dinosaur island.

Realizing the show needed a theme song, I—who'd been out of professional music since the late Sixties—came out of retirement and wrote that song, the original "Dinosaur Tracks." No doubt, it was greatly inspired by the First International Symposium on Dinosaur Tracks and Traces which I had attended in Albuquerque, New Mexico, the previous year, and which was largely responsible for renewed interest by many scientists in this specialized branch of paleontology (called ichnology).

The song's title had a threefold meaning, referring to 1) the individual instrumental and vocal "tracks" that would come together to make up a single recorded song; 2) the individual songs (sometimes called "tracks") on an album; and 3) the footprints or "tracks" (technically called ichnites) made by dinosaurs and preserved today as fossils.

The song written, I phoned up friend Pete about the possibilities of us joining forces to record it. We would play all of the instruments ourselves, recording each "dinosaur track" separately; I would also tackle the vocals. A rough "demo" tape was made at Pete's home on his four-track recorder, after which Pete suggested that the song be rerecorded in a real studio under professional conditions. Though reluctant at first (and cost-conscious, as the TV show had a *Compsognathus*-sized budget), I finally agreed that a professional recording was the way to go.

Getting started off utilizing some good initial advice from music-arranger Robert Bryant, Pete and I recorded our original "Jurassic classic" at Resnik One Studios in Los Angeles, with engineer/singer Jeannie Cunningham (AKA Jae Cie) providing drum programming and also several tracks of background vocals, becoming herself a one-woman backup "group." (She had been a guitar player and singer for popular singer Lionel Ritchie. More recently, she has zoomed from the prehistoric past right into the future to work with the United States space program, some of her cosmic songs making their debut off-Earth as astronauts played them aboard their orbiting spacecraft.) Indeed, it was quite a thrilling experience for both Pete and me, performing in a recording studio after so many years.

When the recording was completed, the consensus was that it should start off with some kind of "dinosaur roar," a sound that would recur at various times in the song. However, a search of the sound-effects library at Resnik One failed to turn up a suitable roar. With the clock ticking away on studio time, I (who had to pay for the session, calculated by the hour) could not afford to go off and try to find the appropriate sound effect at a music shop. Putting our brains together, Pete, Jae Cie and I proved again that necessity is the mother of invention. Ms. Cunningham came up with a recording of a man belching which, when played through a synthesizer, its pitch changed via keyboard, became our now-famous dinosaur roar!

The song having been finished and mixed, Pete and I then named our two-man group the Iridium Band (named after the "band" of the element iridium, usually found in meteorites and volcanic rock, that separates the end of the Mesozoic Era, when the dinosaurs lived, from the beginning of the "Age of Mammals").

Thus, the TV show had its theme song. Kevin Glover, one of the show's co-producers, suggested that, because of the song's catchy title, the show be renamed. Thus, the show premiered in the summer of 1987 as ... *Dinosaur Tracks*.

Two years later, "Cave In" Kevin, by now a video producer with his own company, Popcorn Pictures, approached me with a new plan. Kevin had the idea to shoot a series of music videos based upon the Iridium Band's dinosaur-related music. Unfortunately, we only had one song—or two, if you counted the instrumental version we also produced sans lyrics. Could enough *new* songs be written and recorded to fill an entire album that would then become the basis for the videos?

The challenge was accepted but with reservations. Traditionally most songs about dinosaurs and other prehistoric creatures have been geared mainly toward very young children and were, consequently, avoided by adults as being too juvenile. On a smaller scale, there were also some fairly esoteric dinosaur-related tunes on the market that were directed almost exclusively at "in the know" adults. Remembering that we both had reputations as real rockers to uphold, the two Iridium Band members agreed to produce an album of songs that were, first and foremost, *good rock 'n' roll*—no "Barney" baby songs. At all times the music had to maintain an "edge" that would make it stand out, especially against the more juvenile-oriented product that otherwise dominated the "dino-song" market. The music and lyrics also had to appeal to *all* age groups—sophisticated enough for adults while being "catchy" enough for even very young kids to enjoy.

The intent was also to make the songs *fun* while at the same time having educational content. Whenever possible each song would make at last one valid scientific point, even if one had to listen "between the lines" to know what the song was *really* about. For example, the "point" of "Marooned in the Mesozoic (Without You)" is that the first people and last dinosaurs were separated by approximately 65 million years; "Missing-a-Bone Blues" really explains how fossils are collected and prepared; and the original song "Dinosaur Tracks" tells how these footprints are made and preserved as trace fossils. The songs were to be fun, written with some sense of humor; we didn't want to hit our listeners over the head with some symbolic Stone Age club while pounding in bits of real paleontological information.

The album included the following cuts: "Dinosaur Tracks" (vocal), "Dinosaur Movies," "Missing-a-Bone Blues," "Rock Quarry Rock," "Down in the Tar Pits," "Fossil Fool," "The Unknown Lost Island," "Big Bad Rex," "Marooned in the Mesozoic (Without You)," "Extinction," "Dinosaurs Rule" and "Dinosaur Tracks" (instrumental).

All instruments on that first album, and all those that followed, would be played by Pete and me—no outside or studio musicians were ever used—with Pete playing most of the guitars (lead, rhythm, 12-string, and bass), and I keyboards, some guitars (rhythm and bass), reeds, brass, tambourine, and harmonica. Except for cases in which neither Pete nor I knew how to play (or didn't have access to) a particular kind of instrument (*e.g.*, drums or stand-up bass), all instruments were played *live*. I performed all the male vocals (including backgrounds), with female vocals performed by the Fossilettes (Jae Cie and also Laurisa Stow).

The final step, once the album was recorded and mixed, was to release it—which Pete and I did through the company we subsequently formed. A name for this company came up almost without our thinking about it. Paleontologists often refer to the "fossil record," that is, the known history of ancient life as deciphered from remains preserved as fossils. Appropriately, then, Fossil Records, of Burbank, California, was officially hatched.

Pete would do the artwork—depicting "Big Bad Rex," a realistic appearing *Tyrannosaurus* standing atop a hill marked by dinosaur footprints and holding a guitar—for the cassette's "J card" (the card that fits inside the plastic cassette casing), while I would write the card's liner notes. This end product of that original collaboration, the first *Dinosaur Tracks* album, was released in 1990.

Two additional albums would follow, *More Dinosaur Tracks* (1991)—featuring "Dinosaur Rebels," "Fossil Feud," "Dinosaur Guy," "(He's a) Good Field Man," "Surfin' on the Niobrara Sea," "Trees of Stone,"

"Prehysteria!", "Feelin' Good in the Badlands," "Dragons of the Air," "Nomenclature Blues," "Little Horses" and "They're Not Monsters"—and *Dinosaur Tracks Again* (1994)—with "Rhythm & Bones," "(I'm a) Paleo Man," "Fragmentary Blues," "Earth Shaker," "Last Living Dinosaur," "Jurassic Punk," "Dinosaur Valley Girls," "Keep on Trackin'," "Dinosaur Blues," "I Don't Care (Why They've Gone)," "Dinosaur Invasion," and "The Ultra-Colossal Dinosaur Circus." Both albums featured more of what we called "The 'Rock' of Ages."

The result, one might say, was (pre)history.

The Iridium Band—Track Records

How did the songs come about?

Since I wrote most of the songs, allow me to comment on those:

First off, I get a basic subject idea for a song. Then I try to find some musical style that might appropriately fit that song. Finally I write the song, usually figuring out a chord progression and rhythm along the way, then putting a melody and lyrics to those chords (although at times, lyrics or melodies might come first). Usually I compose the songs on either an acoustic guitar or a piano, although at least one song, "The Unknown Lost Island," was entirely written, both its music and words, while on vacation without benefit of any accompanying instrument. At this point in the process I can already "hear" the song in my mind, complete and finished.

I should stress that, except for the lyrics, these songs are not "written down" on paper. There are no "lead sheets," no musical notes put down on staff paper. Both Pete and I play our parts not by reading sheet music, but by "ear," which is a common practice among many rock musicians. We simply know what to play and we play it.

Next, Pete (who generally *still hasn't heard* the song!) and I book some recording time at Resnik One Studios. There our engineer, either "Jurassic" Jae Cie or "Dromaeosaur" Drake Macy, lay down on our blank master tape a "scratch" or basic programmed drum track.

I then record the song's chords, usually with a piano or organ but sometimes using a rhythm guitar, followed by a "scratch" vocal track. By now Pete has heard the basic melody and chords. Fortunately Pete and I are so musically in tune with each other that it's a simple matter for Pete to walk in and create and play the appropriate guitar parts within just a few minutes of my conveying to him the tune, chords, and general feel.

From that point on it's simply a matter of building up the song, track by track, layer by layer, until it's finished. I then put on the headphones and, with the instrumental tracks blaring away, record the "official" lead vocal track. If the song requires male back-up voices, I or Pete add those, again recording them one track at a time.

When this process has been completed, Jae Cie creates the final drum programming and, where appropriate, adds her own back-up vocals, usually doubling up to create the audio illusion of an entire female singing group.

The last stage of this operation is the mix, which is done by the Iridium Band with their engineer(s). At this stage of the process every track is balanced against the others, until each song has reached the stage it must before the master tape can be sent off to the duplication factory for mass reproduction. The greatest experience for me is to hear a completed song that sounds very much like the one that I'd heard in my mind when I composed it, before even the first "dinosaur track" was "impressed" on tape.

Video Tracking

The original *Dinosaur Tracks* plan—to produce songs for music videos—finally happened.

Dinosaur Tracks, volume one (Simitar Entertainment, 1994), was a half-hour show featuring six songs from the first album of the same name. It was produced by "Cave In" Kevin, and written and directed by myself. The video (intended for ten-years-old through adult) became the first of a projected intended series of six such videos to be shot in the future, each one to feature a half dozen songs from the three albums. It features a cast of attractive and good actors, some original special effects and some famous old movie clips.

This first volume—including live-action, animation, special effects, and (sometimes *rare*) film clips—featured the songs "Dinosaur Tracks," "The Unknown Lost Island," "Missing-a-Bone Blues," "Down in the Tar Pits," "Marooned in the Mesozoic (Without You)" and "Dinosaur Movies." Videotape cameras went to the Natural History Museum of Los Angeles County, George C. Page Museum of La Brea Discoveries, Raymond M. Alf Museum, and the famous Bronson Canyon movie location. Some of the actors and props used in this video may be recognizable (including the original "Time Machine" from the classic George Pal movie, courtesy of movie-memorabilia collector Bob Burns).

The video introduced the Doc Dino character, a joint trademark of Fossil Records, Popcorn Pictures, and Chiodo Brothers Productions, a way cool dinosaur video jock (he's definitely *not* Barney), played by Lenny Rose with voice characterization by Tony Clay, and his pretty and perky assistant Sara Tops, played by Carrie Vanston. Doc's physical character was designed by the famed Chiodo Brothers (Stephen, Ed and Charlie), a team of special-effects siblings whose Chiodo Brothers Productions have also produced their own motion pictures and TV shows, including co-producing the revived children's dinosaur series *Land of the Lost*.

Keeping Track

When Pete and I agreed to (as they say "Down in the Tar Pits") take the "plunge" and produce that original *Dinosaur Tracks* album, we thought it might be fun—as well as challenging—to pay homage to some of the fondly remembered performers (*e.g.,* Elvis Presley, Bob Dylan, Robert Palmer and others), bands (Byrds, Iron Butterfly, *etc.*) and styles of the past by emulating their styles (heavy metal, country, rockabilly, *etc.*), some-times even *combining* totally unrelated styles (*e.g.,* Dave Brubeck Five and Bo Diddley). We followed suit in the next two albums, *More Dinosaur Tracks* and *Dinosaur Tracks Again*. (We *could* reveal which musicians and groups influenced which songs, but that might spoil the enjoyment of anyone listening to them from identifying them on one's own.)

One musical influence that *must* be mentioned, however, though Pete and I did not really imitate his style, was my late good friend "Screamin'" Jay Hawkins. It was "Screamin'" Jay's music, particularly some of his more "off the wall" blues numbers (especially "Constipation Blues"), that impressed upon me the fact that one could write and perform a more or less serious piece of music, even though the lyrics seemed to come from left field or even the Lower Cretaceous. (In other words, if one could write and seriously perform a real blues song about a man being consti-pated, why not one about a paleontologist lamenting about finding a fos-sil skeleton complete except for one bone—hence, the "Missing-a-Bone Blues.")

And I *will* mention a few of the many paleontologists who inspired the various themes of some of the "Dinosaur Tracks" songs:

John R. Horner of the Museum of the Rockies, Montana State Uni-versity, when asked by reporters why he thinks dinosaurs died out, has often emphatically replied in a way as to inspire the song "I Don't Care (Why They've Gone)."

"Trees of Stone" was mostly influenced by work done in the Petrified

Forest by Robert A. Long of the University of California Museum of Paleontology, Berkeley. The late Nicholas Hotton III of the National Museum of Natural History, Smithsonian Institution, when talking about how, for a time, certain animal groups "ruled the show," inspired some lyrics in that same song.

Edwin H. Colbert, for all around discovering and collecting fossils, is just one of many paleontologists known to be a "Good Field Man."

Work on the large carnivorous dinosaur *Allosaurus* in the Morrison Formation by James H. Madsen, Jr., of DINOLAB and Dan Chure of Dinosaur National Monument led to "Jurassic Punk," while studies of the huge sauropod dinosaur *Seismosaurus* in New Mexico by David D. Gillette, then State Paleontologist of Utah, inspired "Earth Shaker."

Michael K. Brett-Surman of the National Museum of Natural History and Georgetown University is just one worker who can proudly state that "(I'm a) Paleo Man."

The sometimes radical pronouncements of Robert T. Bakker and other modern paleontologists inspired "Dinosaur Rebels."

A classic old book about pterosaurs, or flying reptiles, written by Harry Govier Seeley, ignited the spark for "Dragons of the Air."

James O. Farlow, Martin G. Lockley, Giuseppe Leonardi and William Sarjeant, among other modern workers in the field of ichnology (the study of fossil footprints), all inspired our entire concept of "Dinosaur Tracks" and also the follow-up song "Keep on Trackin'."

Of course, "Fossil Feud" had its origins in the infamous and sometimes quite ugly rivalry between paleontologists Edward Drinker Cope and Othniel Charles Marsh during the late 19th century.

And a particular East Coast museum's once meager dinosaur-fossil collection inspired "Fragmentary Blues."

Other paleontologists may also find something of themselves hidden away in lyrics of the various "Dinosaur Tracks" numbers.

Inside Tracks

There is a kind of "secret origin" and evolution of the third album. *Dinosaur Tracks Again* started off as a rather specialized project. The original intent was to put out an album for "Trackers" that preferred 1950s-style rock 'n' roll, the blues, rhythm and blues, and related kinds of music. The album was to feature a half dozen "old" songs from the first *Dinosaur Tracks* and *More Dinosaur Tracks* that fit this mold, and also six new songs with the same basic feel. Pete thought up a title for the album, *Rhythm*

& Bones, after which I proceeded to write the lead-off song with that same title.

The new songs having all been written, the Iridium Band went back to Resnik One Studios to record them. However, well into the recording phase, Pete began to feel that it was too early to come out with an album recycling six old tunes that were otherwise available on two still-in-print albums. Pete suggested that the "Rhythm & Bones" theme be scrapped in favor of simply charging ahead with a new "Dinosaur Tracks" album containing nothing but original songs.

After some deliberation, I finally agreed with Pete, and brought out a few songs I'd written for a future third "Dinosaur Tracks" album, and for which Pete had already written a "rap" song about "wrapping" fossil bones in burlap. Don suggested that Pete also write a song based on his imaginative "Ultra-Colossal Dinosaur Circus" book project for which some of the artwork had already been completed. During the last stretches of the recording phase, both Pete and I decided that, for various personal, professional, and strictly commercial reasons, we didn't want to do the rap song. Thus, I filled out the suite of 12 numbers with a song based on a title I'd been thinking about (the reasons being obvious) for more than a year—"Jurassic Punk."

And so, the Iridium Band had its new album!

But Fossil Records would not only produce music albums.

A Different Trail

"Dinosaur Talks" was the second series to hatch from our company. And no, it wasn't about talking dinosaurs! Rather, it was what we believed to be an important series of audio albums in which the listener could learn about famous paleontologists and their lives and work as related *in their own words.* It was our aim to preserve bits of "living history" through this series of recordings.

The logical choice to spearhead this series was Dr. Edwin H. Colbert, a man known both to scientists and laymen alike, and who had made some significant discoveries and contributions to the field of vertebrate paleontology. Indeed, "Ned" influenced many readers of his works to pursue professional careers in this fascinating field or simply to become interested in fossils and prehistoric life.

For the (fossil) record, one night in November of 1993 I rode a train to Flagstaff, Arizona, where Ned and his wife Margaret lived, and spent two days with the Colberts enjoying their wonderful hospitality. Ned was professionally recorded by a local crew on videotape, speaking for two hours in his office at the Museum of Northern Arizona. The 90-minute audio album was edited down from those two hours of Ned speaking. We titled the album *Dinosaur Talks: Edwin H. Colbert.*

Ned later had this to say about the album: "I have the *Dinosaur Talks* audios, for which my sincere appreciation and many thanks. I think you did an excellent job with this tape of the meanderings of an old geezer. *Congratulations* ... I want to distribute the tape to certain members of my family, and a few friends."

In addition to the two-hour professional office shoot, I followed Ned around with a camcorder, getting footage of the paleontologist at work at his typewriter, walking about in the lab and just going about his everyday activities. This was for the hour-long video documentary about Dr. Colbert, starring Ned himself. The video, titled *Fossil Hunter*, included material not featured on the longer audio cassette, so both were unique items. Kevin Glover and I produced the video through Popcorn Pictures. It included rare photos from Ned's own collection, historical motion-picture footage, video of Ned at the famous Ghost Ranch quarry (shot by paleontologist George Callison) where he discovered thousands of specimens of the small meat-eating dinosaur *Coelophysis*, and a very special appearance by Colbert's wife and artist collaborator Margaret.

Future "Dinosaur Talks" albums would feature the voices of paleontologists Elmer S. Riggs (1869–1963) and Charles M. Sternberg (1885–1981).

Sidetracking

Our "Dinosaur Tracks" tunes eventually (like the critters that left all those footprints) were on the move, some of them turning up in places other than Fossil Records albums and Popcorn Pictures videos:

Various songs from the original *Dinosaur Tracks* were played in 1990 at the Minneapolis Planetarium as people entered its theater for the show "Dinosaurs in the Dark of Night." Songs from all three "Dinosaur Tracks" albums have likewise been played in museum auditoriums before a lecture or other program, and also inside various "dinosaur shops" to attract customers' attention.

"Dinosaur Movies," a song from the first album, was used in *The Hollywood Dinosaur Chronicles* (Rhino Home Video, 1990), a video documentary in which I appeared, hosted by movie star Doug McClure. (McClure had starred in the Edgar Rice Burroughs/prehistoric-world films *The Land That Time Forgot*, 1974, *At the Earth's Core*, 1976, and *The People That Time Forgot*, 1977.)

That same song was also a basis (along with my lecture "Fantasy Dinosaurs of the Movies") for the feature-length video documentary *Dinosaur Movies* (cover title: *Dinosaurs!*, Simitar Entertainment, 1993), that I directed and co-hosted with actress Christy Block. Kevin Glover and I produced it through Popcorn Pictures. Featured in the video were stop-motion animators Jim Danforth and Ray Harryhausen, Forrest J Ackerman ("Mr. Science Fiction"), and lots of (sometimes rare) old movie clips. Highlighted is an original dinosaur scene shot especially for this documentary (also used in the *Dinosaur Tracks* video) by Oscar-nominated Danforth.

"Prehysteria!" a song on *More Dinosaur Tracks*, came out before the hit direct-to-video movie picture *Prehysteria!* (Paramount 1993), which was co-produced by Fossil Records' own Pete Von Sholly. Pete had an earlier idea and screenplay for the movie, with an accompanying poster painted by noted "paleo-artist" Mark Hallett. This version of the project was quite different from the movie that Paramount would actually release. For that original project, Pete asked me to try to come up with a pop song titled "Prehysteria!" reflecting the current popularity of dinosaurs, and which might be worked into the movie. However, the film that was eventually made featured the "King Tyrant Lizard," a *Tyrannosaurus rex* named "Elvis." Consequently the film was scored with original music suggesting that other "King." The movie, about miniature dinosaurs—and which spawned two sequels—became the biggest money-maker in the history of direct-to-video movies, *despite* its not using our song.

Excerpts from a number of "Dinosaur Tracks" tunes were featured in two travelog-documentary videos—*Dinosaurs Next Exit: A Discovery Guide to America's Dinosaur Attractions*, Volumes I, "Dinosaur Parks," and II, "Dinosaur Digs and Museums" (Cleval Films, 1994), with cover art by Pete and my appearances. There were also different versions of these shows edited, one for TV broadcast, another directed toward children.

The tunes "The Unknown Lost Island" and "Dinosaur Valley Girls," from the first and third albums, respectively, were conceived as theme songs for two upcoming comedy motion pictures. *Journey to the Unknown Lost Island (That Time Forgot)*, which may get made someday by Cine-Zoic Films, with co-producers Don Glut and David (*Star Trek*) Stipes, is an *Airplane*-type spoof of dinosaur movies about a group of castaways stranded you-know-where. It sends up many dinosaur movies old and new alike. *Dinosaur Valley Girls*, about a young actor who is magically zapped back to an impossible prehistoric world where cave people and dinosaurs co-exist, was filmed by Frontline Entertainment in 1995, released to television in 1996, and released on home video in 1997 and on DVD in 2000.

Popcorn Pictures may also put out a new and improved video version of the original *Dinosaur Tracks* TV series. Its featured guests include movie special-effects wizard Isadoro (*Baby … Secret of the Lost Legend*) Raponi, cartoonists Scott (*The Flintstones*) Shaw!, Mike Van Cleave and "Prehistoric" Pete, Von Sholly, Mark Hallett, and vertebrate paleontologists Robert A. Long and Marc R. Gallup.

Pete Von Sholly worked up his theme for "The Ultra-Colossal Dinosaur Circus" into a major children's book for which he has produced a minimum of 17 marvelous paintings. This is a fantasy story about the ultimate circus experience of a young dinosaur buff. Keep watching the stores!

Our final word will be from that dino-dude, Doc Dino himself:

> Awwwright, all you Dino-Trackers!! It's ol' Doc Dino, that "Last Living Dinosaur" himself, getting in the last dino-word, reminding you to keep your pineal eyes focused on Fossil Records. "Dinosaur" Don and "Prehistoric" Pete, each one a "Fossil Fool" and okay "Dinosaur Guy," are cooking up some really lava-hot projects. Each one's a volcanic blast from the prehistoric past, and you don't want to be left behind in the crater when they erupt.
>
> Like some rad reptiles I know, Fossil Records just keeps on growing, and that's no croc! So be there or be extinct! Like those first dinosaurs used to put it way back in the Triassic, this is just the beginning!
>
> And so, 'til next time, then … "Keep on Trackin!"
>
> —Later, 'Gators!

DINOSAUR VALLEY DINOSAURS

Just as the first article in this section of the book has historical (as well as "prehistoric") significance for me, so does this next to last. The following piece marks my first "journal-style" article to appear in a professional paleontological symposium volume (*Dinofest International: Proceedings of a Symposium Held at Arizona State University*, edited by Donald L. Wolberg, Edmund Stump, and Gary Rosenberg, published in 1997 by The Academy of Natural Sciences of Philadelphia). Articles written in this format are generally peer-reviewed before their acceptance and subsequent publication in a credited scientific journal or symposium book.

The subject of this article combines science with popular media, focusing upon the fantasy motion picture *Dinosaur Valley Girls™* which I wrote, directed, cast, and co-produced for Frontline Entertainment, a production company I own with equal partners Daniel J. Mullen and Kevin M. Glover. The movie was released to cable television in 1996, to the home video market the following year, and on DVD in 2000.

The reader will notice that this article differs in various ways from others presented in this volume. Journal articles almost always follow certain rules of format. These include opening the piece with an "abstract" or brief summary of what the article will be about and ending with a section concluding what was discussed in the article. References within the article, noted by an author's name in parentheses followed by a publication year, relate directly to a bibliography appearing at the end of the piece. I trust the reader will catch on quickly to this format, have no trouble understanding how it works, and be inspired, I hope, to seek out such articles by other authors, though of a more scientific nature.

The movie itself has since been discussed by the author extensively in *Dinosaur Valley Girls: The Book* (McFarland & Company, Inc., Publishers, 1998). However, that book's sections on the movie's dinosaurs and special effects are not covered with such detail as in the article that follows. The movie was released on video in two versions ("general audience" and the more adult-oriented "director's cut") by EI Independent Cinema and is, like the book on the film's making, available from McFarland.

The following article appears, with very few changes, through the courtesy of Donald L. Wolberg and Dinofest™, "The World's Fair of Dinosaurs."

ABSTRACT—Dinosaurs have been subjects for motion pictures since the earliest days of the medium. However, most films have presented dinosaurs inaccurately or in outdated modes, usually as "monsters." Relatively few movies have treated dinosaurs simply as animals and based their restorations upon current scientific information.

Although a fantasy-comedy in which dinosaurs and "cave people" coexist, the motion picture *Dinosaur Valley Girls* (1996) attempted to portray dinosaurs, most prominently an *Allosaurus*, and other Mesozoic creatures, accurately in both appearance and general behavior. The extinct animals in the film were designed, made, and given screen "life" by Thomas R. Dickens. Dickens worked from the "bones up" to create his finished model animals. The step-by-step processes by which Dickens produced his creatures and then animated them for the film will be discussed.

The various Mesozoic animals featured in *Dinosaur Valley Girls* are, the author believes, among the most accurate ever to appear in an entertainment motion picture to date of this film's original release.

Introduction

Within a few years following the invention of the Kinetoscope by Thomas Alva Edison in 1889, dinosaurs (as well as other extinct animals) have been popular subjects for motion pictures. Prehistoric animals were featured on the moving-picture screen as early as 1905 (*Prehistoric Peeps*) and 1908 (*The Prehistoric Man*). In fact, the earliest classic character designed for an animated cartoon was an amiable *Apatosaurus* (then popularly known as "*Brontosaurus*"), drawn and animated by cartoonist Winsor McCay for his short film *Gertie* (1912), aka *Gertie the Dinosaur*.

Traditionally, the majority of motion pictures featuring dinosaurs and other extinct animals have been in the science-fiction and fantasy genres. Such films are usually set 1) back in some imaginary and catch-all "prehistoric time period" wherein dinosaurs and so-called "cavemen" coexist (*e.g.*, *When Dinosaurs Ruled the Earth* [1971]); 2) in the present, but in some isolated location such as an island (*e.g.*, *Unknown Island* [1948]), a jungle (*e.g.*, *Jungle Manhunt* [1951]), or atop a plateau (*The Lost World* [1925]), cut off from time and where dinosaurs still live; or 3) in a modern metropolis, where some usually overly gigantic Mesozoic reptile, somehow brought back to life in the modern world, goes on a destructive rampage (*e.g.*, *The Beast from 20,000 Fathoms* [1953]). Occasionally, movie dinosaurs and other prehistoric reptiles have inhabited such exotic locales as realms beneath the Earth's surface (*e.g.*, *At the Earth's Core* [1976]) and even other planets (*e.g.*, *Planet of Dinosaurs* [1977]).

In most of these films, dinosaurs have been portrayed in the familiar yet outmoded image of sluggish, slow-moving, tail-dragging creatures existing only to menace the hapless humans who encounter them, or to engage each other in spectacular battles. Sometimes, dinosaurs have even been depicted by photographically enlarged iguanas, monitors, tegu lizards, and other modern day reptiles (*e.g.*, *One Million B.C.* [1940]), oftentimes adorned with rubber horns, fins, or other accouterments to make them appear "prehistoric" (Glut 1980).

Unfortunately, motion-picture producers and the creators of movie special effects have generally regarded dinosaurs as "monsters" or creatures of fantasy (occupying the same world as vampires, dragons, and space aliens), rather than real animals subject to the laws of science. Even when relatively rare attempts at authenticity have been made, the reference materials used for the animals' design are too frequently outdated popular (sometimes children's) books or the inaccurate subjects of earlier dinosaur films. One error, thereby, leads to another and possibly more. Oftentimes, movie dinosaurs have been designed with incorrect contours to accommodate a human actor wearing a rubber costume (*e.g.*, the *Apatosaurus* in *Baby ... Secret of the Lost Legend* [1985]), or have been reconfigured into entirely imaginary creatures (*e.g.*, *Gorgo* [1961]).

Very rarely, over a span of almost a century, have dinosaurs been treated in motion pictures with any serious attempt at accuracy and based on up-to-date information. A relatively rare exception, the 1993 movie adaptation of Michael Crichton's novel *Jurassic Park*, presented dinosaurs as basically real animals (instead of monsters) founded upon current data, although a number of liberties were invoked in both dinosaurian design and behavior. Unfortunately, such liberties (*e.g.*, the flaring neck frill and venomous saliva of the *Dilophosaurus*), springing purely from the imagination, were accepted by many viewers as founded in scientific fact.

More recently, *Dinosaur Valley Girls*, made by Frontline Entertainment, Inc., and released in 1996, was an atypical movie in that it featured a group of Mesozoic creatures intended to appear and, in most cases, behave as accurately as possible, based upon present scientific information.

INSTITUTIONAL ABBREVIATIONS—AMNH, American Museum of Natural History, New York City; MACN, Museo Argentino de Ciencias Naturales, Buenos Aires; MOR, Museum of the Rockies, Bozeman; USNM, National Museum of Natural History, Washington, D.C.

Discussion

MESOZOIC BESTIARY—*Dinosaur Valley Girls*, as should be evident from its title, is a fantasy comedy combining Mesozoic creatures and "cave people." Its storyline follows the adventures of a modern day movie star who, via a magical icon, is hurled backwards through time to "Dinosaur Valley," a mythical realm where, through unknown and unexplainable forces, creatures from different time periods and places coexist. In "high concept" vernacular, the basic theme can be somewhat regarded as "*A Connecticut Yankee in King Arthur's Court* meets *One Million B.C.*"

Although *Dinosaur Valley Girls* is a whimsical movie, it was the present author's intent, as co-producer, writer, and director of the film, and whose name has been linked over the years to various more serious dinosaur-related projects, to portray its dinosaurs with accuracy. Dinosaurs are *not*, after all, monsters or fanciful creatures but *real animals*, some of which are known from quite complete fossil remains. There is no logical reason to portray inaccurately *any* animal, extinct or extant, which can be portrayed correctly.

For the record, the picture included a small "menagerie" of Mesozoic animals, including the horned theropod, *Carnotaurus sastrei*, the titanosaurid sauropod, *Saltasaurus loricatus*, and the camptosaurid ornithopod, *Camptosaurus dispar* (apparently the first appearance of any of these three dinosaurian taxa in a "Hollywood" movie), the stegosaur, *Stegosaurus stenops*, and also two species of the giant pterosaur: *Pteranodon* (the more familiar *P. ingens* and also the high-crested *P. sternbergi*). The animal given the most screen time in the movie was the theropod, *Allosaurus fragilis*, a pesky character referred to in the film (and in a featured song of the same title) as the "Jurassic Punk."™

Thomas R. Dickens's one-fifth scale "animatronic" model of *Allosaurus fragilis* ("Jurassic Punk"™), used in the movie *Dinosaur Valley Girls*™ (1996). Photograph by Alfred Florez, ©Frontline Entertainment, all rights reserved.

Also included in the film were two giant lizards, a tegu and an ornate Nile monitor, photographed in slow motion to give them a sense of great mass. These animals were *not* intended to represent dinosaurs. Their accuracy as lizards, however, cannot be questioned.

CREATURE DESIGN—The Mesozoic animals of *Dinosaur Valley Girls* were all designed, created, and then brought to "life" on screen by Thomas R. Dickens (through his special-effects company Integrity Productions), an artist and sculptor known for his accurate re-creations of extinct animals. Like other respected "paleo-artists," Dickens bases his life restorations upon current scientific data, beginning work with the skeleton of the animal to be restored. Musculature is built up over this skeletal framework, after which integument, then finally color is added. (Some of Dickens's sculptures of extinct creatures have been made available as assembly kits through such companies as Saurian Studios and Monsters in Motion.)

Although Dickens is certainly quite capable of doing accurate life restorations on his own, I felt that a qualified dinosaur expert should be involved in the project, both as a more objective critic and also to lend some paleontological authority or legitimacy to the production. Therefore, Gregory S. Paul, a paleo-artist himself, as well as a published vertebrate paleontologist, was brought onto the project in its early stages of preproduction as the film's "Dinosaur Consultant."

Paul sent Dickens various illustrations depicting skeletons, musculature, and the animals in life, most of these having been drawn or painted by Paul himself. From these source materials, Dickens produced his own detailed life restorations of the animals, drawn in pencil, which he submitted to Paul for changes, suggestions, and criticisms.

All drawings, having been approved by Paul, were then submitted to the author for final approval. Generally, I tend to remain rather conservative in my views concerning theories and notions about dinosaurs that have not, at least in my opinion, been convincingly demonstrated. In the few instances where Paul and I disagreed as to certain details of an animal's external appearance—as in his preference to include dorsal spines on *Saltasaurus*, based on an idea proposed by Czerkas (1992) that all sauropods may have born such spike-like growths—I exerted my right as co-producer and director of the movie to reject them.

Dickens studied the best reference materials available to him. For example, Bonaparte's (1985) description of *Carnotaurus*, as well as Paul's skeletal drawings, comprised the foundations for that dinosaur's design. Because the coloration of dinosaurs cannot be known from fossil evidence and is therefore open to speculation, Dickens made use of artistic license and educated guesses, basing their colors on those of extant animals occupying possibly similar niches. Dickens speculated that *Carnotaurus* could have been black like a panther.

As the titanosaurid sauropod *Saltasaurus* is known from incomplete fossil remains, Dickens was given some artistic freedom in its design. The basic, reconstructed skeletal structure was sketched by Paul, based somewhat on what is known of the anatomy of other titanosaurid genera. Because titanosaurids seem to have been fairly wide animals, Dickens gave it a rather wide mid-section. The skull of *Saltasaurus* is mostly unknown; but since the teeth in this genus are peg-like as in diplodocids, Dickens gave it a rather generic sauropod head somewhat patterned after that of the Mongolian diplodocid *Nemegtosaurus*. As titanosaurids are known to have whiplash tails, one was given to *Saltasaurus* (which this dinosaur swings defensively in one scene against the attacking *Allosaurus*). Armored scutes were placed on the dorsal and lateral regions of the body, as originally suggested by Bonaparte and Powell (1980) and Powell (1980).

Because sauropods were large herbivorous animals, Dickens studied pictures of elephants' skin (Kunkel 1981) as a basis for the skin wrinkling of his *Saltasaurus*, and also colored the skin based on that of an elephant or giraffe. Subtle yellow and black stripes were added to the tip of tail, serving as warning colors (as in wasps). The sauropod's eyes were colored yellow to impart a birdlike effect.

Although still a somewhat controversial idea, the sauropod was depicted in one scene rearing up on its hind legs to feed on tall trees.

The *Camptosaurus*, based upon skeletal reconstructions by Paul, was given a fleshy dorsal frill, and also a "dewlap" on the ventral area of the neck. Although these epidermal accouterments, if present in camptosaurids, have not been preserved in collected specimens of *Camptosaurus*, similar features have been observed in various specimens of related hadrosaurs, including the so-called "mummy" (AMNH 5060) of *Edmontosaurus annectens* (Osborn 1912), the holotype (AMNH 5240) skeleton of *Corythosaurus casuarius* (Brown 1916), and a tail section (MOR V 007) of a presumed *Edmontosaurus* (Horner 1984). The *Camptosaurus* was given a tannish color based on that of some African grazing animals.

The *Stegosaurus* design was inspired by Paul's (1987) painting of this genus, which had been based on the "roadkill" holotype (USNM 4934) of *S. stenops*, first described briefly by Marsh (1887), and then in detail by Gilmore (1914), and also on two more recently collected *Stegosaurus* specimens discovered, respectively, by Donna McKowen in Utah and by Bryan Small in Colorado. All three of these specimens clearly show an alternating plate arrangement, which is, consequently, the way *Stegosaurus* appears in this film.

The flying reptile, *Pteranodon ingens*, was depicted with wing membranes having wing-strengthening fibers. Based on a relatively recent idea, the membranes were shown attached to the two tips of the very short tail rather than to the legs, the legs remaining free of the wings; this idea may, however, prove incorrect after all, as small pterosaur specimens have been subsequently found showing the membranes attached to the legs (G. S. Paul, personal communication 1996). The color was based on that of some birds, the body dark gray on top and light gray (for camouflage) underneath, the beak bright red and black. The pterosaur sported small hair structures except on its legs, beak, crest, and hands. The flight pattern of the *Pteranodon* was based upon diagrams published by Bramwell and Whitfield (1974) and redrawn for Wellnhofer (1991).

Allosaurus was selected as the dinosaur to be most prominently featured in the film for various reasons. As an active theropod, it would provide the required menace for the human characters and other dinosaurs. It was not as large as some other theropods (*e.g.*, the gigantic *Tyrannosaurus rex*), which made its interaction with humans more feasible and visually practical. The animal could also be quite accurately restored, known, as it is, from a wealth of collected fossil remains, primarily those collected at the Cleveland-Lloyd Dinosaur Quarry in central-eastern Utah (Madsen 1976).

The film's *Allosaurus* was based on a number of sources, primarily the following: 1) the restored composite skull (measuring approximately 92 cm, representing a very large *Allosaurus* growth stage), a composite *A. fragilis* skeleton mounted at the Utah Museum of Natural History, and various skeletal elements figured by Madsen (1976); 2) my own cast of that former skull, obtained from Madsen's DINOLAB in Salt Lake City (another cast of that skull, provided by Mary Jean Odano's Valley Anatomical Preparations of Canoga Park, California, was used as a prop in the movie; and 3) skeletal and muscle-restoration drawings of *A. fragilis* drawn by Gregory S. Paul (1987, 1988), as well as life restorations of this species by Paul (1988).

Since no skin impressions of *Allosaurus* have yet been found, Dickens patterned this dinosaur's integument upon that seen on Stephen A. Czerkas's sculpture of *Carnotaurus*, exhibited at the Museum of Natural History of Los Angeles County, which Czerkas had made from skin impressions preserved in the holotype (MACN-CH 894) skeleton of *C. sastrei*. The skin of Dickens's pet ornate Nile monitor lizard also served as a model. Birdlike scales were added to the tops of the hands. Although no hard evidence exists supporting the fleshy, spike-like dorsal "scutes" shown on the *Allosaurus's* neck, back, and tail, Paul approved them, noting that such a frill was certainly possible, perhaps consisting of large "scales" which may have had a display function. As I was attempting to distinguish the *Allosaurus* in various ways to trademark the "Jurassic Punk" character, I also approved this frill.

Rather than assign the *Allosaurus* the traditional lizard-like or serpentine tongue flicked-out by so many movie dinosaurs, Dickens turned to the dinosaurs' closest living relatives, crocodiles and birds, for inspiration. Dickens designed a broad tongue, similar to the tongues of crocodiles and some birds (*e.g.*, parrots) that could facilitate the swallowing of large chunks of meat, and colored it based on the tongues of some skinks and birds. Following an illustration by Paul (1988) of an open-mouthed *Dilophosaurus*, Dickens also showed the internal nostrils and the opening of the trachea, which can be seen when the *Allosaurus's* mouth opens wide enough and the angle is appropriate.

Dickens, as do some vertebrate paleontologists, believes that theropods were active, endothermic animals, and chose his paint scheme to depict this dinosaur accordingly. Although lizards are not analogous to dinosaurs, Dickens attempted to suggest a living *Allosaurus* by looking to various extant lizards (*e.g.*, his pet monitor) and birds (*e.g.*, hawks) in similar predator niches for possible color schemes. Dickens gave his *Allosaurus* a basic monitor-green coloration including a striped tail, while making the legs yellowish green for an avian effect.

The "lightning bolt" markings were added to the face to meet certain identification demands dictated by the script, and also, again, to distinguish the dinosaur for trademark purposes.

Creature Construction and Animation

Because *Dinosaur Valley Girls* was filmed at a very low cost, its budget could not afford such state of the art special-effects techniques as the computer graphics imagery (CGI) perfected in *Jurassic Park*. It was decided that traditional methods, like those used in movies since the earliest days of the medium, were more affordable and still acceptable. Dickens brought his prehistoric creatures to "life" following storyboards—a chronologically arranged sequence of drawings representing individual shots to be filmed, some indicating character movement and also camera directions— sketched by the film's "Dinosaur Illustrator," Frank Brunner.

Most of the animals were given movement through stop-motion photography or dimensional animation, a process almost as old as the movie industry itself. Stop-motion animation was perfected by various artists during the 1920s, including paleontology buff Willis O'Brien, who created some surprisingly accurate (given what scientific information was available at the time) prehistoric animals for such fantasy films as *The Lost World* (1925) and *King Kong* (1933). The process is simple yet effective and works by the same principle as does the animated cartoon. A jointed model is moved a fraction of an inch and one frame of motion-picture film is exposed. The model is again moved and photographed in the successive frame. This process is repeated again and again until the desired length of footage has been taken simulating, through the incremental movements of the model, a certain action. When this sequence of single-frame exposed frames is then projected, and thanks to a phenomenon of the eye popularly known as "persistence of vision," the model seems to be moving (Glut 1978; Goldner and Turner 1975).

Dickens made all of his stop-motion creatures one-twelfth scale (a convenient scale for this special-effects process) basically using the following steps:

1. Joints were plotted out by Dickens over the skeletal drawing. Machinist Peter Marinello then fashioned together an articulated ball-and-socket armature from steel, brass, and aluminum pieces, following the correct dimensions of the skeleton. When finished, the armature was wrapped in tin foil for protection.

2. The animal was sculpted by Dickens, using a plasticine clay molded over a metal frame attached to a wooden base, many details (*e.g.*, scalation) being added individually.

3. The completed sculpture was cast in plaster.

4. A latex "positive" of the animal's epidermis was pulled from the mold and worked over the metal armature.

5. Finally, the completed model was painted.

Dickens animated the models frame-by-frame on a miniature set, with a 5 by 2.4-meter background painting by him suggesting the Pearblossom, California, desert location where much of the film's live-action footage was shot, and with miniature trees and other vegetation. Most of this miniature flora was based on illustrations published by Stewart and Rothwell (1993), sculpted by Dickens, cast and made by his assistant Laurie Hyatt, then painted by Dickens and Hyatt.

Combining scenes of the animated dinosaurs with live-action human actors was accomplished by use of the "blue screen" process. Stop-motion creatures photographed in front of a special blue screen could then be "married" with virtually any background scene, providing the scene did not contain any of that same color. In one instance (apparently a first for this film), a live-action monitor lizard shared a scene with a stop-motion *Pteranodon* via blue-screen compositing.

However, as the stop-motion process is both a time-consuming and expensive one, we decided to find a faster and more practical way of dealing with the numerous shots required of the *Allosaurus* by the film's script. Dickens suggested a method which solved the problem—the construction of a realistic "animatronic" (mechanical) *Allosaurus* model built approximately one-fifth the size of a large (approximately 10.5-meter long) individual.

The one-fifth scale *Allosaurus* was constructed over a mechanical, steel "skeleton," built by Ken Walker to fit inside a styrofoam core of the animal's shape made by Dickens. Featured in this "skeleton" were eyes molded in silicone over correctly-sized ball bearings, then cast in transparent polyester resin and painted with elliptical pupils similar to those in crocodiles and venomous snakes. Dickens chose this design not only to suggest the dinosaur's affinities, but also to identify it as a predator and give the animal a "dignified" look.

When completed under Dickens's direction, the mechanical *Allosaurus*, outfitted in the latex hide which he had sculpted in minute detail and then cast, was capable of numerous movements. Two servo motors in its head worked the eyes (which could move back and forth) and the eyelids. The rest of the body was cable-driven. The mouth could open to 70 degrees (the maximum range, according to Paul). The neck could go up, down, move to the right or left, even pitch and yaw. The main neck movement occurred at the atlas, other movements of the neck being slighter. Two latex gloves in the lung region, connected with rubber bands and surgical tubing (and requiring a human to inhale and exhale), allowed the model to breathe. The arms and elbows were operated by rods and cables. The jointed legs could be moved from below. In short, the animatronic *Allosaurus* could perform most movements except for actually walking (although it did simulate that action in one brief shot).

The animatronic *Allosaurus* was combined with human actors using a very old and simple camera trick known as "forced perspective," which makes such combinations possible without having to resort to costly and often complicated optical effects. Forced perspective was probably used to best effect in the movie *Darby O'Gill and the Little People* (1959). The process allows a relatively small object, such as our *Allosaurus* model, to appear much larger in a frame occupied by a human actor. It is based upon a depth-of-field phenomenon, whereby, if the sunlight is bright enough and a wide-angle lens is used, two objects, though in reality some distance from one another, appear to occupy the same dimensional plane by maintaining sharp focus. In other words, the *Allosaurus* model, rigged up close to the camera, can appear to be bigger than the human actors, who are actually standing some distance away from the camera and the model.

To complete the illusion of a live dinosaur, Dickens also sculpted and cast, in rubber, a full-sized *Allosaurus* forearm and hand, the claws modeled over manual phalanges belonging to this genus obtained from DINO-LAB. This highly detailed forearm could be worn like a huge rubber glove (in one shot, by the author) and directly interact with human actors (*e.g.*, knocking the spears out of the cavemen's hands), with no requirement for blue-screen or forced-perspective trickery, as long as the actor wearing this appliance was kept out of frame. For additional accuracy, Paul informed Dickens how the forearms and hands of the *Allosaurus* were positioned alongside the body and probably moved.

Over the decades, most movie dinosaurs have roared with the sounds of lions, bears, elephants, or other recognizable animals, sometimes slowed down or speeded up, dubbed into their gaping mouths. Eschewing that clichéd route, I proposed that the living relatives of dinosaurs might again provide an interesting analog in creating their vocal sounds. Thomas Morse, who designed many of the film's sound effects (and also composed its musical score), slowed-down a crocodile's roar, which worked as the growl of the *Allosaurus*. When the dinosaur roared, Morse combined a slowed-down and extended hawk's cry with the crocodile sound. The resulting sound, the audio signature of the film's *Allosaurus*, is unique.

Conclusion

Though the motion picture *Dinosaur Valley Girls* is a comedy/fantasy, its Mesozoic bestiary was designed to be as accurate as possible, based upon current paleontological data. Artistic license in creature design was employed only in cases wherein a taxon was known through incomplete skeletal material, *e.g.*, *Saltasaurus*, and missing parts had to be imagined based upon related taxa or when "educated guesses" were made regarding certain details, *e.g.*, frills, coloration, *etc.*, not preserved in the fossil record. Those thoughts considered, the makers of *Dinosaur Valley Girls* believe its dinosaurs to be among the most accurate and up to date ever to appear in a Hollywood movie.

Acknowledgments

Thanks are due to Thomas R. Dickens for spending a considerable amount of time discussing with me the step-by-step process by which he created and gave cinematic "life" to the various Mesozoic animals of *Dinosaur Valley Girls*. I also thank vertebrate paleontologists Michael K. Brett-Surman, James H. Madsen, Jr., John S. McIntosh, and Gregory S. Paul for critically reading, correcting, and, consequently, improving the manuscript.

NOTE: All *Dinosaur Valley Girls* imagery is copyright © 1996 by Frontline Entertainment, Inc. "Dinosaur Valley Girls" and "Jurassic Punk," including names and likenesses thereof, and all related indicia, are trademarks (™) of Fossil Records (Burbank, CA) and Frontline Entertainment, Inc.

References

Bonaparte, J. F., 1985, "A horned dinosaur from Patagonia": *NGR*, Winter, pp. 149–151.

_____, and J. E. Powell, 1980, "A continental assemblage of tetrapods from the Upper Cretaceous Beds of El Brete, Northwestern Argentina (Sauropoda-Coelurosauria-Carnosauria-Aves)": *Memoires de la Société Géologique de France, Nouvelle Serie*, pp. 19–28.

Bramwell, C. D., and G. R. Whitfield, 1974, "Biomechanics of *Pteranodon*": *Philosophical Transactions of the Royal Society, London*, 267, pp. 503–592.

Brown, B., 1916, "*Corythosaurus casuarius*: skeleton, musculature and epidermis": *American Museum of Natural History Bulletin*, 35 (38), pp. 709–716.

Czerkas, S. A., 1992, "Discovery of dermal spines reveals a new look for sauropod dinosaurs": *Geology*, 20, pp. 1068–70.

Gilmore, C. W., 1914, "Osteology of the armored dinosauria in the United States National Museum, with special reference to the genus *Stegosaurus*": *Memoirs of the United States National Museum*, 89, pp. 1–316.

Glut, D. F., 1978, *Classic Movie Monsters*. Metuchen, N.J.: Scarecrow Press, xviii, 442 pages.

_____, 1980, *The Dinosaur Scrapbook*. Secaucus, N.J.: Citadel Press, a division of Lyle Stuart, Inc., 318 pages.

Goldner, O., and G. E. Turner, 1975, *The Making of King Kong*. Cranbury, N.J.: A. S. Barnes and Co., Inc., 271.

Horner, J. R., 1984, "A 'segmented' epidermal tail frill in a species of hadrosaurian dinosaur": *Journal of Paleontology*, 58 (1), pp. 270–271.

Kunkel, R., 1981, *Elephants*. Hamburg: Hoffman und Campe, 255 pages.

Madsen, J. H., Jr., 1976, *Allosaurus fragilis: A Revised Osteology. Utah Geological and Mineral Survey, Utah Department of Natural Resources*, Bulletin 109, xii, 163 pages.

Marsh, O. C., 1877, "Principle characters of American Jurassic dinosaurs, pt. 9. The skull and dermal armor of *Stegosaurus*": *American Journal of Science*, Series 3, 34, pp. 413–417.

Osborn, H. F., 1912, "Integument of the iguanodont dinosaur *Trachodon*": *American Museum of Natural History Memoirs* (new series), 1, pp. 33–54.

Paul, G. S., 1987, "The science and art of restoring the life appearance of dinosaurs and their relatives," *in*: S.J. Czerkas and E. C. Olson (ed.), *Dinosaurs Past and Present*. Volume II. Seattle and London: Natural History Museum of Los Angeles/University of Washington Press, pp. 4–49.

_____, 1988, *Predatory Dinosaurs of the World*. New York: Simon and Schuster, 403 pages.

Powell, J. E., 1980. "Sobre la presencia de una aramadura dermica en algunos dinosaurios titanosauridos": *Acta Geologica Lilloana*, 15 (2), pp. 41–47.

Stewart, W. M., and G. W. Rothwell, 1993, *Paleobotany and the Evolution of Plants* (2nd Edition). New York: Press Syndicate of the University of Cambridge, xii, 521 pages.

Wellnhofer, P., 1991, *The Illustrated Encyclopedia of Pterosaurs*. New York: Crescent Books, 192 pages.

JURASSIC PUNK™

It had long been my dream to spin-off the movie *Dinosaur Valley Girls* ™ into various lines of merchandise, creating a kind of "mini-franchise." Among the many ideas bandied about—including comic books, a "novelization" and trading cards—was a projected series of model assembly kits of the movie's prehistoric creatures, starting off with our "Jurassic Punk™" or *Allosaurus*.

The time was correct for a model assembly kit. The 1990s was a sort of renaissance for the model kit hobby. Assembly kits had become quite popular again, but on a higher level. These were no longer the simple, mass-produced plastic kits of decades past, created by nameless staff workers, and often slapped together with "airplane glue" by the hobbyist in a matter of minutes. These were highly detailed resin models sculpted by oftentimes renowned artists. This new breed of assembly kit required skills and patience; such kits were usually expensive and could take months to put together. They were usually reviewed in such publications as *Prehistoric Times* and *Dinosaur World*, or even in magazines entirely devoted to kit-building.

The *Allosaurus* was, of course, the logical choice to be the flagship critter in this *Dinosaur Valley Girls* series. The "Jurassic Punk" was the movie's primary Mesozoic menace, occupying more screen time than any of the other animals. It figured most prominently in the storyline, both in the prehistoric as well as modern-day sequences. It was also a visually appealing dinosaur and its name was among those best known to laypersons as well as to scientists and serious students. This allosaur was also the subject of the song "Jurassic Punk," which was featured first on the cassette album *Dinosaur Tracks Again* (Fossil Records) in 1994, and which was the basis for a musical sequence in *Dinosaur Valley Girls*.

After discussing the project with several model-kit companies,

we settled on going with Valley Anatomical Preparations of
Canoga Park, California, a company whose main product line is a
series of resin fossil cast reproductions. Intended for inclusion
with the kit was a brochure written by the present author. With
only minor changes, the text of that brochure follows.

Dinosaur Valley Girls (Frontline Entertainment, Inc., 1996) may very
well be the first Hollywood dinosaur movie in which Mesozoic reptiles
are depicted with complete anatomical accuracy, based upon up-to-the-
minute paleontological information.

The movie's main (and most pesky) dinosaur, the so-called "Jurassic Punk," is an *Allosaurus fragilis.* The animal proves to be the most ubiquitous menace of Dinosaur Valley—a mythical realm wherein dinosaurs
and "cave people" mysteriously coexist—finally giving up and walking
away when facing the modern-day ingenuity and resourcefulness of the
film's hero, ex-movie star Tony Markham.

Allosaurus was a genus belonging to the Carnosauria, a group of
theropod (*i.e.,* mostly bipedal and carnivorous) dinosaurs. Adult *Allosaurus*
individuals ranged in size from about 20 to perhaps more than 40 feet in
length. The creature had a narrow head with small "lacrimal" horns above
its eyes, powerful forearms bearing prominent three-clawed hands, three-
toed birdlike feet and a very long tail. This dinosaur may have been the
top predator of its Late Jurassic world (about 140 million years ago). It is
known from numerous specimens, representing many growth stages, collected from Upper Jurassic rocks in Utah, Colorado, New Mexico, Okla-
homa, Wyoming, Montana, and South Dakota.

The "Jurassic Punk," as well as all the other prehistoric reptiles living in Dinosaur Valley, were created and brought to life on screen by
noted sculptor and special-effects creator Thomas R. Dickens through his
company Integrity Productions.

Tom based the film's *Allosaurus* directly upon a number of fossil specimens, mostly material collected from the famous Cleveland-Lloyd
Dinosaur Quarry in central-eastern Utah. This material includes a three-
foot skull cast prepared at (vertebrate paleontologist) Dr. James H. Madsen Jr.'s DINOLAB in Salt Lake City (currently available for purchase
from Valley Anatomical Preparations of Canoga Park, California). As no
skin impressions of this dinosaur have yet been found, the scaly integument was patterned after that known to belong to *Carnotaurus*, a very
large horned theropod that appears briefly in the film.

Working from the "bones up," Tom reconstructed the allosaur's musculature, producing some final sketches of the fleshed-out animal. These drawings were subsequently mailed to paleontologist and "paleo-artist" Gregory S. Paul, the movie's "Dinosaur Consultant," for approval. The present writer, also the film's director, had the final word as to the creature's design. The color of the *Allosaurus* resulted from logical choices based upon the color schemes of modern animals. The distinctive "lightning" marking on the allosaur's face (perhaps a natural marking, or even a scar from some earlier, as of yet unrecorded adventure) would figure significantly into the movie's plot. (For the complete account of how Dickens and his special-effects crew accomplished movie miracles on a very low budget and in very little time, using stop-motion models and also a seven-foot-long animatronic *Allosaurus*, see the preceding article).

This assembly kit, which was also designed by Tom Dickens, is an exact and only slightly restored reproduction of the *Allosaurus* from *Dinosaur Valley Girls*—a veritable "clone," molded from the one and only stop-motion model used in the movie. It is, therefore, the closest a collector can ever come to owning the original special-effects model itself. In addition to its value as a piece of movie "prehistory," however, the model also shines as a scientifically accurate sculpture created by a fine and renowned artist.

When completed, the "Jurassic Punk"—the first model figure in our *Dinosaur Valley Girls* intended collection—should occupy a place of honor in your home, studio, or paleo-lab.

Following are the complete lyrics to the song "Jurassic Punk," heard in the movie *Dinosaur Valley Girls* and available on the cassette album *Dinosaur Tracks Again*.

"Jurassic Punk"

Way out West are bony clues of many an ancient clash,
Preserved by pebbly sand and mud and dark volcanic ash,
These Late Jurassic sediments, the Morrison Formation,
A record of the *Allosaurus*, prince of all predation.

A yard-long head with three-inch teeth, small horns above his eyes,
'Least thirty feet from front to back, scares creatures twice his size.
Balanced by his long, stiff tail, he's got some attitude.
Strutting fast on birdlike feet, he's one bad dino-dude.

Jurassic Punk, Jurassic Punk,
He takes the lead, he's out to feed.
Jurassic Punk, Jurassic Punk,
He gets his way, he rules okay.

He strides through seasons wet and dry, his turf a hunter's dream,
Stalking over floodplains, passing rivers, lakes and streams,
Ignoring ferns and conifers and horsetails growing 'round.
Sniffing out the scent of prey with which his world abounds.

Sauropods with serpent necks look down and spot him coming,
Hope a crack of whiplash tail will send the hunter running.
Stegosaurs with spiked-up tails may do some deadly damage.
But more than not his fangs and claws create their crimson carnage.

With rapid steps of three-toed feet, the *Allosaurus* prowls.
He craves a meal, perceives his prey, his hungry stomach growls.
An unsuspecting camptosaur is browsing on all fours.
A flash of teeth, a slash of claws, there's one less dinosaur.

With grasping hands and three big claws, he tears through hide and
   muscle,
Then pressing hard with taloned feet, he quickly ends the tussle.
His head juts down on hawk-like neck, he's clearly Number One,
He gulps his food, then feeds again, he rules the Morrison.

Explore the *Dinosaur Valley Girls* world at its Website at www.FrontlineFilms.com.

THREE

MESOZOIC MEDIA

TOR OF
1,000,000 YEARS AGO

As a child, and later as an adult, I loved both prehistoric animals and comic books. Naturally some of my most pleasurable reading time as a kid, living in Chicago during the 1950s, was spent with comic-book tales about dinosaurs and other extinct creatures.

My favorite comic book at that time—as well as one of my favorites as an adult—was the usually difficult to find (for me anyway) book that would come to be known as *Tor*, starring an atypically noble caveman hero living in an anachronistic world of dinosaurs, pterosaurs, fin-backed pelycosaurs, and other animals long extinct before the emergence into the world of the first human beings. Tor's adventures were always written and drawn by the very talented Joe Kubert, who was probably the first comic-book creator whose name and also face were familiar to me as a child. The comic book was, in this writer's opinion, the best of its kind ever published.

Indeed, *Tor* would prove to be a major influence on me as a child, really exciting my early interest in prehistoric life. I spent much of my time rereading the stories and copying their dramatic illustrations. In my later professional career as a writer of comic books, *Tor* would become a major inspiration for projects including *Tragg and the Sky God*, a comic-book series I created and wrote for Western Publishing Company in the 1970s (as well as various non-series stories for other publishers), and *Dinosaur Valley Girls*™, a 1996-released movie I wrote and directed for Frontline Entertainment.

As a side note, collecting the comic book's "scrapbook" pages of various prehistoric creatures was a major inspiration that eventually lead to three of my books—*The Dinosaur Dictionary* (1972), *The New Dinosaur Dictionary* (1982) and the more extensive outgrowth of those two books, *Dinosaurs: The Encyclopedia* (McFarland, 1997) and its subsequent supplementary volumes.

Tor, issued by St. John Publishing Corp. and edited by Kubert and Norman Maurer, was, in many ways, eons ahead of its time in sophistication and rather adult-oriented themes, which may account, at least in part, for its relatively short life. Its appeal may not have been to audiences mostly attracted to books about gaudily-costumed superheroes, non-prehistoric jungle lords, cowboys, detectives, and other more familiar comic-book good guys. Since the book was often rather violent in its portrayal of Stone Age man, Tor included, it also became one of the many casualties of the newly instituted Comics Code Authority in the mid–1950s, basically a censorship board established to regulate certain kinds of comic books—mostly the violent, horrific, and sexy ones—which were believed, at the time, to be a direct cause of juvenile delinquency and other social problems.

I had missed some of the original *Tor* issues as they came out on the newsstands (there were no comic-book shops in the '50s) and, therefore, had to acquire them years later, and at higher cost than their original dime cover price, through used book dealers. It was a thrill, two decades after the series folded, finally to meet Joe Kubert at the San Diego Comic Convention, and also to write TV animation scripts for Norman Maurer while he was a story editor at Hanna-Barbera Productions.

Joe Kubert did not let his brainchild *Tor* die with the cancellation of its final issue. He would revive the concept a number of times and in a variety of formats, presenting both new stories and reprints (and re-drawings) of the classic originals over the years in various incarnations—including comic books, newspaper comic strips, and graphic novels—and for several different publishers. But to me, at least, that first series of the 1950s remains the best. Kubert would also go on to bring dinosaurs into various other comic-book tales such as his "War That Time Forgot" and Edgar Rice Burroughs-based stories done for DC Comics.

The following article about *Tor* was originally titled "Stone Age Perils" in its first presentation; it was also crudely illustrated by me in those days when I had notions of becoming a comic-book artist like Joe Kubert. The piece first appeared in *Shazam Annual!*, a mimeographed fanzine I published and edited in 1963.

It was the world of a million years ago, not one that actually existed, but an imaginative "what if" kind of world, where man walked in the shadow of the dinosaur...

Kal-El, the future mighty Superman, had not yet been born on the dying super-planet Krypton. Wealthy Lamont Cranston still had to learn "the strange and mysterious secret" that would allow him to "cloud men's minds" as the crime-fighting Shadow. Young John Clayton had not met the Great Ape Kala in Africa and become Tarzan, Lord of the Jungle.

Nevertheless, this planet had one hero, a single defender of and fighter for the weak. He was Earth's first champion, who fought his way through adventures set one million years past. He was Tor the Hunter.

Tor, the ax-toting caveman hero of a romanticized "Stone Age," destroyer of prehistoric monsters and brutish human villains, appeared, courtesy of editors Joe Kubert and Norman Maurer, in a tragically short-lived comic magazine which premiered with a cover date of September, 1953, and the title *1,000,000 Years Ago*. According to Kubert, he got the idea for the book while flying in an Army plane over Korea in 1950. The name and theme of the comic were seemingly inspired, in part at least, by *One Million B.C.*, a hit movie made only seven years earlier, set in the same imagined time-frame and featuring its own heroic caveman, Tumak (played by actor Victor Mature).

All of the stories featuring Tor (and also some of the book's other serious features) were written and illustrated by the prolific and highly talented Kubert. Page one of the first issue depicted both Kubert and Maurer themselves, lecturing to us, the readers, about how the Earth may have been formed from a flaming ball of matter flung off by the sun. And as we turned that page, we met, for the first time, the Hunter himself.

In this premiere tale, Tor is seen trudging confidently through entanglements of prehistoric foliage, eyeing the fantastic displays of animal violence around him. He is puny in comparison to the towering mammoth, the scaly dinosaurs and the soaring *Pteranodon*. Some of the animals, more intent upon eating their freshly slain prey, barely notice him. In one way, however, Tor is the superior of the great beasts. His one advantage—his intelligence—allows the Hunter to continue his seemingly almost insignificant existence.

Of the type of man Tor is, the story does not specifically mention. His general build and facial appearance could be Cro-Magnon, although he retains a Neandertal-like ridge of bone over his eyes. But for all practicality, he may be considered to represent the more advanced species of the two.

In this first-issue "origin" tale, Tor rescues a small, monkey-like creature from a slithering plesiosaur (this scene boldly recreated on the cover) inhabiting a swamp. The bulbous eyed mammal befriends the caveman and, due to its characteristic chattering of "chee-chee," it is so named by Tor.

Tor and Chee-Chee return to the Hunter's tribe. There, bitter feelings arise between Tor and Klar, the ruthless Leader of the Hunt. The roar of a hungry *Tyrannosaurus* interrupts the argument.

Responding to the saurian bellows, Tor and his band of primitive warriors find another caveman, Zul, being pursued by the giant meat-eater. Basically a coward at heart, the brutal Klar advises the group not to interfere. Tor, of course, is somehow different from the other men. It is against his nature to see the weak suffer. Thus, Tor risks his life in battling and finally killing the menacing dinosaur.

Klar, shamed by the prowess and heroism of Tor, then sets a trap for the Hunter, who falls into the villain's tiger pit. As Klar raises his spear at Tor, gazing up at him from the pit, Zul sees the nefarious goings on and tackles the evil caveman, only to meet the smashing end of Klar's stone-headed ax. Tor finally escapes from the pit, dashes to the scene and kills Zul's murderer. But Tor is accused of killing the Leader of the Hunt and is therefore banished from the tribe.

And so began the adventures of Tor, alone save for the company of his tiny friend Chee-Chee, in the world of a million years ago.

The brief 3D-comics craze struck, and therefore, one month after Tor made his bow on the printed page, he and his primitive companion found themselves appearing in two consecutive issues of *3D Comics*, as the book was then officially called, printed in the red and green three-dimensional process (developed for the medium by Kubert and Maurer, and requiring the use of special glasses included with the books), the second of these attempting rather unsuccessfully a 3D rather than "flat" cover. Each of these 1953 issues was labeled as "volume 1, number 2," but the covers, identified as October and November, respectively, eliminated any confusion.

Unlike the original *1,000,000 Years Ago* book, wherein Tor himself only appeared in one story (save for a single-paged monkey-English dictionary titled "Chee-Chee's Glossary"), the caveman hero graduated to three full stories in each of these three-dimensional issues. Within these red-and-green pages Tor vanquishes another *Tyrannosaurus* and also a titanic serpent in a forbidding cave; battles to the finish with a menacing prehistoric turtle; observes a fight between the horned dinosaur *Triceratops* and plated dinosaur *Stegosaurus*; defeats the deformed and crazed "Killer Man"; saves a cavegirl from her savage human pursuer; and at last comes to grips with the stalking "Giant One," a villainous brute of which readers were forewarned in the original *1,000,000 Years Ago* issue.

And so, Tor battled his way through his prehistoric realm, eventually returning to his original two-dimensional color format, fighting primitive monsters and men along the way. Almost always the central focus was on Tor the man himself. The animals and other prehistoric trappings were included more as incidentals, human nature being the real theme of these tales. Human nature, readers were told, was the same in ancient times as it is today.

Tor was never reluctant to aid those who needed him. Those people who benefited from his strength, courage and willingness to help them included the fearful cavemen in the magnetic valley of meteorites; captives of the chalky-skinned lava people; children who were being sacrificed to vicious human huntresses; those subjugated during a time of drought by the possessors of water; the enemies of the more-powerful lizard-men; and victims of the vicious dire wolves.

The caveman hero ended his career in these comic books after, Tarzan-like, destroying the ferocious Man-Beast, a furry terror more simian than human.

However, Tor did not steal the entire spotlight of his comic book himself. True, with the return in 1954 to the 2D format following the demise of the 3D-comics fad the title of the book was changed to *Tor in the World of 1,000,000 Years Ago*. But his magazine was still shared by other characters and features.

Of major interest was the "Danny Dreams" feature, a series of stories about Danny Wakely, a young boy interested in prehistoric life, who had a habit of sleeping at inopportune times, during which he dreamed of some possible past life as a caveboy. At the end of each story Danny would learn of an actual event that had taken place a long time ago which he had just participated in during his dream. The endings of these stories were basically the same: "Gee, did it really happen?"

1,000,000 Years Ago, number one, offered the first story in this series, with Danny drifting off into slumber while attending a school lecture at the local museum (patterned after New York's American Museum of Natural History). He arrives in the prehistoric past to witness a gripping duel between a sabretooth cat and a cave bear, escaping from them on a crude rock-wheeled device of his own invention as the two fighting mammals kill themselves. Danny then awakens to find, on display in the museum, the remnants of the vehicle he had constructed and also the mummified remains of the cat and bear, still locked together as if in battle.

"Danny Dreams" was featured in every issue of the magazine, pitting the youth against a charging bison, an avenging *Pteranodon*, a freakish giant on an island of pygmies and a thundering, splashing *Tylosaurus*, a kind of "tyrannosaur" of the deep. Each story left the reader wondering: Was it really a dream, or was Danny a reincarnation of some former self? Joe Kubert, whose drawn countenance often introduced and commented upon the stories published in *Tor*, revealed that young Danny Wakely's body existed "in two places at one time," transported through time and into the past via his dreams. But it is doubtful that Danny was originally intended to be a reincarnate, since his Stone Age self always retained full knowledge of his future life. The coincidences, though, still kept the reader intrigued. Perhaps the truth here remains Kubert's own "little secret."

"The Wizard of Ugghh" (subtitled "Wuz a Wiz of a Wiz, If Ever a Wiz There Wuz"), a feature created by writer and artist Norman Maurer, was, quite obviously, a humorous feature that lasted for only three issues—the first, and then the two 3D follow-ups. The hero of this bit of prehistoric satire was the pompous and unpredictable Wizard, a type of caveman version of comedian W. C. Fields. The Wizard was accompanied by a caveboy assistant (resembling a comical version of Danny Wakely) named Kluck, son of Dripp the Stupid. Inane prehistoric characters and monsters rounded out the rest of the cast.

Another regular *Tor* feature was the two-page text "filler" offering more or less science-based content. However, official issues numbers three and five featured Tor himself. Surprisingly these pieces were well written when compared with the usual brand of comic-book fillers published in other titles. The third issue featured "Snow Trap," in which Tor is taken into bondage by the fierce Flatnose slavers. This tale was written in the first person, Tor being the narrator and speaking in a quite fluent and natural English. In the comic-book stories his language had been more the "flowery" jargon typical of comic-book jungle heroes. *Tor* number five (July 1954) gave readers "Avenging Waters," unique in that Tor rescues from a turbulent river the very men who were instrumental in his banishment from his tribe. Tor shows no hatred for the men. They implore his forgiveness and bid him to return to his people. But Tor tells them that he has found the life that better suits him—that of giving help where it is needed.

A final regular feature was the "true" one-page histories of prehistoric creatures. These treatments were fairly straightforward and accurate, based on information culled from books, although many errors still managed to creep into the text: For example, *Dimetrodon*, a sail-backed reptile of the Permian period, was incorrectly referred to as a dinosaur, even

The 4th issue (cover dated July, 1954) of Joe Kubert's classic comic-book series *Tor.* ©St. John Publishing Corp. and Joe Kubert, all rights reserved.

though the Permian predated the beginning of the Mesozoic or dinosaur era by many millions of years.

Most of the artwork in the *Tor* books was done by the versatile Joe Kubert. The first issue's inside cover was devoted to a short biography of both Kubert and Norman Maurer, and the two managed to pop into many of the stories in various places to comment upon any number of things. Though Maurer handled the "Wizard of Ugghh" tales, Kubert's masterful pencil and ink work brought to life the majority of the adventure-based sections. Both artists even advertised their own mail-order course in comic art, which also made use of caveman Tor.

To many of his fans, the present writer included, Joe Kubert never surpassed his work in *Tor* (and, indeed, he has been quoted numerous times stating that *Tor* was his all-time favorite feature). His dinosaurs and other extinct animals are distinctly his own and are easily identifiable, even in such later non-*Tor* comic-books as *Hawkman, Viking Prince, Rip-Hunter—Time Master,* and others. It is true that Kubert based some of his ancient creatures on earlier works by such paleontological artists as John C. German, Frederick E. Seyfarth, and the dean of them all, the great Charles R. Knight; but Seyfarth also copied from Knight, and Kubert's "swipes" were done at a minimum, his own creativity and originality more than compensating for this artistic "shortcut."

Joe Kubert may have been uncertain as to the precise physical appearance of some of his prehistoric animals, or he may sometimes have digressed slightly from the true course of nature for purely his own artistic or dramatic reasons. For example, in different stories he depicted the two-fingered *Tyrannosaurus* with anywhere from two to four fingers on each hand, while the great toothless and tailless flying reptile *Pteranodon,* at least in the earlier issues of the series, inaccurately sported razor teeth and swinging, spaded tails. Still, such inaccuracies never detracted from the overall greatness and visual power of the artwork.

Kubert's name appeared on every Tor yarn and on every cover, except for the third (3D) issue, and on the "Danny Dreams" installments in the first issue and two three-dimensional books, the latter two unsigned but unquestionably the work of Kubert. Subsequent issues were illustrated by such noted comic-book artists as Alex Toth. At any rate, the artwork in this book was always of top quality, sometimes going slightly experimental as with the occasional use of zip-a-tone to provide, via a series of dots, gray-tone shading.

From a scientific standpoint the stories in the various *Tor* books cannot, of course, be considered accurate. Cave people, whether Neandertal or Cro-Magnon, did not live a million years ago, nor did they, or even more primitive kinds of early humans, coexist with the mighty dinosaurs. A facsimile reproduction of the first issue, appearing in an advertisement for various St. John comics, bragged, "It's true!" Some readers began to write in commenting on or complaining about the anachronisms.

Responding in the third issue, the editors were drawn explaining that it was only "theory" to assume that people and the dinosaur did not ever meet in the flesh. It was also just theory that certain human beings *might* have lived while the last great saurians were still dying out, as presented in this comic book. Kubert and Maurer, in this illustrated editorial, pushed the idea of presenting stories which proved that human emotions are basically the same now as they were in very ancient times. Human nature, they contended, was ... and forever will be ... human nature.

The fifth issue of *Tor* comics brought Joe Kubert and Norman Maurer to the forefront again, this time to discuss something which, as far as the survival of their comic book was concerned, was more immediate than discussions regarding the age of the Earth and what-if scenarios pitting humans against dinosaurs. Now they were discussing the anti-comic-book crusade spearheaded by a psychiatrist named Dr. Frederick Wertham. This was 1954, and, thanks to Wertham's campaign, would be the last year of the era to feature comic books offering violence, gore, horror, and sex.

The two editors rightfully defended their books, Maurer stating that they were "the type of magazines that we wouldn't be ashamed to allow our children to read."

Kubert followed his partner's statement with his own: "Our aim is to produce the very best the medium of comic books has to offer!!!"

And this they both accomplished grandly with *Tor*. But Tor was a caveman hero who lived in an oftentimes violent world, where the solution to a problem could only be resolved with the hard swing of a stone-headed ax.

Sadly, to the distress of the book's fans, *Tor* number five ended the series—the final issue of one of the comic-book medium's greatest entries.

There was no decline in quality by this last issue. *Tor* ended as it began. The book went in glory.

ONE MILLION B.C.
(THE ORIGINAL)

The following article occupies a very special place in my memory, as does the motion picture it discusses. The article's original publication is quite important to me, for its appearance marked my rite of passage into the arena of professional writing. This was the first article I ever wrote for which I was paid—not a tremendous amount of money, that's for certain—and which appeared in a professional magazine having real newsstand distribution.

But first, the movie: *One Million B.C.*—one of many science-fiction and fantasy movies to combine, anachronistically, prehistoric people with dinosaurs—was one of the first movies, if not *the* first, I saw on nighttime television. This major event occurred during the prehistoric days of TV (*i.e.*, the early 1950s) at a time when I, as if it were possible, had not yet really become interested in extinct creatures. Our family was still listening to the radio, and so my first exposures to "the tube" were at the homes of neighbors and relatives, and in appliance and department stores.

I saw *One Million B.C.* for the first time in the home of a next-door neighbor. The movie ran on a local Chicago TV channel. Images from this film would remain with me for years before I became "formally" introduced to dinosaurs and other prehistoric creatures through other sources. Oddly enough, none of the movie's fantastic animals stuck in my memory during that early time—only those of the cave people and the volcanic eruption. It wasn't until I saw the film again on TV in the mid–1950s that I realized what else it offered in the way of fauna.

I would see *One Million B.C.* many times over the years, on TV, at home screenings, on home video, and finally, during the 1990s, in a new and beautifully restored 35mm print screened at UCLA.

Always I would love this movie, which would inevitably inspire various professional projects of my own. Indeed, the first feature-length movie I would direct, *Dinosaur Valley Girls™*, shot in 1995 and released to TV the next year, would be based in many ways— including the character names, "cave lingo" and all-around acting style—on *One Million B.C.*

This article itself, originally titled simply *"One Million B.C.,"* was one of three—the others on stuntman Eddie Parker, and on the Republic Pictures movie serial *The Adventures of Captain Marvel* (I don't remember which of the three was written first)—were all published in the third, August 1966, issue of *Modern Monsters.* This magazine was one of many that followed in the wake of Forrest J Ackerman's popular *Famous Monsters of Filmland*, making a failed attempt to usurp the original's success.

I had discovered the first issue of *Modern Monsters* during a vacation from Los Angeles, where I was now living, to my hometown of Chicago. Reading through it, I concluded that I could write better and more informative articles than those published in that magazine. Noting that the magazine originated with a Hollywood company called Prestige Publications, upon returning to California a few days later, I rang up its president, publisher Jim Matthews and, with frequent partner Larry M. Byrd, visited him in his office in the Playboy Building on the Sunset Strip.

Inspired in part by the magazines edited by Forry Ackerman and also Ron Haydock (*Fantastic Monsters of the Films*), Larry and I attempted selling Matthews on the idea of publishing a couple of original magazines which we would produce for him. One of these was a black and white, magazine-sized comics publication featuring offbeat superheroes, among them *Man-Lizard, Stone Age Avenger*, to feature artwork by then relative newcomer Jeff Jones. A full script would soon be written and a "splash page" drawn and inked by Jones, with lettering by Bill Spicer. The magnetic-powered Man-Lizard wore a costume of sorts made from a *Ceratosaurus* skull and skin and mammoth hair. His character was based, in many ways, on Joe Kubert's non-superheroic Tor. The series would have been the first comic-strip prehistoric superhero ever published.

While Matthews submitted our proposals to his distributors, Kable (they'd eventually be turned down), I also sold Jim on the idea of my writing some material for the next available issue of *Modern Monsters.* Since the second issue was already completed and at the printer's, the three articles Matthews bought from me would go into the third (with Larry, beginning with that issue, painting the covers and later also handling the interior layouts).

Almost as thrilling to me as the expectation of seeing my writing printed in a "real magazine" was Matthews writing me a check.

I wrote the *One Million B.C.* article at a time in which monster-movie fans were eagerly waiting Hammer Films' color remake *One Million Years B.C.*, the main sources of interest of which were the stop-motion special effects by master animator Ray Harryhausen, and equally the spectacular physical effects contributed by new-comer star Raquel Welch in the role of Loana. In those days before home video, the text of the article was largely based upon my own memories of *One Million B.C.*, seen over the years in various television reruns.

With *One Million Years B.C.*, master animator Ray Harryhausen's spectacular motion picture for Hammer Films of England, a popular topic among monster-movie and dinosaur lovers the world over, this writer thought it appropriate that we not lose any fond memories we might have of that original black-and-white "epic," *One Million B.C.*, of which Hammer's color melodrama (about cavemen trying to survive in a hostile world made more so by deadly dinosaurs) is a remake.

In 1940, Hal Roach, a movie producer known mainly for his comedy films (including those of Our Gang and Laurel and Hardy), produced the original *One Million B.C.*, a motion picture that has remained a classic of its kind—one of a subgenre featuring stories about sometimes brutal cave people trying to survive in their hostile prehistoric world.

The story of *One Million B.C.* begins, not in the period suggested by its title, but in modern-day Europe, possibly in the Swiss Alps. A storm ushers a group of mountain climbers into a large cave where they take shelter. Inside the cave they encounter an hospitable archaeologist (played by well-known actor Conrad Nagel) who invites them to sit down before the warmth of a fire which illuminates the interior of the rocky room. In the light from the flames, they see the inscriptions on the cavern wall which have been the object of the scientist's studies—paintings of men and extinct animals produced by a primitive human hand.

Sitting among the climbers are a young man and woman, played respectively by actors Victor Mature (in only his second movie role) and Carole Landis. The archaeologist points out that the pictures on the cave wall constitute a story about a young man, like Mature, whom he will call Tumak, and a young woman, like Landis, whom he will call Loana.

Tumak, the scientist explains, belongs to the warlike Rock Tribe, and Loana to the peaceful Shell Tribe.

With that introduction, the film dissolves back in time one million years—*One Million B.C.* ...

Crudely armed with staffs, the Rock Tribe hunting party, led by Akhoba (Lon Chaney, Jr.), spot their quarry at the base of a canyon—a *Triceratops*, a three-horned ceratopsian dinosaur, which is grazing on some foliage. The *Triceratops* is small for its genus (because it was portrayed by a live pig) and Tumak, son of Akhoba, is granted permission by his father to attack the animal himself. Savagely, the youthful caveman leaps upon and wrestles the dinosaur until he has the chance to club it to death with his staff.

The carcass of the dinosaur is carted to the caves. There Akhoba satisfies his own hunger first—then tosses chunks of meat to his hunting dogs. Next, the hunters attack and tear their own portions from the animal's corpse. Finally, the women and children are allowed to eat. Tumak attempts to steal an additional chunk of meat from Akhoba and a battle ensues, the outcome being the young caveman's banishment from the tribe for daring to attack his chieftain father.

Out on his own, Tumak is chased by a charging woolly mammoth, a shaggy extinct elephant, to the edge of a cliff. The caveman plunges off the cliff, landing unconscious in the river below.

As great saurians swim by, Tumak, out cold in a makeshift boat, drifts peacefully into the hands of Loana, who is spearing fish near the bank of the river.

Tumak is taken into the Shell Tribe's cave, where their strange customs, such as passing equal shares of food to all individuals, confuse his violence-oriented mind. Eventually, however, this Rock tribesman begins to succumb to his hosts' way of life.

Subsequently, Tumak experiences other wonders of the Shell People—including edible vegetation, social order, and a new kind of weapon, the spear.

A *neecha* stalks toward the Shell Tribe. (*Neecha* is the cave people's word for monster, in this case a lumbering carnivore, an unusually small *Tyrannosaurus*.) With borrowed spear clutched firmly, Tumak furiously battles the dinosaur, vanquishing it with repeated stabbings. For his heroism, Tumak is now looked upon favorably by the Shell People.

That night, Tumak, rather than make his own spear, attempts to steal one belonging to Ohtao (John Hubbard), apparently Loana's brother. But Tumak is discovered in the act and, as before from his own people, banished. Obviously attracted to Tumak, Loana follows him.

On their own now, Tumak and Loana trudge through the steaming prehistoric jungle, meeting one dangerous *neecha* after another: A towering "cave bear" (though publicized as a bear, in reality a photographically enlarged coatimundi, a mammal resembling a raccoon) yanks a gargantuan python from a tree. A giant monitor lizard with a smacking tongue crawls amid the foliage. A giant mammal (apparently supposed to represent a glyptodont, an extinct relative of today's armadillo, this one sporting clearly rubber horns) chases the two cave people into a tree.

Meanwhile, Akhoba and his band of cave warriors have once more entered a canyon to hunt. From their high vantage point, they see several mammoths and musk oxen (hairy horned denizens of the Ice Age). Again armed only with a crude staff, Akhoba engages in deadly combat with a musk ox. The caveman is promptly gored, to become a crippled remnant of a one-time great warrior.

Shakana (Edgar Edwards), one of the other hunters, raises his staff, signifying his ascent to Akhoba's rocky throne. In submission to their new leader, the other hunters drop their weapons.

Continuing to make their way across the prehistoric landscape, Tumak and Loana halt their trek as they become the potential target of two approaching reptilian hulks. From one side, a gigantic *Dimetrodon*, a carnivorous fin-backed reptile, nears them menacingly; from the other, a crawling, monstrous tegu lizard. The humans take refuge in a crevasse and the huge reptiles lock together in frantic combat. Over and over the battling monsters roll, teeth gnashing, claws tearing, until the *Dimetrodon*, victorious, slowly makes its way to the nearby lake to nurse its wounds. The tegu lizard quivers and dies on its back.

But Shakana and the other Rock Tribe hunters have entered the area and attempt to capture Loana. Tumak rushes to her rescue, battles his human enemies, and returns with them and Loana to his former home. Loana, unwelcome at first by Tumak's erstwhile tribe members, does at last manage to influence the Rock People and teach them some of the advancement made by the Shell Tribe.

Later, Tumak and Loana are playing with Wandi, the small daughter of the Rock Tribe woman Nupondi (played by Mamo Clark), and possibly of Tumak, also, when an all-too familiar rumbling sound is heard—the volcano.

Spewing forth fire, smoke, rock, and lava, the steaming volcano erupts with cataclysmic ferocity. The earth splits apart, swallowing up trees, monsters, and whatever else gets in the way. Lava bubbles and rumbles down the sides of mountains like flaming gravy. Landslides rain down boulders on fleeing cavemen. All is pandemonium! In the confusion,

Outfitted in its prehistoric best, this Chuck-Walla lizard appeared behind the opening titles of the original movie *One Million B.C.* (1940). Courtesy the late Fred Knoth, ©United Artists.

Wandi is separated from her mother. The almost-maddened parent runs after her fleeing child, only to be covered by an engulfing river of molten lava. Loana heroically manages to scoop up the child before the lava has a chance to claim her, too; but in performing this rescue, the blonde-haired cave woman loses her sandal in the sticky and smoking mud.

Soon afterwards, Tumak finds the lone sandal, thereby believing that Loana has been killed.

The eruption reaches its conclusion and the turmoil finally subsides. Again the world of one million B.C. is relatively tranquil.

Shortly afterward, Ohtao is spotted approaching the Rock Tribe's cave. Tumak rejoices as the caveman communicates to him that Loana is still alive with the Shell People. But there is one major difficulty in Tumak's being reunited with her—a *neecha*! Tumak immediately starts to set off to rescue her, when the messenger stops him, indicating with his hands that this *neecha* is much larger than the *Tyrannosaurus* he had defeated before.

With the support and manpower of his fellow cave-dwellers, Tumak and his band of warriors march off to save the Shell Tribe. What awaits them is a gigantic lizard (actually, a "blown up" rhinoceros iguana), its snapping, barking head trying viciously to devour the Shell folk trapped behind the mouth of their cave. Loana is among the hapless primitives. Tumak sees her, and she him.

Futilely, the Rock warriors attempt to kill the saurian terror with their spears, but the stone tips do not even prick the scaly hide. One warrior meets a horrible death between the closing jaws of the monster. Then, the now weak and mutilated, but still alert, Akhoba relates a plan to Tumak, and the young man proceeds to put it into effect. Bravely hurling a rock at the snout of the creature, Tumak diverts its attention, the angered reptile turning to chase its arrogant, two-legged foe. Tumak begins to climb the mountain wall with the lizard in ascending pursuit. Then, working together, warriors from both the Rock Tribe and Shell Tribe roll down huge boulders. As the boulders bounce down, they start a landslide, which buries the giant reptile in a mass of rocky debris. Cheering follows, and the Rock Tribe and Shell Tribe are at last united.

Soon afterward, Tumak and Loana accept Wandi as their own.

One Million B.C. was shot in black and white, required no dialogue (except for the opening scenes with the archaeologist and mountain climbers), and utilized mostly real lizards and other live animals rather than animated models for its extinct animals. And yet, this original movie still remains one of the most entertaining and exciting prehistoric-monster epics (and movies in general) ever made.

In its day, in fact, *One Million B.C.* was a bona fide *epic*, with a scope so wide, so vast, so titanic that its original choice of director was no less than D. W. Griffith, the director of such triumphs of the silent screen as *The Birth of a Nation* and *Intolerance* (as well as some earlier moves set in the Stone Age). Because *One Million B.C.* was basically a silent movie, since real dialogue was not required to tell its simple and basic human story, Griffith would have been perfectly suited to direct it.

Reasons for Griffith's not directing the movie, however, remain clouded. Apparently personal and business difficulties between him and producer Roach inevitably forced him to withdraw from active participation in this project, his main contributions to the film being the suggestion of macho actor Victor Mature (in his second movie part) and the beautiful Carole Landis for the lead roles and the use of his name in some of the publicity. In truth, *One Million B.C.* was an entirely *visual* movie, as were most silent pictures, and could also have been effective if released 20 years earlier without the benefit of sound.

Unfortunately, when shown on television and allowing time for commercial interruptions, *One Million B.C.* has frequently been cut drastically by local-station film editors in order to fit the picture into a prescribed time slot. It is not unusual, then, to find entire chunks of footage gone— usually either the *Triceratops* segment at the beginning of the prehistoric story, or the sequence in the jungle involving the "cave bear," armadillo, monitor, and so forth. However, the less exciting scenes with the archaeologist and his audience are almost always left intact.

Most monster-movie fans have been unwilling to acknowledge the positive qualities of the original *One Million B.C.* because of its use of live reptiles rather than animated miniatures. However, *One Million B.C.* arguably features the *best* sequences ever filmed in which lizards and other extant reptiles paraded across the screen posing as prehistoric species. Their actual battle scenes (before the American Society for the Prevention of Cruelty to Animals rightly banished such goings on), staged by special-effects ace Fred Knoth and photographed by Roy Seawright, surpassed, in many film fans' opinion, such later efforts in the same vein as *King Dinosaur* (1955), *The Cyclops* (1957), *Journey to the Center of the Earth* (1959), *The Giant Gila Monster* (1959), and *The Lost World* (color remake version, 1960). Shot in slow motion, and with dubbed-in sounds made by real animals (including dogs, lions, pigs, monkeys and speeded-up elephants), the *One Million B.C.* reptiles were indeed convincing as prehistoric monsters.

Attempting to re-create some of the denizens of Earth's past, the special-effects creators at Roach Studios, led by Knoth, dressed up some of their nonhuman performers in suitable "costumes":

A dwarf alligator was given an artificial section of back hide, made from rubber, to which was attached a flexible dorsal fin. The result—a *Dimetrodon*, one of the sail-backed pelycosaurs from Earth's Permian period. However, the real animal's fin, consisting of skin stretched across a series of elongated dorsal spines, would not have bent as seen when the film's version rolled over during the battle against the tegu lizard.

Curved tusks and shaggy hair were used to adorn Indian elephants, transforming them into woolly mammoths.

Great winding horns and coarse fur comprised the costuming worn by the great Brahma bulls, making them appear to be musk oxen. Actor Glenn Strange, who did not appear in *One Million B.C.*, related to the author an accident that occurred during the filming of the scene involving the Akhoba character and a musk ox. Stuntman Yakima Cannut (a frequent stunt double for John Wayne), filling in for Chaney, struck the bull with his staff, as assistants out of camera range executed what was called a "running W." A wire attached to the animal's legs was pulled, yanking the legs together, the legs forming a sort of letter "W." As "Yak" pretended to fight the bull, the animal got out of control. The stuntman

Tumak (Victor Mature) defends cave-mate Loana (Carole Landis) from an attacking *Dimetrodon* (really a dwarf alligator wearing a rubber dorsal fin) in *One Million B.C.* (1940). ©United Artists.

was really gored, but escaped alive, working for decades following this film.

About the filming of the *Triceratops* scenes, Lionel O. Comport, who ran an animal rental service to the Hollywood movie and television studios, remembered in the author's now defunct fan publication *Shazam! Annual*:

> In filming, they ran a goat [actually, a pig] through heavy undergrowth, just out of sight, so you could only see the brush agitated by some animal. Then Victor Mature leaped after the goat and pretended to kill it. But in the movie the sound department dubbed in the squeals of a wild boar!

The animal had been outfitted with three horns, a neck-covering frill, and a thick reptilian tail. Comport supplied many of the animals in *One Million B.C.*, including some vultures. Commented Comport, "Vultures are the ugliest creatures in the world. They really looked like they came from one million B.C."

Aside from live animals, stuntman Paul Stader, formerly an action double for Johnny Weismuller in the old Tarzan movies, stalked about in a rubber *Tyrannosaurus* costume (explaining the dinosaur's short stature, the rubber suit loosely based on Charles R. Knight's original painting of this dinosaur done in the early teen years of the 20th century) in similar fashion, but far more convincingly, than later attempts as in *Unknown Island* (1948), *Godzilla, King of the Monsters!* (1956), *The Land Unknown* (1957), *Gorgo* (1961), or *Varan the Unbelievable* (1962).

The spectacular volcano eruption effects, and also the very *creative* use of rear-screen projection (with actors timing their movements perfectly to the projected miniature backgrounds), added to the ingredients in making *One Million B.C.* the minor classic it remains today.

One Million B.C. has the distinction of being one of the relatively few "monster" movies to contribute numerous stock scenes, outtakes, and alternate shots to a great number of later, usually low-budget films—perhaps more such films than any other. How familiar that *Dimetrodon* versus tegu lizard has become over the years, as well as the volcanic eruption and other scenes.

A list of some of the feature-length motion pictures, serials and theatrical short subjects featuring *One Million B.C.* footage includes the following titles:

Tarzan's Desert Mystery (1943), *Superman* (1948), *Atom Man vs. Superman* (1950), *Two Lost Worlds* (1950), *Lost Volcano* (1950), *Jungle Manhunt* (1951), *Voodoo Tiger* (1952), *Smoky Canyon* (1952), *Untamed Women* (1952), *Robot Monster* (1953), *The Lost Planet* (1953), *Devil Goddess* (1955), *King Dinosaur* (1955), *Space Ship Sappy* (1957), *Teenage Caveman* (1958), *She Demons* (1958), *Valley of the Dragons* (1961), *Los Fantasmas Burlones* (1964), *Aventura al Centro de la Tierra* (1966), *Isla de los Dinosaurios* (1967), *Journey to the Center of Time* (1967), *One Million AC/DC* (1970), *Horror of the Blood Monsters* (1970), *Terrorvision* (1986) and *Attack of the B Movie Monster* (1989).

One Million B.C. footage has also turned up in various 1950s-era television series, including *Jungle Jim* and *Soldiers of Fortune*, as well as several TV commercials.

Despite the color, Ray Harryhausen's stop-motion dinosaur effects and the natural attributes of star Raquel Welch in Hammer's remake *One Million Years B.C.*, the original *One Million B.C.* deserves not to be overlooked—as an epic, and a classic.

KING KONG AND
THE WAR EAGLES

By the fourth issue, October-November 1966, of *Modern Monsters*, I had assumed full editorship of the magazine, although I was listed on the masthead as an assistant editor, with publisher Jim Matthews taking credit as full editor and Larry Byrd officially the art director. Since I was, by now, writing most of the magazine's text, I preferred using a number of pen names, so that my own name would not become too ubiquitous within a single issue.

Among the favorite subjects of monster-movie magazines was the 1933 RKO classic film *King Kong*—that modern "Beauty and the Beast" fable featuring a gigantic prehistoric gorilla that ruled over an island inhabited by dinosaurs and other animals that should otherwise have been extinct, all animated one frame at a time by Willis H. O'Brien and his special-effects crew.

I wrote the following article about *King Kong*, originally titled "*King Kong*—a Double Take," under one of my pseudonyms "Rod Richmond," an in-joke melding of the names of two actors—Rod LaRoque and Kane Richmond—who had played the part of The Shadow, that famous radio and pulp-magazine crimefighter, on the screen during the 1930s and 1940s.

In the years following the publication of this piece, *King Kong* would become the subject of countless in-depth articles, reviews, interviews, and even entire books, while videotapes of the restored film—some colorized—would be almost mandatory additions to every film buff's and collector's home library.

Back in the 1960s, however, writings about *King Kong* had to be based upon the occasional television broadcast of the (often edited down) movie, the less frequent theatrical showing, or the screening of some private collector's "bootleg" print. They also had to rely on memory.

Directly following on the hairy heels of the *King Kong* article, in that same *Modern Monsters* issue, was a very short piece published without my byline, real or pseudonymous, about one of many prehistoric animals-related projects that had been planned by Willis O'Brien but that never saw completion. This "Obie" project was entitled *War Eagles* and would have been a spectacular and unusual RKO show. Only some of its scenes were actually filmed in 1939. Had the movie been completed it would have been the first movie of its kind shot in full color. The article itself, as far as the author can determine, was the first to be published about *War Eagles* in a popular movie magazine.

The two articles are so similar in theme that the *War Eagles* piece, titled simply "The War Eagle" in its original magazine publication, will follow the *King Kong* article below.

Without a doubt the greatest and most beloved "classic giant monster" movie ever to roar out of Hollywood and into movie theaters the world over—from the earliest days of filmmaking and even decades after it was produced—was *King Kong*. The present writer believes that most fans of classic motion pictures will agree with this assessment.

There have been, over the years, myriad adventures preserved on celluloid about huge monsters, removed from their original environments, to run wild in some modern metropolis and inevitably create chaos. These include movies about dinosaurs and other prehistoric creatures that have somehow survived or returned from the Mesozoic Era, or "Age of Reptiles"; of gigantic insects from the dawn of time or created in the test tube of a mad super-scientist; or about alien behemoths, some possibly having ancient origins, invading the new territory of Earth for a target of conquest. These are such movies as *Rodan the Flying Monster, The Deadly Mantis,* and the *Giant Claw* (all coincidentally released in 1957).

And yet, none of these or other of the many films about giant rampaging monsters really deserves to be mentioned in the same breath with *King Kong*.

Even those well-appreciated movies about giant beasts, animated frame by frame by stop-motion wizards like Ray Harryhausen—for example, *The Beast from 20,000 Fathoms* (1953), *It Came from Beneath the Sea* (1955), and *20 Million Miles to Earth* (1957)—are, regardless of the artistry of their visual effects, just shadows of the overall majesty that was *King Kong*.

Released in 1933 by RKO Radio Pictures, *King Kong* was as perfect a film of its type as could be made in its day. The dramatic pacing of its scenes, the build-up in the opening of the story with the suggestions of some mysterious presence called "Kong" prior to the King's first appearance, the sequences set on Kong's Skull Island, the thrilling climax, all of these were done "just right." The special effects were masterfully executed and hold up quite well even after so many years have passed since the film was made. The final product resulting from all the care and work that went into *King Kong* has become common knowledge to anyone interested enough in fantastic films to purchase and read a publication devoted entirely to them. The movie is, in fact, a four-star cinematic masterpiece.

The following brief summary of *King Kong's* plot is recounted herein for reference (and can also inform anyone reading this article who might not yet have experienced this motion picture classic): Movie producer Carl Denham is determined to make an on-location "true" story using the "Beauty and the Beast" theme. He hires a crew, acquires a leading lady, Ann Darrow, and ships off to the uncharted Skull Island, a large piece of land where a Great Wall was once built to keep out a legendary, but real, beast-god, Kong.

Ann is captured by the island's natives and tied to Kong's altar. A gong summons the creature from the jungle, and Kong, the huge gorilla, steals her. Denham, first mate Jack Driscoll, and part of the crew go after the monster and its captive. While in Kong's domain, they encounter various menaces from Earth's Mesozoic Era, including the plated dinosaur *Stegosaurus*, giant dinosaur *Apatosaurus*, giant carnivorous dinosaur *Tyrannosaurus*, snaky-necked marine reptile *Elasmosaurus*, and the huge flying reptile *Pteranodon*, as well as other prehistoric reptilian forms.

Driscoll manages to save Ann; Kong, angered at his loss, attacks the wall—killing, stomping, and crushing natives and crew members. Denham knocks Kong out with gas bombs, then transports him to New York.

In the city, the great gorilla is placed on exhibition as "King Kong, the Eighth Wonder of the World." But flashbulbs from the cameras of over-eager newspaper photographers excite him. Kong breaks loose, runs wild in the city, recaptures Ann and carries her to the summit of the Empire State Building, from which he is shot down by airplanes. As Denham succinctly explains, "It was beauty killed the beast."

Robert Armstrong portrayed Carl Denham in the film, Fay Wray was Ann Darrow, and Bruce Cabot played Jack Driscoll.

It was the intent of the present writer, when contemplating this article on the so-called "Eighth Wonder of the World" (since the movie is so well known and has already been covered extensively in other publications), to approach *King Kong* from a somewhat different perspective. I decided to look back on *King Kong*—to give it a kind of "double take," and discuss the movie in a different way than it has generally been written about in the past.

To begin this "double take" on *King Kong*, a few of the less obvious fine details can be pointed out, some of which, no doubt, have rarely, if ever, been noticed, especially in inferior-quality prints of the film shown on the small TV screen, even after repeated viewings:

Recall the sequence before Kong battles the plesiosaur *Elasmosaurus* that slithers snakelike out of the misty pool in Kong's Skull Mountain sanctuary. The titanic ape first enters the cave in the background of the shot, while the pool is seen in the foreground. If the viewer watches very closely, a trail of bubbles—the plesiosaur breathing—can be noticed steadily moving across the pool. Also seen in the foreground is hero Jack Driscoll (actually a stop-motion model) swimming across the pool toward the rocks. These subtle details were injected into the shot by the genius behind the special effects, Willis O'Brien. Rarely do they seem to be noticed by viewers, and rarer still written about.

Now call to memory the sequence in which the raging Kong pounds on the massive door of the Great Wall, erupting with furious hatred against the tiny humans who stole his blonde-haired prize, Ann Darrow. When this shot flashes upon the screen, minute (to Kong, anyway) windows can be seen cut into the lower portion of the door. Through those windows can be observed the tiny men (the real actors projected into the spaces on the miniature door) moving about through those openings.

Often also missed are the pterosaurs and birds flying about in the distance in a number of the shots set in the King's primeval jungle.

Another fine detail is the *Tyrannosaurus* scratching its "ear" as the dinosaur pauses prior to the dramatic battle with its simian enemy.

Few viewers also seem to notice the people (again very small in the film frame when compared to the large figure of the giant ape) falling from the windows of the overturned L-train, as Kong battles this serpentine mechanical adversary.

Details such as the above, apparently not necessarily intended for obvious notice but simply as "background," added immeasurably to the overall greatness of *King Kong*.

Continuing this "double take," let us now compare the dinosaurs and other assorted saurians indigenous to Skull Island with their actual counterparts from the Mesozoic Era, a stretch of our world's prehistory

The Monarch of Skull Island meets a *Stegosaurus*, an encounter (staged for this photograph) that never occurred in the movie *King Kong* (1933). ©RKO Radio Pictures and Turner Entertainment, courtesy Ronald V. Borst/Hollywood Movie Poster.

beginning approximately 248 million and ending some 65 million years ago.

Despite the beautiful design and fine construction of the models used to represent these animals, their lifelike appearance, and the fine animation that made them move on screen, these survivors from the Age of Reptiles appeared quite different from their creature counterparts that existed in the past. The animals will be looked at and commented upon, one by one, in the order of their appearance in the movie, and some of the differences between them and their authentic counterparts will be noted:

Stegosaurus: Looking at this dinosaur from the viewpoint of the paleontologist, the animal in *King Kong* is wrong in various respects. In actuality, *Stegosaurus* was a non-aggressive herbivorous animal of the Late Jurassic period (Triassic period preceeding it, Cretaceous succeeding) that would not have sought out and attacked its foes. *Stegosaurus* is now believed to have had two rows of alternating plates and two pairs of tail spikes. In *King Kong*, the *Stegosaurus* has more or less paired plates and eight tail spikes. Of note here is that the movie's version resembles in basic body shape a very early life restoration of the animal drawn by artist Charles R. Knight for a *McClure's* magazine article published in 1897, and also a painting by an unknown artist that was published by paleontologist E. Ray Lankster in 1905. Both illustrations portrayed this dinosaur with eight spikes, and with apparently paired anterior smaller plates followed by a single row of larger plates. Knight, however, had also made a more scientifically correct sculpture of *Stegosaurus* in 1903, showing alternating plates and a total of four spikes, this reconstruction apparently escaping the notice of *King Kong* model designer Marcel Delgado.

Apatosaurus (popularly known as *Brontosaurus*): In *King Kong*, the swamp-dwelling *Apatosaurus*—Delgado's model based directly on a popular Knight painting of 1898 made for the American Museum of Natural History in New York—which upsets the raft and pursues the fleeing Denham and crew members is apparently an aggressive carnivore, as demonstrated by the scene wherein the huge sauropod dinosaur chases a sailor up a tree, then snatches him out of it with its very toothy jaws. From a paleontological perspective, mere curiosity would probably not inspire an *Apatosaurus* to go after even animals, since it was a peaceful herbivore. Moreover, future paleontological discoveries would show that the head on the model of this animal is really that of *Camarasaurus*, while a reevaluation of the dinosaur's habits would result in regarding it as a mostly land-based animal, not a water-dweller.

Tyrannosaurus: This gigantic Late Cretaceous theropod dinosaur—the model based on an early 20th century Knight painting, again done for the American Museum—only possessed two fingers on each scaly "hand," while the one in *King Kong* (as would many movie tyrannosaurs) is portrayed with three. There are other anatomical inaccuracies, also, in the creature appearing in the film—*e.g.*, body too squat, eyes not positioned correctly on the head, tail too long, *etc.*, than on the real animal some 65 million years B.C.—but these would only be known to be in error in later years following subsequent fossil discoveries, and these mistakes do accurately reflect the visual information incorporated into Knight's painting.

Elasmosaurus: Although this creature has usually been called a "snake" in conversations and articles about *King Kong*, the serpentine creature in the movie is really one of these very long-necked plesiosaurs (note the paddles). Delgado portrayed this Mesozoic marine reptile as relatively longer and thinner than it really was. Apparently the model was based upon a Knight painting of 1897 in which a very flexible *Elasmosaurus* was shown twisting about like a serpent.

Pteranodon: Although the *King Kong* version possesses a beak lined with sharp teeth, this giant pterosaur or flying reptile, in reality, was toothless. The creature portrayed in the movie flies by flapping its wings. For decades, including the 1930s when *King Kong* was made, it was largely believed that pterosaurs did not really fly, but were merely able to glide with those batlike, skin-stretched wings. Later research, however, would show that reptiles like *Pteranodon* did, in fact, fly; and so the portrayal of this pterosaur in *King Kong*, at least in this respect, would someday prove accurate.

In general, all the prehistoric animals in *King Kong* were depicted as too large, this because of an edict by producer Merian C. Cooper, upon seeing the designs for each creature, to "Make it bigger!"

Finally, in this double take of *King Kong*, let us consider some apparent facts and fallacies concerning this movie about the mightiest of screen gorillas:

The so-called censored spider sequence is a typical example of the kind of misinformation that has, over the years, circulated about this classic film. The consensus has long been that the scene, in which Kong shakes the sailors off a log into a pit of creeping spiders and crawling prehistoric reptiles, was too terrifying for 1933 audiences, and was consequently cut from the original release prints. That is what is commonly believed, this conclusion being an easy and logical one to arrive at when the true facts are not known.

We can be confident that the spider scene was, in fact, shot. For example, it appears in the *King Kong* novelization that came out before the film itself was released, written by Delos W. Lovelace based on the original story by mystery writer Edgar Wallace and producer Cooper (published as a hardcover book in 1932 by Grosset and Dunlap). In the book version, an octopus-monster is one of the denizens sharing the pit with the spider:

> Something which would have been a lizard except for its size lay warming itself on a sunny ledge. The spider moved toward it, then thought better of the impulse and looked about for smaller prey. This was provided by a round, crawling object with tentacles like those of an octopus. The spider crawled to the attack. Both octopus-insect and spider vanished into a fissure.

In the movie, we know there are living things inhabiting the pit into which Kong shakes the crewmen. Driscoll, spared from the fall, looks

Giant "prehistoric ape" Kong versus the giant *Pteranodon*, portrayed as a "flapper" ahead of its time, in *King Kong* (1933). ©RKO Radio Pictures and Turner Entertainment, courtesy Ronald V. Borst/Hollywood Movie Poster.

down into the pit and reacts with an expression of nausea, witnessing whatever horrible activity is happening down there offscreen. And a strange lizardlike reptile—apparently with no hindquarters, unless the model was not intended to be seen in its entirety—climbs up a vine hanging down into the pit, its ascent cut short as Driscoll's knife sends it plunging back to where it came from. Furthermore, preproduction drawings of the scene (showing both the spider and the novel's octopus creature), as well as a photograph of the scene itself (showing the spider and other horrors in the pit), have already been published, in *Famous Monsters of Filmland* magazine.

Yes, there really was a giant-spider scene cut from *King Kong*, but, contrary to most accounts, this scene never made it into theaters; moreover, it was *not* deleted by the censor.

According to Merian C. Cooper, whom the author briefly questioned about the missing spider scene in 1966, the reason for its deletion is as follows: The action around this part of the film is rather quickly paced. Kong is being chased, the crew members are running, much is going on and quite rapidly so. But the spider scene ... well, it moved so slowly that it interrupted the overall pacing of the film at that point. For that reason only, the scene was cut—voluntarily by Cooper and the film's editor, and not by the censor.

It could have been for the same reason that some of the other prehistoric animals intended for the film—including the large, spike-frilled horned dinosaur *Styracosaurus*, which appears in some production and publicity photographs (the latter obviously paste-ups), and also the giant horned mammal *Arsinoitherium*—are also missing from release prints of *King Kong*. Originally, the *Styracosaurus* was supposed to chase the crewmen onto the pit-spanning log, where they find the great ape waiting for them at the other end. The dinosaur would, however, eventually make it into the sequel *The Son of Kong*; the mammal, alas, would not.

Contradicting what many fans of the movie have long been led to believe, there was also no human actor inside a gorilla costume playing the colossal simian in the distant shots in which Kong climbs the Empire State Building. Over the years, various actors have claimed to have played Kong in this scene, including a virtually unknown performer named Carmen Nigro (AKA Ken Roady), and also noted gorilla impersonator Charles Gemora, whose greatest ape performance was arguably that of Sultan the gorilla in the 1954 3D horror movie *Phantom of the Rue Morgue*. In Nigro's case, the claim seems to have been simply fraudulent; in Gemora's, the inaccurate claim was apparently based on the actor's memory of playing a giant ape in a never-completed *King Kong* spoof entitled *The Lost Island* (Christie Studio, 1934), and also a huge "missing link" in the Abbott and Costello comedy *Africa Screams* (1949). An existing photograph, however, plainly shows O'Brien assistant Buzz Gibson animating the stop-motion Kong up the side of the famous building.

Our *King Kong* "double take" ends with some brief notations about the movie: In 1966, Hollywood's Lytton Center presented a special-effects exhibit that displayed what purported to be an original stop-motion model of King Kong. Visitors to the center were, however, misled. For within its glass exhibit case, next to a *King Kong* screenplay, advertisements for the movie, artwork, stills and related paraphernalia, was, in reality, the remains of a Kong successor—the ape star of *Mighty Joe Young*. (All the existing miniature Kongs are now only armatures, or jointed metal skeletal frames, the rubber long having rotted off.) In a screening room at the Lytton Center, the Empire State Building sequence from *King Kong* was frequently screened during the exhibit, and it was at one of these screenings that the author had the opportunity to question Cooper about that spider sequence.

King Kong was parodied a number of times on screen, some of the parodies released the same year that the original movie premiered. One of the most memorable of these spoofs was the animated Walter Lantz cartoon *King Klunk* (Universal, 1933). The short film depicts a giant ape's adventures with prehistoric monsters, his capture and exhibition in New York, with the expected results. Among other notable spoofs, Kong was also parodied in the 1933 Mickey Mouse cartoon *The Pet Shop* (United Artists, 1933), about an escaped gorilla that imitates Kong—inspired by a picture of the authentic Kong shown in a magazine—by climbing on top of a bird cage suggesting the you-know-what building.

Decades following the original movie's release, Kong was the subject of various kinds of merchandising, including trading cards, model kits and comic books, with an animated-cartoon series starring the giant gorilla premiering on television in 1966.

King Kong was a product of its Depression Era times. It can never be remade in a way that truly captures the positive qualities of the original.

There would be, however, numerous sequels and remakes and imitations over the years. But despite their sometimes good intentions, movies like *Africa Screams, Konga* (1961) and *King Kong vs. Godzilla* (1963), and even the better efforts such as *The Son of Kong* (1933) and *Mighty Joe Young* (1949), there will always be only one real *King Kong*.

War Eagles!

Willis O'Brien, whom some film critics and buffs regard as the never-surpassed animator of three-dimensional models, is famous for a long list of motion pictures enhanced by the wonders of his special effects.

When O'Brien's name is mentioned, immediately titles such as *The Son of Kong* (1933), *Mighty Joe Young* (1949), *The Black Scorpion* (1957), *The Animal World* (1956), *The Giant Behemoth* (1959), and others come to the minds of his legion of fans.

And, of course, there remains his masterpiece, the one and only *King Kong* (1933).

In addition to the films he did complete, there is also a fairly substantial list of planned, sometimes started but unfinished, films that had brewed in the imagination of Willis O'Brien—movies which, for one reason or another, never reached completion. A good percentage of these tantalizing titles—including *Creation* (1931) and *Gwangi* (1942)—involved dinosaurs and other extinct creatures.

Creation, for example, would have been about a submarine crew that

Allosaurus models for Willis O'Brien's intended but never filmed *Gwangi*: (*left to right*) original clay sculpture by Marcel Delgado, ball-and-socket animation model, and bronzed cast of sculpture. Courtesy of the late Darlyne O'Brien.

gets stranded on a prehistoric promontory. Surviving test footage shows a beautifully designed and animated *Triceratops* family (original models sculpted by Marcel Delgado, of *The Lost World, King Kong,* and *The Son of Kong* fame), the mother of which pursues one of the crew (played by actor Ralf Harold) after he shoots one of her young. Some of the *Creation* models would later be used in *King Kong*.

Gwangi would have starred an *Allosaurus* that has inexplicably survived into a "lost valley" in the American West, the plot pitting cowboys against dinosaurs. Production art and models (again sculpted by Delgado) were made, but the movie itself was not. Nevertheless, at least some story elements from *Gwangi* seem to have entered O'Brien's original story for the 1956 movie *The Beast of Hollow Mountain,* in which a carnivorous dinosaur resembling an *Allosaurus* is killing (and of course eating) cattle, only to be lured to its death in quicksand, eventually, by an heroic cowboy (played by Guy Madison).

Another such ambitious, started-but-not-completed "Obie" project was *War Eagles.*

The movie was to have been made by RKO Radio Pictures, the same studio that had given the world *King Kong* and its same-year sequel *The*

Son of Kong, and also another epic to feature Willis O'Brien's effects, *The Last Days of Pompeii* (1935). *War Eagles* was to have been produced by Merian C. Cooper, who had produced the two "Kong" pictures. Marcel Delgado, another alumnus of the "Kongs" and also the 1925 O'Brien classic *The Lost World* (who would go on to create similar dinosaurian models for such movies as *The Beast of Hollow Mountain* in 1956 and *Dinosaurus!* in 1960)—and O'Brien were again to team up to create the special effects.

The story of *War Eagles* was different from any that had ever been projected onto a motion-picture screen.

The "War Eagles"—there would be a number of them in the planned movie—were enormous eagles of some presumably unknown prehistoric species. Natives living in their prehistoric world, existing in the present though in some remote part of the globe, have learned to tame the gigantic feathered creatures, riding them mounted on saddles made from the hides and horns of the huge ceratopsian dinosaur *Triceratops.*

Atop these living, airborne warships, the natives are able to battle the Mesozoic menaces also living in their time-misplaced world—including the dreaded carnivorous dinosaur *Tyrannosaurus*. Photographs and various single nitrate-film frames survive from the project, some of them showing the angry *Tyrannosaurus* roaring defiantly, another with this meat-eating dinosaur in physical conflict with a War Eagle ridden by a native, another with the *Tyrannosaurus* the target of an obviously harmless native spear.

With great ambition in mind, the natives decide to invade new frontiers. They settle upon attacking no less than New York City!

The titanic flying monsters from a lost world invade the metropolis, only to be fought off by the current mechanized wonder of civilized man—the dirigible. Thus, a battle between two ages is waged in the skies above Manhattan.

War Eagles went into production about the same time that its producer entered the armed services, during which time the project waned. Years later, upon his return to civilian life, Cooper, believing that the concept of using dirigibles for defense had since become outmoded, shelved the project.

Although *War Eagles* will never be seen on any local motion-picture theater screen or turn up on late-night television, at least some traces of it remain in the photographs and other fragments yet extant—all of which give a hint of what fans of dinosaur films in general, and Willis O'Brien's work in particular, have unfortunately missed.

Godzilla— Tokyo's Greatest Nemesis

Godzilla, a gigantic mutated prehistoric reptile that first appeared in "made in Japan" movies during the early 1950s and was immediately dubbed "King of the Monsters," was probably the most popular movie creature of the 1970s, outdoing even Count Dracula and the Frankenstein Monster in the fan ratings. The decade was indeed a good one for film monsters in general and the "Big G" (as he is affectionately known) in particular, and was also a prosperous time for new magazines devoted to fantastic movies.

One publishing outfit to jump onto the beastly bandwagon was Magazine Management Co., which was basically the same as the Marvel Comics Group. Marvel generally offered comic books, some of them starring monsters (though most of them featured superheroes), but often experimented by going off in different publishing directions. (For a while during the late '70s the company would even publish a comic book titled *Godzilla, King of the Monsters*.)

Monsters of the Movies, edited by Jim Harmon, was Marvel's response to the successful *Famous Monsters of Filmland*. I was, along with Ron Haydock, listed as an associate editor, both of us having had previous experience editing monster-movie magazines.

The following article about one of Japan's biggest stars appeared in *MoM*'s fifth (February 1975) issue, which also featured the towering Godzilla on its cover.

This article is about the *original* series of Godzilla movies. In 1984, Toho decided to start afresh with a new group of Godzilla epics, based on the premise that none of the original stories, with the exception of that of the first movie, ever occurred. The new

196

series, starting with 1984's *Gojira* (American title: *Godzilla 1985*), picked up 30 years after the original *Gojira*. Actor Raymond Burr reprised his role as reporter Steve Martin, but for the American-release version only. The new movie proceeded to launch yet another string of six sequels. Eventually this new series was also put to cinematic rest, with Godzilla apparently being destroyed forever, so that a mega-budgeted American interpretation of this monster character, much different from its Japanese predecessors in both appearance and powers, could debut in 1998. Toho's *Godzilla Millennium* started another new series in 2000.

In Japan, the superstars of the motion-picture screen are not necessarily of the stock of Paul Newman or Clint Eastwood. Even the former Emperor of Japan's equivalent of "Mr. Hollywood," the late Toshiro Mifune, was aced out of his top star billing position by some rather interesting rivals. For the Tokyo-based stars that draw the most fan mail are not even human. Instead, they comprise a corps of behemoths from out of time and outer space—monstrous reptiles, insects, and mammals.

Greatest of all the Japanese monster-film stars is undoubtedly Godzilla, a 400-foot-tall, amphibious prehistoric reptile, with a spiked back and breath of radioactive fire. The residents of Tokyo must have forgotten how many times the mighty creature has leveled their crowded metropolis, or at least forgiven him for his destructive behavior. For the more Godzilla demolishes this city on screen, the more his fans love him.

Godzilla's history goes back to the studios of Toho International (now Toho Co. Ltd.) in 1954. Director Ishiro Honda and special-effects wizard Eiji Tsuburaya had formed a team that would make an indelible mark on the giant-monster film genre. Together, Honda and Tsuburaya created a somber, black and white science-fiction/horror epic about an enormous legendary monster from prehistoric times, reborn in the modern-day world.

The film these men made was entitled *Gojira* and became a sensation in Japan.

Not until 1956 was the movie released in the United States. Motion picture mogul Joseph E. Levine, through his company Embassy Pictures, booked an American version of the film into the United States (with new footage of Raymond Burr portraying a foreign correspondent whose expository narration eliminated the need to dub the entire picture into English). The celebrated Japanese monster was given a new name—one that would sound more formidable to American ears. Thus, the two-year-old film *Godzilla, King of the Monsters!* was unleashed to neighborhood theaters all across the country.

Godzilla, King of the Monsters! has the standard giant-monster-on-the-loose plot. The real action in the film starts with a series of ship and other disasters, perpetrated by some huge unseen menace, which prompt an investigation. The natives of Odo Island, a body of land near the area where the disasters have taken place, believe that Godzilla, a monster out of their legends, is responsible for the trouble. Naturally, reporter Steve Martin (Burr) and paleontologist Dr. Yamani (well-known Japanese character actor Takashi Shimura) go to the island to investigate. Godzilla himself raises his reptilian head over the hillside. Pandemonium follows as the towering horror, lumbering along on his powerful hind legs, returns to the sea, leaving behind a trail of enormous footprints.

Later, at an evening gathering of scientists, Dr. Yamani presents his theory that Godzilla is actually a prehistoric monster—a hybrid of land and marine reptile—revived from its millions of years hibernation by (not surprisingly, as this was the 1950s) repeated H-bomb tests.

In an attempt to destroy the gigantic monster, the authorities drop a series of depth bombs into the ocean off Japan. They realize how successful their bombings are when Godzilla rises to his full 400-foot height in Tokyo harbor. What follows is the part of the film the eager audience has been awaiting—Godzilla's spectacular raid upon Japan's greatest city.

Effortlessly, Godzilla stomps his way through Tokyo, leaving only destruction behind him. His enormous jaws chomp through whole train cars. His fiery breath sets the city ablaze. Buildings crumble and topple with his every step. Certainly, the Japanese fight back with all the defensive weapons at their disposal. Yet nothing available to them—neither bullets nor electricity—can stop the raging colossal creature.

It is not long before Steve Martin despairingly accepts that Tokyo—and the world—is doomed.

These scenes of grand-scale destruction are a sheer visual delight to behold for fans of giant-monster movies, despite Honda's rather slow-paced direction. The Godzilla character itself was sometimes brought to screen life in the form of a remote-controlled miniature puppet that represented the creature from about the chest up. But usually the "King of the Monsters" was actor Harua Nakajima wearing a stiflingly hot rubber costume which, when photographed with the proper low angles as Godzilla stomped through Tsuburaya's skillfully constructed model city, are entirely convincing. The movie's low-key black and white cinematography and the predominance of night scenes added to the realism, demonstrating to the present writer at least that a dinosaur-like monster can be convincingly brought to life on the screen without stop-frame animation (generally considered one of the best special-effects methods for this kind of film). Some of Tsuburaya's finest miniature work appeared in this original *Godzilla* movie, establishing him as a true master of his art.

The salvation of the world from the rampaging Godzilla becomes the task of an eye-patched scientist named Dr. Serizawa (Akihiko Hirata), the inventor of a device called the Oxygen Destroyer. The invention removes oxygen from water and reduces any living creatures in the vicinity of its operation to bones—and then to atoms. Dr. Serizawa has vowed never to make his discovery known, lest it be used for evil purposes (an allusion to the use of the atomic bomb in World War II). Only after much coaxing is the scientist convinced that his device could destroy Godzilla.

Beneath the waters off Japan, Dr. Serizawa places his Oxygen Destroyer near the submerged resting Godzilla. Then, to ensure that his secret can never surface again, the scientist commits suicide. The water begins to bubble. Moments later, the roaring Godzilla emerges from the surface of the churning waters, then sinks back to the bottom of the sea. Within seconds the monster's bones are stripped of all flesh … then dissolve to nothingness. Godzilla, the "King of the Monsters," is undeniably dead as this minor classic of the 1950s comes to its end.

Godzilla, King of the Monsters! was made for a basically adult audience. The subject matter, though fantastic and in many ways outlandish, was handled with complete sobriety, the mood often quite depressing. Godzilla himself was depicted as no more than a titanic, virtually brainless prehistoric monster. Had Godzilla remained no more than atoms flowing with the waters of the sea, this original image would have remained thus. But Toho—as well as director Honda and special-effects expert Tsuburaya—soon realized that even Dr. Serizawa's Oxygen Destroyer could not forever "destroy" a monster that made as much money for the studio as did Godzilla.

Yet, if Godzilla were to endure through more films without becoming a colossal bore by repeating his original act, the monster's "personality" would have to change. Godzilla needed to be more than simply a near-mindless lumbering behemoth.

The year following the Japanese release of *Gojira*, Toho made its first sequel, *Gojira no Gyakushyu* (translated as "Godzilla's Counterattack," according to the second volume of Walt Lee's *Reference Guide to Fantastic Films*, published in 1973). This new production presented *a* Godzilla (not the *original*, disintegrated Godzilla); by the time the film went through its Warner Bros. release in the United States in 1959, his name was changed to correspond to the new American title *Gigantis the Fire*

Monster. (Paul Schreibman, an attorney who represented Henry G. Saperstein, the American producer who would eventually control the Godzilla rights in the United States, and later also to Tsuburaya Productions, once told this writer that Godzilla's name was changed so that the public would not assume that the new film was just a reissue of the original.)

The Godzilla costume had been somewhat revamped for this sequel. Certain close-ups of the modified head almost have a comical look, and already can be seen the beginnings of the humorous aspects of the character that would soon become a part of the Godzilla mythos.

The plot of the new movie, again, is relatively simple. A pair of Japanese fliers discover two huge prehistoric monsters battling for survival on a remote island. The monsters, as later identified, are Gigantis (or Godzilla) and the quadrupedal armored reptile Angurus (Angilas in the original Japanese version), "fire monsters" from Earth's prehistory so-called because of their incendiary breaths. The two behemoths continue their ancient war into the streets of another Japanese city where, after reducing most of its buildings to rubble, Gigantis finally kills his reptilian adversary. Eventually, Gigantis is confronted on a snow- and ice-blanketed island. Airplanes bomb one of the white slopes, burying the monster under an avalanche of ice and snow.

One aspect of *Gigantis the Fire Monster* unique to the Godzilla movies is that it contains a scene of genuine stop-motion special effects, although this scene only appears in the American version of the film. As part of a "newsreel" film that shows the Godzilla from the first movie (stock footage from *Gojira*) attacking Tokyo, there is also a sequence depicting the Earth in various stages of development. For one brief shot, two sauropod dinosaurs appear battling via some extremely jerky puppet animation. This tantalizing scene has an old, "silent-movie" look to it and, to date of this writing, has still not been identified.

Gigantis the Fire Monster was the last motion picture in the series to maintain a basically serious approach to its lead character. It was also the last Godzilla epic to be filmed in moody black and white. When the prehistoric giant next appeared it would be in full color, with a sense of humor and with his original (and more famous) name restored.

Monster-film buffs cringed when the title *King Kong vs. Godzilla* was announced in 1962 (original Japanese title: *Kingu Kongu tai Gojira*). In fact, many fans were almost on the verge of riot when the advance publicity stills for the film revealed a human actor wearing a quite shoddy appearing gorilla costume purporting to be the venerable King Kong. "*Blasphemy!*" some fans shouted, perhaps as loud as Godzilla's own roars, even when learning that the movie was made in a tongue-in-cheek comedy

Two famous prehistoric monsters made their comebacks in *King Kong vs. Godzilla* (1963), the first color outing for both. ™ and ©Toho Co., Ltd., all rights reserved.

style. The movie was to be played largely for laughs. In fact, Godzilla himself would partake of the fun; when he virtually laughed after singeing the giant anthropoid with his fiery breath, the tone of most future entries in this original Godzilla series was established.

The legendary ape monster King Kong (no explanation is given as to how he escaped his plunge from the Empire State Building or left New York) is discovered by a pharmaceutical company expedition on a distant island and, after a fight with an enormous (and quite convincing) octopus, is brought back to civilization. Godzilla (continuing where *Gigantis the Fire Monster* left off) is freed from the iceberg that imprisons him. There soon follows a scene (in the American version only) in which an American paleontologist holds up a copy of a children's book about prehistoric animals (a familiar volume this writer had on one of his own bookshelves), then laughably goes on to explain that Godzilla is actually a combination of the carnivorous dinosaur *Tyrannosaurus* and plated *Stegosaurus*, a scientific impossibility akin to combining a panther with a pig.

Now freed, Godzilla begins his usual destructive journey south, while King Kong smashes his way northward. The two behemoths meet in the city of Nikko, where yet another earth-shaking battle commences. The usual Tsuburaya spectacle follows, this time with much humor interjected into the action, with the two monsters finally plunging into the sea. Although it has commonly been stated in publications that only Godzilla survives in the Japanese version and Kong in the American, both editions have the same ending—Kong surfaces and swims away, seemingly to his island, while Godzilla, after a final roar, returns to apparent hibernation underwater.

I went to see *King Kong vs. Godzilla* at a Hollywood theater during its first-run American release in the summer of 1963, not really knowing what to expect. What I discovered in that dark auditorium was an action-filled monster movie aimed at a mostly juvenile audience. Certainly that intent was a valid one. The movie was fun, entertaining, at times exciting; in short (and risking the wrath of highbrow fantasy-film connoisseurs), I loved it and stayed to see it twice. Yes, the much revered Kong was made fun of; but then, no one and no-*thing*—not even the great King Kong himself—is beyond healthy spoofing.

Toho now had their formula for success fairly well established. Godzilla would return again ... and again, in movies aimed at younger audiences. And like some of the horror films made by Universal Pictures during the 1940s, Godzilla would share his star billing with other famed monsters that would be dragged out of Toho retirement.

Mothra (Japanese title: *Mosura*) was a Toho production released in the United States in 1961. The fantasy production was about, as one may guess from its title, a gigantic moth. Mothra became the first of the "old" Toho monsters (as opposed to an original like Angilas, or a creature licensed from another studio, like RKO Radio Pictures' King Kong) to co-star with the towering reptile in 1964's (years subsequently listed being for the American releases) *Godzilla vs. the Thing* (Japanese title: *Gojira tai Mosura*). The rather odd American title was presumably intended to capitalize on the old yet still popular RKO science-fiction classic of 1951, *The Thing*. A new Godzilla costume was designed for the picture and the Nipponese superstar again terrorized another big city.

In *Godzilla vs. the Thing*, an enormous oval object is washed ashore during a hurricane. This "thing" is actually the egg of the flying "monster-god" Mothra. When the rampaging Godzilla threatens to destroy the egg, Mothra attacks the scaly brute, going so far as to pull him by the tail while he futilely claws at the earth in an attempt to keep himself upright. Godzilla's hot breath eventually destroys Mothra. But the reptile is soon confronted by Mothra's twin caterpillar offspring, who hatch from the giant egg and vengefully trap their much bigger foe in a wispy cocoon.

With the next film, *Ghidrah the Three-Headed Monster* (1965; Japanese title: *San Daikaiju Chikyu Saidai no Kessen*, translated as "Three Giant Monsters, the Greatest Battle on Earth"), Godzilla began to change his status from "villain" to "hero," as he teamed up with Mothra and also the giant pterosaur Rodan (recycled from *Radon*, a movie released in the USA in 1957 as *Rodan the Flying Monster*) to battle Ghidrah, a giant winged creature from outer space. Ghidrah (or Ghidorah, in Japan), "born" from an extraterrestrial stone, is larger than Godzilla, more powerful and meaner. The three-headed space monster can also fly, with Rodan-like wings, and shoot death rays from each of its heads. Within minutes, Ghidrah can decimate an entire major city.

Godzilla and Rodan are fighting it out in a kind of slapstick battle, when Mothra (larval version) intervenes and *talks* to them (in "monster language," naturally), somehow persuading them to unite and drive their common enemy Ghidrah off the Earth. The inevitable super-battle occurs on Mount Fuji, proving that three heads are not better than three adversaries like Godzilla, Rodan, and Mothra.

Toho executives decided to maintain a sizable cast of monsters in the studio's succeeding entries in the Godzilla series. In addition to more than one monster, there were more juvenile plots and more laughs. *Monster Zero* (1965; Japanese title: *Kaiju Daisenso*, or "The Great Monster War") firmly established Godzilla and Rodan as Earth's *heroes*, while space monster Ghidrah would forever act the part of *villain*. In this film, a group of aliens capture Godzilla and Rodan (their other ally apparently having been returned to mothballs) and transport them bodily to their Planet X, there to battle Ghidrah, the so-called Monster Zero (all monsters having been numbered by the extraterrestrials) of the title. Only later do the aliens reveal their true evil motives, whereupon they release all three monsters to destroy the people of the Earth they intend (not surprisingly) to conquer.

Godzilla vs. the Sea Monster (1966; Japanese title: *Nankai no Dai Ketto*, or "Big Duel in the South Seas") introduced Ebirah, the "Horror of the Deep," a gigantic shrimp, to use an oxymoron, that guards an island occupied by would-be world dictators. Godzilla, also on the island, is aroused from sleep and again teams up with Mothra (now in moth form) to destroy Ebirah and also the faction of human villains.

The Godzilla movies reached a new level of appeal for juvenile audiences in 1968 with *Son of Godzilla* (Japanese title: *Gojira no Musuko*). On

Special-effects wizard Eiji Tsuburaya (in hat) checks out a relaxing "Godzilla" (Haruo Nakajima) between takes on *Monster Zero* (1965). ™ and ©Toho Co., Ltd., all rights reserved.

an island in which giant plants and insects thrive, Godzilla's son hatches from an egg. (The question has never been answered as to just *who* laid this egg; if "our" Godzilla, then the famous movie monster must actually be a female.) Disturbingly, Godzilla's offspring, named Minya, has a face more closely resembling some deformed human child than Godzilla himself. Minya playfully blows smoke rings and hitches rides on his daddy's scaly tail. Godzilla displays his fatherly instincts (quite unlike most *real* reptiles) and saves Minya from some giant mantises and spiders before a group of scientists force both family members into a snowy hibernation.

Destroy All Monsters (1968; Japanese title: *Kaiju Sohingeki*, meaning "March of the Monsters") was Toho's equivalent of multi-monster rallies like Universal's *House of Frankenstein* (1944). Not only did this epic feature Godzilla, Minya, Rodan, Mothra, and Ghidrah, but also these familiar Toho creatures: Angilas, from the *Gigantis* movie; Spiega, the giant spider from *Son of Godzilla*; Varan (Baran in Japan), the prehistoric reptile from *Varan the Unbelievable* (1959); Manda, the possibly prehistoric sea serpent from *Atragon* (1963); Baragon, the prehistoric burrowing reptile from *Frankenstein Conquers the World* (1964); and Gorosaurus, a more or less generalized theropod dinosaur who first showed up in *King Kong Escapes* (1967).

The story is set sometime in the future when all of the Earth's giant creatures have been grouped together on a kind of "Monster Country Safari" or "Wild Monster Park" called Monster Island. Once again, a band of aliens with Earth conquest in mind gain control of the monsters and set them against the people and cities of our world. When the Earth monsters finally regain control of their own diminutive "minds," the aliens unleash their monstrous ace in the hole—old reliable Ghidrah—who is summarily defeated by the planet's band of bizarre heroes.

Godzilla's Revenge (1969; Japanese title: *Oru Kaiju Daisingeki*, or "All Monsters Attack") was a unique entry into the series of Godzilla sagas. The story is a child's fantasy, set not in the shiny, super-scientific Tokyo of the other monster films, but in the smog-ridden Tokyo of the real world. The story is that of a young boy, pestered by a neighborhood bully named Gabera. Unable to deal with Gabera, the boy flees from his unhappy life into a world of daydreams. In his fantasies, the boy goes to Monster Island, where he watches Godzilla battle such creatures as Ebirah and Spiega and the giant mantises (all appearing again courtesy of stock footage from earlier Godzilla films). He also meets Minya, who shrinks down to the boy's size, at the same time gaining the ability to speak. Minya demonstrates to the youth how Godzilla and he defeat a new towering monster, thereby inspiring courage in the lad for his dealings in his own real world. The child gives this new creature the name of the bully, then proceeds to defeat his human adversary.

Undoubtedly, the above plot condensation sounds silly in the extreme. But to the very young audience for which the film was made, *Godzilla's Revenge* is a thoroughly delightful and sometimes inspiring fantasy, sensitive yet exciting, and showing that Honda can be a masterful director. Again, at the risk of offending serious fantasy-movie fans, the author would classify this picture as one of the best monster films ever made strictly for children. Unfortunately most Godzilla aficionados seem to regard this film as one of the most ridiculous in the entire series. Eiji Tsuburaya regrettably died about the time *Godzilla's Revenge* went into production, which may account for the extensive use of stock footage from past films including *Godzilla vs. the Sea Monster* and *Son of Godzilla*.

Godzilla and his monster cohorts kept on coming.

In 1971, the now heroic monster battled Hedorah, a slimy horror spawned in pollution and feeding on it, in *Godzilla vs. the Smog Monster* (Japanese title: *Gojira tai Hedora*). That same year Godzilla and Angilas (who *talk "human"* in this film) returned to fight more evil alien invaders and their slaves, Ghidrah, and the obviously large space monster Gigan, in *Godzilla on Monster Island* (Japanese title: *Gojira tai Gigan*). Gigan is a flying creature with a birdlike beak, hooked claws, and (quite literally) a *buzzsaw* on its stomach! *Godzilla vs. Megalon* (Japanese title: *Gojira tai Megaro*) was the 1973 entry in which Godzilla teams up with superhero robot Jet Jaguar to defeat a monster from under the Earth.

Where would all of these monsterfests end? Other films in this series would promptly follow, including *Godzilla vs. the Cosmic Monster* (Japanese title: *Gojira tai Mechagojira*) in 1977 and *Terror of Godzilla* (Japanese title: *Mechagojira no Gyakushu*) the following year, both featuring robotic versions of this favorite monster. Seemingly, Godzilla is destined for many new battles, many romps through the perpetually reconstructed Tokyo. The big lizardlike monster might still not have reached his zenith in popularity. Japan's department stores are continually flooded with new Godzilla merchandise—including toys, model kits, comic books, music albums, *etc.*—not unlike that associated with the contemporaneous *Star Trek* and *Planet of the Apes* crazes in this country. There are even books and catalogs about giant monsters published in Japan in which Godzilla and his brood are taken quite seriously. (Consider that some of these books feature cutaway illustrations of the monsters, detailing their skeletons and all of their supposedly functioning internal organs!)

Godzilla has made many other appearances—in movies and on TV— apart from the original Toho series of films. Among these, during the mid–1960s, Godzilla was unsuccessfully disguised with a *Styracosaurus*-style spiked frill around his neck, for an episode of Tsuburaya Productions' *Ultraman* television series. Now called by a different name altogether, the moonlighting monster fights Ultraman until the skyscraper-tall alien superhero finally defeats him with brute force and humanoid cunning, ripping off the frill (and exposing his true form) in the process.

Godzilla has also made appearances in several amateur-movie shorts made by independent filmmakers in the United States. While living in Chicago, Illinois, the present writer borrowed Godzilla for two such amateur productions featuring stop-motion plasticine clay models, *The Fire Monsters* (color, 1959) and *Son of Tor* (part-color, 1964). In *The Fire Monsters*, Godzilla (here called "Gigantis" again) and sparring partner Angilas (once more, "Angurus") fight it out in the Windy City. *Son of Tor*, a sequel to *Tor, King of Beasts* (1962) and a loose remake of *The Son of Kong*, guest-starred Godzilla along with a number of other famous giant monsters, pitting the Japanese giant against Ray Harryhausen's dinosaur-like Venusian "Ymir" from the 1957 movie *20 Million Miles to Earth*.

The most unusual of all "unofficial" Godzilla titles is unquestionably *Bambi Meets Godzilla*, a 30-second animated-cartoon short made by Marvin Newland in 1969. The student film received considerable attention during the early 1970s, with advertisements on the radio and screenings in theaters and on television. There is but one scene: Bambi the young deer happily munches grass to pleasant classical music until an enormous reptilian foot suddenly comes down to squash him. The picture is brief—yet hilariously effective.

Godzilla has often been derided by monster-movie fans who scoff at the idea of human actors wearing dinosaur costumes and who believe that humor has little or no place in a horror or science-fiction film. In defense of Godzilla and his gigantic sparring partners, this writer states that for what his films have been—spectacular action fantasies made essentially for kids—they serve their purpose. Some are extremely entertaining. Godzilla's popularity attests to the reality that young audiences appreciate what the people at Toho have done for them. Even discounting the use of giant-monster costumes, most of Toho's miniature work is more than competent—while much of it is masterful.

Regardless of one's personal opinion as to what Godzilla evolved (or perhaps *de*volved) into, the original movie *Godzilla, King of the Monsters!* remains one of the most memorable creature films of its type from the Fifties, earning its titled star his niche in the upper echelon of enduring creatures.

Personally, I enjoy the Godzilla movies—and many years have passed since I was a kid.

THE CREATURE FEATURES

The most popular movie monster of the 1950s—indeed, the most singular monster to represent that era, despite its lack of atomic-energy spawned origins—was a fictitious prehistoric being called the Gill Man, or Creature from the Black Lagoon.

The Creature was one of a number of film monsters that supposedly originated in some vague prehistoric age but had no basis in any kind of scientific reality. His history followed none of the known or logical evolutionary family trees and, therefore, could never have existed in the real world at any time. Nevertheless, the Gill Man was a beautifully designed and appealing—as far as monsters can be—character destined for the usual sequels, homages, ripoffs, spoofs, and merchandising.

I was one of countless young fans who responded to the character in the correct ways when his films were first released to theaters back in the '50s. As with many fans of about the same age, the Gill Man became "my Creature," my personal monster of that era.

The following article appeared, along with the preceding Godzilla piece, in the fifth issue of *Monsters of the Movies* in 1975. In the years following the article's first publication, the Creature or variations of it would appear in other movies, with at least two major film directors, John Landis and John Carpenter, announcing at various times plans to do a big-budget remake of *Creature from the Black Lagoon*.

Universal-International, the movie studio that the former Universal Pictures had become, was seeking a new movie-monster character, one the company hoped would have the enduring appeal of their "old school" horrors that had once made such great profits for the studio in decades past.

But these were the 1950s. Such fiends as Count Dracula, the Frankenstein Monster, and the Wolf Man were, to the studio executives' thinking, already out of date. After all, hadn't the studio already admitted on screen that this former staple crop of horrors had run its course by casting the monsters as straight men opposite comedians Bud Abbott and Lou Costello? Besides, in this modern age, artificial men stitched together and brought to life by mad scientists, as well as supernatural fiends of the night, were "known" to be passé.

The Fifties was a new kind of era. It was an era of the monster spawned by testings of the atomic bomb, a time of prehistoric *things* awakened from their millions-of-years hibernations by the interference of puny humankind. The horrors of the 1950s were usually monsters in every sense of the word—beasts, human or otherwise, bent upon destruction, usually without even a semblance of humanity.

Nevertheless, *some* traces of humanity—at least some kind of humanity toward which the character may have been evolving—crept into the scaly and finned monster known as the Gill Man, or "Creature," the amphibious star of Universal-International's gem of 1954, *Creature from the Black Lagoon*. Like many such monsters, the Gill Man's inevitable downfall resulted from that modicum of humanity.

Creature from the Black Lagoon began as an idea in the mind of motion-picture producer William Alland. According to the studio publicity, at least, Alland had learned of an obscure South American legend concerning a prehistoric monster still living in the Amazon. Allegedly this "creature" was some kind of hybrid of man, fish, turtle, and alligator, and was a supposed survivor of the Devonian period, the ancient age of fishes. According to this probably specious and studio-fabricated story, Alland then telephoned the Universal-International make-up department and informed its chief, Bud Westmore, that if an appropriate monster suit could be delivered, he would have a script written around the prehistoric character.

The so-called "Gill Man" outfit was not to be, however, the usual phony-looking rubber monster costume. It had to be totally convincing, allowing the actor wearing it the freedom to breathe, to make its gills flare and pulsate, to walk on the land and also to swim with the grace of a human fish.

Westmore and his crew, consisting of Jack Kevan and Bob Hickman, promptly accepted Alland's challenge and went to work. Since the only bust with a neck in their make-up studio happened to be in the image of actress Ann Sheridan, that was where they began their monster-making process, building over Sheridan's lovely features with modeling clay.

The Creature's look was largely designed by Millicent Patrick. Westmore, however, contended that a monster lacking a nose was always more menacing than a monster with one; thus, the Gill Man, by necessity of breathing with gills, would appear even more formidable. The chin and mouth were based on a frog. Various designs were considered; originally, Westmore and crew intended to give their Gill Man crab claws and a mechanical tail strong enough to knock a man off his feet. However, both of these innovations were eventually abandoned to give the actor having to wear the outfit more freedom, both on land and in the water.

The final design of the Gill Man turned out to be one of the make-up studio's (as well as Universal's) finest creations—a scaly, finned, dark-green amphibian in the general shape of a man, with a gaping mouth framed by full lips. After the costume had been sculpted, by various workers (Chris Mueller sculpting the head), then the various pieces cast in foam rubber from plaster molds and finally painted, the cost for the outfit had reached a total of $12,000, certainly a very large sum in 1954. When such a relatively large amount was invested in a monster suit, and after so much care went into its design and construction, it would be an understatement to say that its creators were proud of their work.

Alland was, not surprisingly, pleased with the Gill Man that was created for him, and proceeded to commission a script from writers Harry Essex and Arthur Ross to bring the legendary Creature to life. The next logical step was finding a suitable actor to portray the unbilled Gill Man.

One of the earliest choices for the part was mostly Western actor Glenn Strange, best known to monster-film buffs as the Frankenstein Monster in the Universal films *House of Frankenstein* (1944), *House of Dracula* (1945), and Universal-International's send-up *Abbott and Costello Meet Frankenstein* (1948). Glenn Strange was a rugged and tall man (6 feet 3 inches) with a good physique, having once been a wrestler, rodeo rider and, in the 1930s, also a movie stuntman (John Wayne being among the actors he'd doubled). He was also a fair swimmer, and had been tested for the role eventually played by Olympic swimming champion Johnny Weismuller in MGM's original *Tarzan, the Apeman* (1932).

"...I just swim," Strange told me back in 1965. "I was supposed to originally play the Creature from the Black Lagoon, too, but that was another underwater hazard. They told me how much water stuff there was, and I said, 'No, I don't want it.' It turned out they used a swimming double after all, Ricou Browning from Hawaii."

For the scenes of the Gill Man performing on land, the actor who was finally chosen for the role was, appropriately, an ex-United States Marine named Ben Chapman, who would learn that his most grueling experiences were not to be had on screen or in the "Black Lagoon," but in Bud Westmore's studio make-up shop.

Chapman found that the Gill Man outfit was not a simple slip-on affair, but had to be built around him so that it could function as a second layer of skin and would not fit any other actor. Stripped down to his underwear, Chapman would lie motionless upon a clay slab, while the skilled monster-makers built an exact mold of his body. The various sections of the Gill Man costume—the head, torso, hands, and feet—were baked in an oven inside the various molds. After these sections were completed, the claws, fins, and scales were added, completing a Creature suit that only Chapman could wear in scenes shot at Universal City, California.

Another costume was made to fit Chapman's double, the above-mentioned Ricou Browning—not tall enough to play the character on land, where he could be visually compared with the other actors—who performed, in Florida, the underwater scenes in the movie. Browning developed his own individualistic swimming style for the Gill Man. He would twist his body from side to side to make the Creature's underwater movements even more believable. These movements also became a kind of signature or trademark, not only for the Gill Man, but for Browning also. Once he perfected this style, Browning never seemed to swim out of it, even when performing in non-Creature projects. (The reader should take notice when watching reruns of the television series *Sea Hunt* and *Flipper*, or the episode of TV's *Voyage to the Bottom of the Sea* in which a miniature "gill man" is enlarged to the size of a man; with a bit of imagination, in these instances, the Creature can be seen all over again.)

Creature from the Black Lagoon was made in the three-dimensional process that was so popular (but relatively short-lived) back in the 1950s. Director Jack Arnold made good use of the 3D Polaroid process, offering his audience enough chills, with the Gill Man leaping and clutching at them from the screen, to elicit their telling their friends to go and see the picture. In part, as a result of this word-of-mouth publicity as well as the studio's own promotion, the movie was an explosive success, grossing an impressive $3 million (a substantial amount in those days) by the end of 1954. Much of this success can also be attributed to the realistic Gill Man costume itself and the audience's ability to suspend its disbelief and accept it as real. But perhaps more of it was due to the direction of Jack Arnold.

In his book *Science Fiction in the Cinema* (A. S. Barnes & Co., 1970), John Baxter devotes an entire chapter to director Arnold, hailing him as an unsung genius of the science-fiction film genre. In many respects, Baxter is certainly correct in this opinion. Arnold managed to take a property like *Creature from the Black Lagoon*, with its rather obvious and lurid title and which could have been utterly ruined by some other, less caring director, and created a minor Fifties classic, featuring a monster that is surely part of a pantheon in a spot just below that of the undying Frankenstein Monster, Count Dracula, and the Wolf Man. Arnold presented the Amazon's Black Lagoon as a world of eerie and sinister beauty, dominated by the lingering presence of a creature not entirely man or monster. His handling of the prehistoric Gill Man resulted in *the* classic monster of a mostly undistinguished era populated by giant crabs, alien conquerors, and teenage horrors.

Creature from the Black Lagoon opens with the discovery of a fossil claw embedded in a bank of South America's Amazon river (in reality, the location was Florida), the bones suggesting something part man and part fish—perhaps some previously unknown species of "missing link" bridging both groups of vastly disparate animals. Shortly after this discovery, a living incarnation of the fossil raids the camp of the expedition that found the claw.

The discovery of the fossilized claw brings another expedition to the Black Lagoon area, this one including two scientists who are also adept frogmen, played by Richard Denning and that perennial star of science-fiction films of the 1950s, Richard Carlson. Adding glamour to the group was Universal-International starlet Julia (later Julie) Adams, playing the character who would finally lead to the Creature's downfall.

As Ms. Adams's character Kay innocently goes for a swim in the dark waters of the Black Lagoon, she is observed from below by the Gill Man. The monster takes an immediate fascination (or, if his buried humanity is stronger than one might suspect, something more sublime) with the beauty in the alluring white swimsuit. He follows her from below, mimicking her graceful movements underwater and, thus far, remaining unnoticed.

Later on in the film, the Gill Man is caught in the net of the expedition's boat, the *Rita*. In tearing himself free, the Creature leaves behind a single claw (which later, mysteriously and without explanation, appears to have grown back). The frogmen scientists don their scuba gear, grab spearguns, then seek out the thing that left its claw by plunging into the lagoon waters. At last, the Gill Man confronts them head-on, engaging the frogmen in a savage battle until the humans' spearguns drive him away.

Still desiring the dark-haired woman, the Gill Man blocks the *Rita*'s

Actress Julia Adams reacts appropriately in the presence of the prehistoric Gill Man (Ben Chapman) in the original *Creature from the Black Lagoon* (1954). ©Universal-International/Universal Pictures.

passage out of the lagoon with a barricade of branches. Then, while the boat's crewmen focus their attention on the blockade, the monster steals aboard and abducts the screaming Kay.

The film climaxes in the misty lair of the Creature, where Carlson's character emerges via an underground stream to find the woman he also loves draped across a rock like a sacrificial victim (or honeymoon bride). But even as the scientist embraces her, the Creature stalks toward them, infuriated over the human male's trespassing into his dark domain. The final struggle of man versus monster occurs, the scientist wounding the Gill Man with his knife, then forcing the monster into the open air. Unable to breathe for long on the surface, the Gill Man staggers back into the waters that presumably spawned him, as the humans fire after him with their guns. Riddled with bullets, the Creature sinks back beneath the waters of the Black Lagoon, apparently dead.

Dead?

A Universal-International monster costing 12,000 1954 dollars to build, and starring in a movie that grossed $3 million, *dead*? Frankenstein's Monster, Dracula, and their fiend friends all survived through a long string of sequel movies. Surely the considerably more expensive Creature would follow their example.

Before the film was released, Universal-International sent their Gill Man celebrity, with Ben Chapman inside the suit, to TV, making live special-guest appearances on shows like *The Colgate Comedy Hour*. Glenn Strange, who had turned down the role, now found himself sharing the small screen (as Frankenstein's Monster) with the Gill Man on the *Colgate* show as well as other programs. "Ricou [Browning] and I did a live show with Sonja Henie and Bud [Abbott] and Lou [Costello] at NBC," Strange told this writer. "I did the Monster and he did the Creature."

In 1955, Jack Arnold assumed the directorial chores again for the first sequel, *Revenge of the Creature*, also made in three dimensions (though mostly released "flat," as the 3D craze was rapidly declining). Ben Chapman was no longer in the Creature suit. Although Ricou Browning again played the character underwater, the Gill Man on land was played by stuntman Tom Hennesy. There were some changes made in the Creature outfit, the eyes now bulging out farther and the upper lip jutting forward a bit more, suggesting more of a fishlike appearance. The coloring was also darker than in the original suit. In this writer's opinion, the new Creature costume lacked some of the realism of the first design.

Not surprisingly, the Gill Man is discovered very much alive in his Black Lagoon kingdom. Perhaps the waters of the Black Lagoon had some curative effect upon the Creature's wounds, interacting with his unique physiology. Besides that, how often could mere bullets permanently put to rest any Universal monster, "International" or otherwise?

In this second adventure, the Creature is captured by another scientist, this one played by John Agar, another 1950s science-fiction movie stalwart, and taken to Florida's Ocean Harbor Seaquarium, where he joins the true fishes as a living exhibit for the public's education and enjoyment. The Gill Man, however, becomes infatuated with another human being, this one in the person of blonde and lovely Lori Nelson. The monster snaps his confining chains and goes on a destructive spree, displaying enough superhuman strength to overturn a car. Inevitably the Gill Man captures his new heart's desire, setting her down long enough to receive yet another volley of apparently deadly bullets.

By the third film in the series, both the Creature character and the 3D fad had waned in popularity. The limitations in dealing with a character that could do little more than walk, swim, growl, kill and carry off pretty human brides-to-be were apparent to the studio. Therefore, Universal-International decided to change the Gill Man—drastically—in the monster's third (and two-dimensional) screen outing, *The Creature Walks*

Among Us (1956). The new movie would be directed by John Sherwood, who seemed to lack much of Arnold's understanding of the character.

The Creature (Browning), inexplicably alive and well, is set aflame during another conflict with humans, this time in the Black Lagoon-like Florida Everglades. The fire does not kill the monster, but merely burns off its outer layer of scales. In an effort to save the Creature, a group of scientists operate on him, the result of their medical tampering being a new, less scaly and aquatic version of the character. He has also mysteriously become larger (including acquiring bulk while on the operating table), and is now played by another *big* actor, usually–Western performer Don Megowan. (I can attest to the size of Megowan. The actor used to manage the apartment building next to one I was living in, and being late paying the rent to him could have been an unsettling experience!)

Without all of his fins and gills, the Creature now looks a bit more human. Not only does he look more like a man, he also acts more like one. Now he is capable of some humanlike understanding and breathes, to the Gill Man's distress, only air. Caged like a wild beast, the new (and supposedly "improved") Creature not surprisingly bursts free, disrupting the electrified fence that confines him, killing his human captor, then striding anxiously across a beach presumably to drown in the ocean. But since we never see the Creature enter the water, we are led to believe that yet another sequel might follow.

There never was a fourth movie in the series, although there were reports that another entry was planned, possibly going so far as the script stage of development. But the Creature, whether he really did commit suicide by returning to the water, or if the water miraculously restored him to his original form, did not entirely disappear.

The Creature's only other appearances in Universal projects were on TV. Among these, the Gill Man was the mysterious and wealthy Uncle Gilbert (played by Richard Hale, wearing a rubber head, hands, and feet made by Don Post Studios, a commercial manufacturer and supplier of custom masks and related items, the "missing parts" hidden by a raincoat) in "Love Comes to Mockingbird Heights," a 1965 episode of *The Munsters* series. Parts of the Gill Man were incorporated into the demon costume of "Pickman's Model" (1971) on the anthology series *Night Gallery*. In 1981 the Creature would also turn up as a mechanical robot in the made-for-TV motion picture *The Munsters' Revenge*. Plans to remake the first movie would be announced for years; although Universal never continued its original Creature from the Black Lagoon series, the studio did make money from the amphibian by licensing numerous masks (as with those made by Post), model kits, toys, comic books, and other items.

Though Universal's Creature series died after its trilogy of films, other studios continued to capitalize on the copyrighted Gill Man character, almost always without its legal owners' consent. For example, a number of Mexican production companies starred the Gill Man in movies that were apparently not affected by United States copyright and trademark regulations (unless Universal simply didn't know about them or bother to take legal action against them). *El Castillo de los Monstruos* ("The Castle of the Monsters"), made in 1957, was a typical newlywed-couple-stuck-in-haunted-castle farce, with Mexican comedian Clavillazo being pursued by shabby versions of American movie horrors, among them a very phony-looking Gill Man. In this instance, the Gill Man is the creation of a mad scientist who makes the monster from a tiny fish. The Creature (played by an actor adding a rubber Don Post mask and appendages to his Gill Man outfit) was one of many recycled Universal fiends (actually robots) in *Chabelo y Pepito contra los Monstruos* ("Chabelo and Pepito Against the Monsters"), a Mexican monster comedy of 1973.

There were also American attempts at profiting from the famed Gill Man.

For example, *The She Creature*, an American-International Pictures B-film of 1957, featured a reincarnated sea monster that seems to have been inspired by the Gill Man. The 92-pound monster foam rubber and latex suit was designed and built by the studio's resident monster creator Paul Blaisdell and his wife Jackie, Paul also playing the title female character. Blaisdell told this writer around 1977,

> The She Creature was never designed to go *underwater*. It could, however, go *into* the ocean, to a limited extent, with some degree of safety. Unfortunately, the foam rubber had a habit of taking on a considerable poundage of water, which slowed you down considerably if you had to make a transition from water to land. On the opposite side of the coin, she did contain a small reserve of air which was never timed, but could probably be rated as one to two minutes. This was handy in dealing with chemical smoke fumes in some of "her" pictures.

The Gill Man's builder Jack Kevan unsuccessfully tried creating his own original but similar horror, even incorporating parts of the original Creature costume and reusing the character's distinctive roar, in the inexpensive movie *The Monster of Piedras Blancas* (1958). Producer/director Roger Corman made a low-budget but funny spoof of the Creature and other genres, *Creature from the Haunted Sea* (1961), featuring a comical version of a Gill Man beast. An amphibious monster simply called the Creature was invited, along with other infamous horror characters, to the castle of Dr. Frankenstein in *Mad Monster Party?*, a 1966 children's movie featuring a cast of animated puppets.

Just a few of the other movies that were obviously inspired by the original Gill Man are *The Horror of Party Beach* (1964), *War-Gods of the Deep* (1966), and *Destination Inner Space* (1966), none of which approached their inspiration in quality.

The original Gill Man was a product of the Fifties, just as Frankenstein's Monster and Count Dracula remain with the monster-film mythologies of the Thirties and Forties. His days of greatest glory encompassed but three brief years. But during those years he became a motion-picture legend—one that endures, preserving the names of "Gill Man" and "Creature" among those of the most famous of all movie monsters.

KING KONG
CLIMBS AGAIN

King Kong, that famous giant gorilla and fighter of Mesozoic reptiles, became an authentic icon following his original screen appearance in 1933. In the years following his motion-picture debut, his recognizable image, particularly standing on top of the Empire State Building amid swarming biplanes, became instantly identifiable the world over.

The following article—about the mighty prehistoric ape's unexpected appearance in an early 1970s television commercial—appeared as "King Kong Kommercial" in the 126th issue, July 1976, of that granddaddy of all magazines devoted to fantastic cinema, *Famous Monsters of Filmland*. Unfortunately my byline was somehow eliminated from the piece, though my name did manage to sneak into a photo caption. The penchant of the magazine's editor Forrest J Ackerman—and the author—for using puns is reflected in some of my text.

The article's subject, when first seen on the tube, was especially startling in those days before colorized versions of classic black and white movies would become commonplace on TV and home video. The commercial was animated by David Allen (1944–1998), who would become a top name in the field of stop-motion animation. Its human star Vickie Riskin had recently appeared with the author in a USC Western short subject made by film student Rick Mitchell, himself a very serious fan of the original *King Kong*. Another participant in the commercial, a very young Rick Baker, would go on to become an Academy Award winning make-up artist and would also create and portray the colossal ape himself in Paramount Pictures' 1976 color remake of *King Kong*.

Although the commercial itself only had a brief "shelf life," it managed to survive, decades later, to become a popular subject for television shows about old commercials, and video compilations of such pieces of TV advertising.

David Allen's name would become, over the succeeding years, associated a number of times with stop-motion creatures, many of them prehistoric. He animated various extinct animals in *When Dinosaurs Ruled the Earth* (1971), assisting the movie's main special-effects creator Jim Danforth. Allen would bring to life a plesiosaur, a Mesozoic marine reptile, for the low-budget yet entertaining movie *The Crater Lake Monster* (1977). He would animate a number of dinosaurs and other extinct reptiles in the slapstick comedy movie *Caveman* (1981), starring Ringo Star, the most memorable among them being a clutzy, overweight *Tyrannosaurus* that gets "stoned" on Stone Age berries. The movie also featured such creatures as an Allen-animated *Pteranodon* and a giant horned lizard. The highlight of the horror movie *Doctor Mordrid* (1992) would be a battle inside the Los Angeles County Museum of Natural History between skeletons of an American mastodon and a *Tyrannosaurus* brought to life thanks to Allen. In 1993 his company David Allen Productions would create the special effects, some of them using stop-motion animation and others cable-operated mechanical models, for the hit direct-to-video movie *Prehysteria!*, co-produced by Pete Von Sholly.

Allen's dream project *The Primevals*—the latest incarnation of his *Raiders of the Stone Rings*—started filming with Full Moon Productions during the 1990s, with Allen creating the stop-motion special effects, writing the script, and directing. The film is being completed posthumously by Allen's friends Chris Endicott and Kent Burton.

King Kong extended a brown and furry hand, reaching for a passing biplane. The gigantic anthropoid maintained his precarious perch, his one-paw grip on New York's famous Empire State Building.

To myriad television viewers across the United States in 1972, what they seemed to be watching in this opening footage—which had faded in from black following the end of a segment of the regularly scheduled programming—was no more than a preview of some familiar footage of possibly yet another telecast of the classic Willis O'Brien "ape-ic" *King Kong*. It was probably not until this sequence cut to a medium close-up of the brown-faced behemoth that most watchers finally realized that something was wrong in "Den(ham)mark."

Scene from the original test created in 1970 by David Allen which evolved into the "King Kong" Volkswagen commercial utilizing the same ape model. Courtesy of the late David Allen.

A *brown* King Kong—?!

While everything else seemed to be in accord with the original 1933 version, right down to the sculpture and animation of the simian stop-motion model seen in this footage, *King Kong* was undeniably colorful ... but it was not made in *color*!

Watching the remaining footage of this short piece of film provided the answer to the puzzlement. Kong reached out again, this time actually catching one of the annoying, *Pteranodon*-like airplanes. But instead of letting it drop to the pavement 102 stories below, he merely tucked it beneath a hairy arm, then descended the once-tallest building in the world.

On the ground, Kong then lumbered toward an equally gigantic Volkswagen 411. He tossed the airplane "trophy" into the spacious trunk of the car, beat his chest several times, then got into the giant "Bug" with his date—a young woman wearing an evening gown and suspiciously resembling actress Fay Wray. Finally, waving "goodbye" to the people gawking at him from the sidewalks, King Kong drove off into the fadeout.

This all had to be a TV commercial, perhaps one of the most imaginative and elaborate yet in the history of the medium. To the average viewer, this Volkswagen 411 plug provided a few moments of nostalgia, bringing to their memories the image of the original black and white Kong protecting Ann Darrow (Fay Wray) from those nasty planes. To a fan of monster films, the commercial (aptly titled "King Kong") proved that someone in TV production or in the advertising business (or both) lovingly recalled the animation work of the master Willis O'Brien, and also possessed the talent and integrity to duplicate some cherished moments from the original.

Who was responsible for the "King Kong" Volkswagen commercial and what was the evolution of his idea?

The origins can be traced back to 1970 when England's Hammer Films, a studio which had enjoyed some impressive profits with the 1966 dinosaur movie *One Million Years B.C.*, seriously considered securing the rights from RKO Pictures to remake *King Kong*. Coincidentally, a young stop-motion animator, prehistoric creature buff, and all-around Kong lover, David Allen took the initiative to shoot his own piece of test footage of Kong battling the ancient airplanes atop the Empire State Building.

Allen built his Kong model to stand approximately 12 or 13 inches tall. The model was virtually identical to one sculpted by Marcel Delgado for the original *King Kong*. On a miniature set at Cascade Pictures of California, in Hollywood, Allen shot four Kong test scenes at his own expense. Afterward he added a soundtrack consisting of effects recorded from the track of the RKO feature. The finished 35-millimeter, with its optical soundtrack, was an example of what could be done if, in fact, this planned *King Kong* remake did go into actual production.

"I made it as a portfolio piece," David Allen told this writer. "I quite keenly enjoyed doing it. I wouldn't have done it if I weren't so overly enthusiastic about the original *King Kong*."

The Hammer version of *King Kong* never went before the cameras. RKO, the Hammer legal department soon discovered, jealously guarded their masterpiece. While RKO would then permit other studios to use their Kong character in original stories (*e.g., King Kong vs. Godzilla* and *King Kong Escapes*, both from Japan and featuring rather shoddy versions of the gargantuan ape, as well as other prehistoric monsters), the studio would not, at the time, permit anyone to film an outright remake. Consequently, Hammer moved on to other projects, some of them with prehistoric themes, while David Allen filmed his test sequence as part of a Cascade sample reel that went out across the country to various advertising agencies.

Three months passed.

At this time a nostalgia craze was sweeping the United States. The 1920s and 1930s were popular again; this era was frequently the setting for many of the advertising campaigns that sold products to trend-following consumers. The advertising firm which handled all Volkswagen promotion thought it might be wise to capitalize on this fad by incorporating the new larger "Super-Bug" into a commercial featuring the mightiest (and biggest) monster of the 1930s, King Kong.

Numerous production companies began bidding for the Volkswagen King Kong account, all of which had planned to utilize simply an actor wearing a gorilla suit. But when the VW executives saw David Allen's test footage spliced into the Cascade sample reel, all considerations of using a monkey-suited man were discarded. Cascade—and Allen—had won the job.

The "King Kong" commercial seemed to have everything going in its favor. Vickie Riskin, the young actress hired to portray Kong's human "girlfriend," was the most suitable choice imaginable for the role. Her mother was the very actress who was once carried away in the gigantic black-and-white paw of the first King Kong, Fay Wray!

There was also the matter of hiring someone to fill in for the non-animated close-up of Kong's hand as it opens the trunk of the giant VW 411, then later grips the floor shift. David Allen had mentioned that Rick Baker, a young make-up artist who was already displaying early signs of genius in his work, had made a mold for a gorilla hand. Cascade, however, was already considering two performers well-known for their ape roles—George Barrows, whose gorilla suit had been used in such films as *Gorilla at Large* (1954) and the *King Kong*-inspired *Konga* (1961), and Janos Prohaska, whose rather unconvincing gorilla suit was most often seen in films and television programs of the 1960s and '70s. Barrows, whose wife Jewell happened to be Cascade's casting director, was not really interested in doing the part; Prohaska, whose ape suit would not have matched Allen's miniature anyway, demanded too much money.

Cascade followed up Allen's suggestion and hired Rick Baker, who worked against deadline time to make the gorilla hand that he would wear himself in the commercial. Baker was pleased with the finished project; it wasn't often that anyone was given the opportunity to appear, albeit briefly, as the celebrated Eighth Wonder of the World.

"King Kong" the commercial went into its month-long shooting period. David Allen would have preferred helming the filming himself, but given the usual bureaucracy involved in large companies, a staff director was brought in to oversee the production. Before much longer, more and more staff people found their way into the production, while Allen, the real creator of the project, performed the animation.

Despite his being aced out of the controlling part of his own brainchild, and despite certain objections he had regarding the design of the commercial, Allen perfectly animated the King Kong model—the very same one he had built for that original test footage—and created one of the authentically memorable highlights in the history of television advertising.

The commercial was extremely well received by the home viewers, although it only ran about three times. Aesthetically, at least, "King Kong" was an unqualified success. To the ad agency, however, it was a dismal Kong-sized flop!

How could such a masterfully executed piece of film have been considered a failure?

There have been a number of reasons given, all stemming from certain uncorroborated opinions on the part of various unnamed Volkswagen personnel. Apparently these people felt that the commercial gave a false impression of the *size* of the VW 411, and that potential buyers might believe that the new Volkswagen was enormously larger than the more familiar VW "Bug."

Another explanation was that the commercial made it seem as if *apes* drove Volkswagens.

A third reason arose from one executive's daughter, who had literally become *frightened* by the giant ape in the commercial.

According to David Allen, all of the above reasons implied that the figure of King Kong was simply too powerful for the commercial. When the commercial ran its 60-second length, one tended to remember the ape more than the merchandise it was attempting to sell.

"King Kong," to the dismay of fantasy film-minded viewers who had seen it only once, or who had never seen it but learned of its existence through hearsay, was abruptly pulled from its network programming. Those viewers who were able to see the commercial, even if only once, were fortunate. It was certainly one of the best and its imagery would be lasting.

David Allen was no newcomer to the field of puppet animation by the time he animated the "King Kong" commercial. Like many of his contemporaries, Allen began his professional career in the field as a monster-movie fan and an enthusiastic maker of amateur horror, science-fiction, and fantasy movies. His work, particularly in this field of stop-motion animation, was recognizably superior to that of many amateurs (this writer included) who struggled to bring miniature dinosaurs, molded from clay, to life on home movie screens. Eventually Allen became a professional, his frame-by-frame creatures enhancing such movies as *Equinox* (1971) and *Flesh Gordon* (1972).

For *When Dinosaurs Ruled the Earth* (1971), Hammer Films' follow-up to its highly profitable *One Million Years B.C.*, David Allen contributed to some of the exceptional stop-animation work that was otherwise done by Jim Danforth, who was Oscar-nominated for the film. Allen's contributions included an exciting scene wherein a primitive man, entering a cave, is suddenly confronted by its occupant—an angry, charging *Chasmosaurus*, a giant horned dinosaur that pursues him. For another sequence Allen animated some giant "prehistoric" crabs that were, no doubt, not to be found in any book about fossil crustaceans.

David Allen's original prehistoric-themed *Raiders of the Stone Rings* was one of the projects seriously considered by Hammer Films in the 1970s. The studio even went so far as to make up a color poster for the planned film under the new title *Zeppelin vs. Pterodactyls*. Though Hammer eventually passed on Allen's project, it would not die, continuing over the years in various revised versions and under new names.

We should all be thankful that the Volkswagen "volks" had the foresight to employ the talents of David Allen to create this full minute of magic that brought the Mighty Monarch of Skull Island back to life again, and this time in full color. Allen's Kong provided monster-movie fans with one of those memorable moments—when a commercial actually transcends in interest the show that it is interrupting.

GODZILLA,
SAURIAN SUPERHERO

Superheroes and shows about them—*e.g.*, *The Six Million Dollar Man*, *Wonder Woman*, and *Shazam!*—were quite the rage on television during the 1970s. At the same time, giant prehistoric monsters, Godzilla being the most prominent of the lot, continued to thrill (mostly younger) moviegoers. It was during the latter part of this decade that a new (and inferior) *King Kong* (Paramount, 1976) was filmed by Dino De Laurentiis, following a fierce competition with Universal Pictures for the remake rights, and other similar towering gorillas starred in their own productions.

It was in this climate of superheroes, prehistoric monsters, and giant apes that writer friend Ron Haydock edited the one-shot magazine *King of the Monsters*, published in April 1977 by Cousins Publications. Mostly capitalizing on the current interest in the Kong character, the magazine also featured the author's article on another "King"—Japan's "King of the Monsters"—and the way that character had evolved to tie into the lucrative realm of the celluloid superhero. In its original publication, the article was titled more topically "Godzilla, Superhero of the '70s."

I can remember cheering the heroes as far back as the middle 1940s and into the 1950s. Superman was flying across the radio waves back then, pitting his Kryptonian superpowers against whatever menaces the writers of his radio series could invent. And, of course, the Man of Steel and other heroes were perpetually waging their singular wars against crime in the four-color pages of the comic books.

There were also the cowboy stars—Roy Rogers, Gene Autry, Hopa-long Cassidy—whose fast guns, hard fists, and sometimes ability to strum a guitar and sing a tune, helped them bring law and order to the old and even the modern West.

Some of the heroes of the Forties stayed on through the 1950s, when Captain Video, Tom Corbett, and a new cast of heroic futuristic charac-ters continued the tradition of battling evil, though the setting was usu-ally another world instead of Hoppy's "Wild West." The Sixties brought us super spy James Bond and the "campy" Batman-style superhero.

But in the 1970s...

The most universally popular superhero of 1977 did not wear a flashy costume like Superman's, and was not the fastest gun on the draw. He wore nothing, in fact, and for that matter, was not even human. Surpris-ingly, he was a 400-foot tall, amphibious reptile with a spiked back and a fiery radioactive breath. In Japan, the country that spawned him, this atomically mutated prehistoric survivor of the dinosaur age was called "Gojira." American audiences knew him as "Godzilla, King of the Monsters."

Godzilla had been around, at least on the movie screen, since 1954, when he starred in his first feature-length motion picture—a moody, black-and-white epic of mass destruction made by Toho International as *Gojira*, and released in the United States two years later as *Godzilla, King of the Monsters!* But Godzilla was hardly a "superhero" in the 1950s. Then he was simply a virtually brainless behemoth with a terrible disposition who stomped, squashed, and seared his way through a doomed Tokyo.

Over decades and myriad film adventures, Godzilla's image changed—or mutated—so that he was no longer Earth's greatest enemy, as he was in the more adult-oriented original movie, but rather the world's most valued protector, especially when our planet became threatened by other monsters or extraterrestrial invaders. Godzilla's reformation was the decision of the head of Toho who wanted to direct the monster's series of films to a very young audience.

By the 1970s, an era perhaps characterized by terrorism and real-life violence, audiences at least unconsciously sought after heroes—not the "campy" heroes of the Sixties, or the antiheroes as portrayed on theatre screens by a Charles Bronson or Clint Eastwood—but authentic heroes like Edgar Rice Burroughs's Tarzan and the legendary Lone Ranger, big-ger-than-life characters who would fight for truth and justice even at the expense of their own lives. Television began to introduce no-nonsense superheroes like the Six Million Dollar Man and the Bionic Woman, who didn't need to wear masks and fancy costumes, but theaters were still mostly lacking in such characters.

In some ways, the "Big G" had already assumed somewhat of an heroic status by the 1960s. By *San Daikaiju Chikyu Saidai no Kessen*, which was released to American movie theaters in 1965 as *Ghidrah the Three-Headed Monster*, Godzilla already teamed up with popular monsters Rodan and Mothra to defend the world against a much larger and more powerful dragon from space. In *Oru Kaiju Daisingeki*, released in the United States in 1969 as *Godzilla's Revenge*, Godzilla not only heroically fought a horde of other monsters, but also served as a scaly role model that inspired a young child to stand up and heroically defend himself against a bully. Indeed, in *Gogira tai Hedora*, whose American version was released as *Godzilla vs. the Smog Monster* (1971), Godzilla mimicks numerous flying superheroes by literally taking to the air, turning his body around and utilizing his atomic breath like a jet exhaust.

Toho International filmed the Godzilla movie *Gojira tai Megaro* in 1973. The movie was released city-wide across the United States three years later by Cinema Shares under the translated title *Godzilla vs. Megalon*. I experienced this movie first-run at a Saturday matinee in 1976, the much revered afternoon of the week that, during my own childhood, was alive with the heroics of any number of movie cowboys, costumed superheroes, and spacemen. Hoppy, Roy, and Gene were no longer dominating those Saturday matinees, but the niche they had left behind was far from vacant.

As first, I—an adult in the company of three other "grownups"—was reluctant to go see *Godzilla vs. Megalon* at a theater that would undoubtedly be filled with restless (and often screaming) children. (After all, I was once very much a part of that scene myself, and knew full well precisely what to expect!) But when the situation was such that the Saturday matinee proved to be the only available time to view the picture, I went ... and discovered something.

Superheroes were not simply the ghosts of past Saturday afternoons, but were still very much alive that day. Only their form, style, and size had changed.

Godzilla vs. Megalon was a "multi-monster" picture in which survivors of the lost empire of Mu (last seen in Toho's science-fiction epic *Atragon*, which had featured an enormous sea serpent named Manda) found their secret world of Seatopia nearly destroyed by the nuclear-bomb tests of the surface dwellers. In retaliation for this destruction, the Mu people unleashed the insect-like Megalon, a huge subterranean monster who drilled up to the surface world and promptly attacked Japan.

Clearly, Megalon was a monster but not a hero—though he may have been one to the citizens of Seatopia—as evidenced by the young audience's (literal) *booing* and *hissing* at his appearance.

Superheroic Godzilla (Haruo Nakajima) and son Minya, role models demonstrating how to handle a giant spider, in *Godzilla's Revenge* **(1969). ™ and ©Toho Co., Ltd., all rights reserved.**

Before Godzilla made his first appearance in the film, we were introduced to a more recognizable hero, Jet Jaguar, a silvery robot made in the metallic style of most of the superheroes (*e.g.*, Ultraman) so popular on Japanese television. But not even this noble, super-powered mechanical man was strong enough to save the world from Megalon. For that Earth required the special talents of Godzilla, who now lives with other gigantic creatures on a remote and isolated body of land known as Monster Island.

Jet Jaguar flew to Monster Island to alert Godzilla that his saurian aid was needed to save the world. To the author's astonishment, the entire audience cheered when Godzilla made his initial appearance—a cheer that, 30 years earlier, might have arisen at the first sight of William Boyd as Hopalong Cassidy, mounted on his white horse Topper. But the cheering *really* commenced in full force once Godzilla followed Jet Jaguar back to Japan for the inevitable conflict with Megalon.

As the battle began, Megalon was joined by Gigan, a gargantuan monster from outer space who was first introduced in the movie *Godzilla on Monster Island*, the previous film in the series. Though the Gigan picture had not yet been released in the United States, the audience immediately knew his identity (presumably after seeing his picture and name in various monster-movie magazines), and was aware of his allegiance to the Seatopian villains. Jet Jaguar, having literally "shot up" to Godzilla-size, and Godzilla then proceeded to battle and defeat the two menacing creatures.

Though *Godzilla vs. Megalon* was already the *13th* Godzilla film made by Toho, the young audience reacted to the main monster's every action as though seeing him for the first time. Each blast of his destructive radioactive breath prompted howls of approval from his fans, each chomp of his toothy jaws and kick of his taloned feet into the hides of his adversaries brought on thunderous applause. The viewers had seen all of this action before in earlier Godzilla pictures. But then, this writer had seen Tarzan swing through trees many times in the past, or watched Roy Rogers bulldog a fleeing cattle rustler, and each time these actions were repeated on the screen, I cheered again.

The motion picture superhero had also become a part of the Seventies. Granted, his costume or cowboy suit had been replaced by scales, claws, and an incendiary breath. But whether human being or monster, he accomplished the same heroic results.

WHO IS ... THE CREATURE?

Science-fiction movies were BIG during the late 1970s, in no small way due to the extreme popularity of such major shows as *Star Wars*, *Star Trek: The Motion Picture*, and *Close Encounters of the Third Kind*.

As with the horror films before them, these high-tech fantastic films inspired numerous enterprising publishers to devote entire magazines to movie spaceships, robots, aliens, superheroes, and, once again, monsters.

The Gill Man, that still-popular Creature from the Black Lagoon, had always been more of a "science-fiction" than "horror" monster, his origins being rooted in science instead of the supernatural. He was, then, an ideal subject for the main theme of the premiere issue (August 1978) of a new magazine entitled *Incredible Science Fiction*. The publication had much going for it, including well-written articles, interior color, and pull-out sections. Apparently the magazine did not have enough "something" to compete with other such publications, primarily the highly successful *Starlog*. There never was a second issue.

When the editors at *Incredible Science Fiction* approached me to do one of the issue's articles about the Gill Man, I set out to tackle the project from a slightly different and, I hoped, new direction. The editors liked the end result, but I'm still waiting to be paid for this essay.

He swam from the prehistoric depths of a South American lagoon and into the mythology of our popular culture. According to the scientists who sought him out and studied him, he was an extinct form of life, some kind of "missing link" hybrid of fish, reptile, amphibian, and man, though a form unknown to paleontologists. In actuality he was the invention of the Universal-International make-up department, which officially dubbed its creation the Gill Man.

To most of us, however, this green and scaly monster, who first appeared on the motion-picture screen in 1954, was simply ... the Creature from the Black Lagoon.

According to the screenplay of the film *Creature from the Black Lagoon*, co-written by Harry Essex and Arthur Ross, the Creature or Gill Man is a throwback to the Devonian period, the so-called "Age of Fishes," a geological expanse of time stretching from approximately 345 back to 395 million years ago (though the script erroneously dates this period as a mere quarter of a million years ago).

Although a Gill Man-like monster was never included in any of the science books, William Alland, the producer of *Creature from the Black Lagoon*, claimed to have heard of such a life form in an obscure South American legend. According to this account, Alland explained, the so-called Gill Man was some weird combination of alligator, fish, and turtle. The fact that the monster also possessed the general shape of a human being made him even more interesting. This "Creature" supposedly still haunted the jungles of South America and existed unchanged in appearance or habits since Devonian times.

Whether or not such a legend really existed is not that important. The significance of the Gill Man is that he—with the arguable exception of the gigantic mutated prehistoric reptile Godzilla, who really became most popular in later decades—was the only movie monster to emerge during the 1950s to take upon himself a kind of classic status. The Gill Man was the real successor to such earlier Universal classic horror characters as the Frankenstein Monster, Count Dracula, the Wolf Man, the Mummy, and the Invisible Man.

He would someday be immortalized, not only through his own series of motion pictures, but also in television-show appearances, in comic books, and a veritable flood of licensed merchandise bearing the character's likeness.

The image of the Gill Man, with his ichthyoid face and fins and his unique style of swimming, has become, over the years, as familiar an icon as the square-headed Frankenstein Monster with the scars and the neck electrodes, and the sinister black-caped Transylvanian with his craving for human blood.

Alland took his ideas for the Gill Man to the head of Universal-International's make-up department, Bud Westmore (of the famous family of

Hollywood make-up artists). It became the task of Westmore and his crew, most notably Jack Kevan, to literally build the Creature from foam rubber, liquid latex, and paints.

After $12,000 was, along with the latex, poured into the Gill Man costume, and after Westmore, along with Kevan, Chris Mueller, and Bob Hickman, finished manufacturing it in their famous studio make-up shop, a former United States Marine-turned-actor named Ben Chapman donned the form-fitting outfit. Chapman possessed the height needed for the Creature's menacing stature; but it became the work of yet another though physically smaller man to bring the Gill Man to life in his own element, the murky waters of the Black Lagoon.

Ricou Browning had the reputation that he could hold his breath underwater for a duration of five minutes. He was also a masterful swimmer and, therefore, a logical choice to portray the Gill Man when the character wasn't stalking about and growling on land. Wisely, Browning understood that the appeal in a monster character lacking any real facial expressions and incapable of even the most rudimentary speech would be extremely limited. For the Gill Man to transcend the legion of other grotesque monsters being churned out by studio assembly lines during the 1950s, he would need a quality other than just the ability to terrify. The Creature demanded some degree of personality and it was Browning's task and ability, at least in part, to bestow it.

The screenplay for *Creature from the Black Lagoon* called for the Gill Man to be attracted to the film's lovely heroine, portrayed by popular Universal-International starlet Julia (later Julie) Adams. Surely this attraction could not be merely physical. Except for some very basic and obvious physical characteristics—the number of limbs, eyes, *etc.*—the Gill Man in no way resembled either Ms. Adams or any other human being.

No, the attraction of this scaly green monster for this beautiful young human woman had to be something deeper. The implication in this very special attraction was that, despite the bizarre appearance of the Creature, a human being existed—albeit a very primitive one buried beneath this grotesque assemblage of gills and fins. Perhaps it will require several hundred million years of evolution to bring to the surface that human being.

But who, certainly not the Gill Man, could wait that long?

For now, Ricou Browning, the real man hidden inside the monster's prehistoric exterior when under water, would have to convey the Creature's latent humanity. Browning developed his own swimming style for his portrayal of the Gill Man, twisting his body from side to side, sometimes almost in rhythm with the film's powerful music of Herman Stein, one of the film's scorers. This swimming style is weirdly sensual, certainly an atypical kind of movement for a non-human character, especially when the monster pursues the swimming Julia Adams.

Director Jack Arnold was most determined to give the Gill Man some kind of a perceived personality. As Arnold once stated, he intended that the Creature be sympathetic, attacking only when provoked, and then capable of any form of violent revenge. The final scenes in *Creature from the Black Lagoon* especially convey this, as the Gill Man bears his captured human "bride" to his damp and gloomy grotto for a purpose even he probably does not yet understand, and as, subsequently, he brutally attacks the human intruders who seek to rescue her from his cold-blooded touch.

The Gill Man could very well have joined the numerous other shambling and snarling horrors of the Fifties, fading out into obscurity. However, thanks to the talent and integrity of those who brought him to "life" on the screen, he remains today, decades later, something considerably more.

THE SEA SICK
SEA SERPENT

For more than a decade, from the early 1970s and continuing until his death on May 2, 1984, Bob Clampett was a good friend. I admired him for his many talents and also the great volume of his work. Our personalities were also quite similar in many ways. Frequently during the 1970s, my then-wife Linda and I socialized with Bob and his wife Sody. More than once Sody told me that Bob and I were two of a kind, which I took as a great compliment. (As a kid I owned a "Beany" propeller cap.)

Bob Clampett, like many of us, loved dinosaurs and other prehistoric creatures. Occasionally these extinct animals found their way into Bob's various animated-cartoon and puppet projects. In fact a fairly large *Apatosaurus* figure was among the many fun decorations and memorabilia treasures from past projects that filled his cheery Hollywood office.

Time for Beany starred a cast mostly consisting of hand puppets. This early–1950s television classic, that remains one of Bob Clampett's most fondly remembered accomplishments, was directly inspired by *The Lost World*, silent 1925 version, which was the first feature-length live-action movie ever made to portray "living" dinosaurs. When Bob revived the concept for the animated-cartoon series *The Beany and Cecil Show* in 1962, dinosaurs and other prehistoric critters sometimes played major roles in the plot lines, some of their sequences again directly inspired by visuals from the original *Lost World*.

The long-necked Cecil the Sea Sick Sea Serpent appears to have been patterned somewhat after either a plesiosaur, a Mesozoic marine reptile, or a sauropod dinosaur like the *Apatosaurus* which had so impressed Bob in *The Lost World*. But whether or

not Cecil possessed flippers, legs and feet, or simply had a long
snakelike body with no appendages whatsoever, we'll never know,
because Cecil's "true" appearance beneath the puppet stage
remained one of Bob Clampett's closely guarded secrets. Some of
his fans, myself included, sometimes wondered if even Bob knew
for certain how Cecil looked below the neck.

When Bob Clampett was selected as guest of honor at the Minneapolis Comic Convention in 1979, I was asked—either by someone associated with the convention, or by Bob himself; I no longer
remember which—to contribute an article about the original
Beany show. I provided a slightly edited-down version of a piece I
had written for *The Great Television Heroes* (Doubleday 1975), a
book co-authored with friend Jim Harmon. The essay was published, along with others about Bob Clampett, in the convention's
souvenir booklet. Both versions were titled, "I'm Comin', Beany
Boy!", which, when exclaimed by Cecil, informed TV viewers that
the big Sea Sick Sea Serpent was coming to the rescue.

All script excerpts and song lyrics appearing in this article are
copyright ©Bob Clampett Productions.

At 6:30 every Monday through Friday evening in the early 1950s,
those of us who were young enough in body or spirit knew what time it
really was. We would sit close to the small screen of our RCA or Zenith
television set as an energetic announcer exclaimed, "And now, it's *Time
for Beany!*"

Time for Beany, a 15-minute-per day puppet show originating from
the Paramount Studios in Hollywood, was seen nationally for an extremely
successful run of nearly a decade. During this time it won three well-
deserved Emmy Awards for its creator, "Bugs Bunny" cartoonist Bob
Clampett.

On the very first telecast of *Time for Beany* in 1950, Clampett's cast
of puppet characters was lost at sea in a small one-sail ship called the
Leakin' Lena. Prop waves tossed the little craft about as Captain Huffenpuff, wearing an explorer's outfit topped by a pith helmet, made his dramatic debut appearance.

With the Captain was his nephew, a cute young boy with a turned-
up nose and a wide grin that never changed regardless of the danger or
his mood. The boy wore a striped shirt, dark blue pants with shoulder
straps, and a beany cap with a propeller on the top. Appropriately, his name
was Beany.

The *Leakin' Lena* crew (*from left*, Hopalong Wong, Beany, Captain Huffenpuff and Hunny Bear) with Cecil the Sea Sick Sea Serpent on TV's *Time for Beany*. Courtesy Sody Clampett, ©Bob Clampett Productions, all rights reserved.

Captain Huffenpuff was a husky blowhard with a penchant for getting his ship into big trouble. Even while the *Leakin' Lena* faced destruction from a violent storm, the Captain could not resist bragging about his supposed past triumphs. Beany never let his uncle know that he did not really believe all of his wild and usually self-serving yarns.

CAPTAIN: Steam the whistle! Mizzun the mast! And put some air in those sails. Thirty-two pounds all around.
BEANY: Nose, nose, sir. (*Salutes.*)
CAPTAIN: Yes, sir, there's nothing like a shipshape ship—what?
BEANY: Nose, nose, sir. (*Salutes.*)
CAPTAIN: Not nose, nose, Beany. You're supposed to say, aye, aye.
BEANY: I can't reach my eye. I can only reach my nose. See? (*Salutes.*)

Beany had all the wide-eyed enthusiasm and belief in wondrous things that any typical young boy might have possessed. And so, when an enormous green head with button eyes and suction-cap nostrils lifted out of the turbulent waters, supported by a serpentine neck adorned by a fantastic dorsal fin, Beany had no doubt that he was seeing an authentic sea serpent. The creature was Cecil, a slightly lisping and admittedly "Sea Sick Sea Serpent" who moaned and hiccuped incessantly. His long neck swayed from side to side as the waves rocked him back and forth.

CECIL: I'm Cecil, the Sea Sick Sea Serpent (hiccup) and I'm seasick. [*Goes into seasick routine.*] Stop rocking the boat! Steady the frame!
BEANY: Oh, you poor boy, you.
CECIL: I gotta go now.
BEANY: You're not gonna go too soon, are you?
CECIL: I gotta. It's gonna storm. And storms make me (hic) seasick! [*Cecil goes under.*]
BEANY: Goodby, Cecil.
CECIL: [*gargling sound*]: Goodby!

Unfortunately the more practical and mature "Uncle Captain" (as Beany called him) did not, like most grownups, believe in sea serpents, seasick ones or otherwise. He was below deck when Cecil looked at the young boy and gave out a friendly "Howdy!" When Beany told his uncle what he had seen, the chubby skipper merely scoffed.

CAPTAIN: You say you saw a singing Sea Sick Sea Serpent named Cecil? I can't even *say* it. How could I *see* it? Beany, you know there's no such thing as a sea serpent and I'm ashamed of you for telling an untruth.
BEANY: It's the truth, Uncle Captain Huffenpuff. [*Puts up hand.*] If I didn't see a Sea Serpent may lightning strike me. See?
CAPTAIN: And I say there was no Sea Serpent! [*Lightning strikes Captain.*] EEEEEeeeeyyyyyyy!
BEANY: See?
CAPTAIN: Never mind the fairy tales about Sea Serpents, Beany. We gotta get this tub into high gear. They're waiting for us at K.T.L.A.—and you know how Landsberg is when you're late.
BEANY: Maybe we're lost. Are you sure you know where we are?
CAPTAIN: Beany boy, I know every wave in this ocean. [*Splash.*] Ha! *There's* one of 'em now!

Uncle Captain Huffenpuff and Cecil the Sea Sick Sea Serpent finally met after several years (and several hundred Monday-through-Friday episodes) of *Time for Beany*. Until then, Beany tried in vain to convince his uncle that the friendly creature did, in fact, exist.

Time for Beany was more than the typical and average children's show featuring puppets. The program was designed to appeal to a full-spectrum

age group. The adventures of Beany, Cecil, and Uncle Captain Huffenpuff
were filled with all the necessary ingredients of danger, action, and thrills,
plus generous helpings of slapstick comedy. But the stories and characters also possessed an underlying sense of adult wit and satire which
appealed to as many parents as to their offspring. Groucho Marx, who at
the time was pulling in television ratings with his comedy quiz show *You
Bet Your Life*, once sent Bob Clampett a letter stating that *Time for Beany*
was the only kids' show on the air adult enough for his young daughter
to watch. Scientist Albert Einstein was also a famous fan of the show.
Much of its adult appeal lay in the fact that the names of its characters
and places were almost always clever puns or other plays on words that
viewers like Groucho and Einstein could appreciate.

Besides Beany, Captain Horatio K. Huffenpuff, and Cecil the Sea
Sick Sea Serpent, all of whose names were descriptive of their look or
personality, the show featured such characters as Hopalong Wong the
Chinese cook, Clowny the Clown, Crowy the Crow, the Fat Bat, Smarty
Pants the Frog (also known as The Brain, a psychiatrist who let his
patients solve their own problems, then inadvertently took the credit himself), Tearalong the Dotted Lion, Peeper Frijole, Mr. Nobody (an invisible man occasionally represented by a floating umbrella), the eccentric
scientist Professor X, Flush Garden, Sir Cuttle Bone Jones, the Little
Goose, Ping Pong the giant ape (this take-off on King Kong played on
different occasions by George Barrows and Walker Edmiston), Mama
Knock Knock Hawk, Oogle, the Hum Bugs, Peg Leg McYegg, Dizzy
Lou and Dizzy II (a take-off on Desilu, the production company formed
by Desi Arnaz and Lucille Ball), the Staring Herring, a robot named
Clank Clank McHank, Tick 'n' Tock the tick birds, the Jimmy Durante-
like Inca Dinca Doo Bird, Mouth Full o' Teeth Keith, and that lovable
(and most popular) villain Dishonest John.

The gang's adventures would take them to such colorful places as the
Fifth Corner of the World, Shangri-La-Di-Da, the Ruined Ruins, Vit-
amin Pill Hill, Tin Pan Valley, Nothing Atoll, Close Shave Cave, Widow's
Peak, and Horrors Heights. These exotic locales were always indicated
on a large map which sometimes filled the television screen for as much
as five minutes, allowing everyone at home to marvel or groan over its
seemingly unending display of puns. Beany and his friends often shared
adventures that were literally out of this world. Once they took off for
the Schmoon, which (unknown to real-life astronomers) is actually the
moon's moon. There was also an adventure on the Square Planet which
had been responsible for all manner of "squarish" phenomena on the Earth.

In one episode set in India, the announcer did his best impression of popular radio announcer Gabriel Heater, opening with, "Ahhh, there's untouchable news tonight." These bits of satire and topical reference provided most of the fun backstage and also appealed to those of us who were presumably too old to believe in the antics of puppets in impossible adventures.

Dishonest John was the archetypal villain of the mustache-twirling, old school of melodrama—almost. He was oily, with slicked-back black hair, sinister-looking eyes, a large nose that hooked over his pencil-thin mustache, and a perpetual toothy grin. His attire was as sinister in appearance as his face, including a black coat, inverness cape and a slouch green hat. But the appearance of D. J. (as he was "affectionately" known) was deceptive, for underneath that leering face was a person not nearly as dastardly as one might have expected. Although he was a charter member of the Villains' Union, with the characteristic laugh that many of his fans imitated ("Nya ha *ha!*"), Dishonest John was really a rather lovable guy. He never really meant to harm anyone, but delighted in leading "Beany Boy" (as Cecil called him) and his friends through one incredible scheme after another. D. J. was the show's "Kingfish" in that he was always attempting to put some fast-buck deal over on his three perennial adversaries. But in attempting to foil Beany and company, it was the villain himself who was inevitably foiled. Even in his worst failures, Dishonest John relished every moment of his villainous life—because there was great fun in being such a rat.

Cecil the Sea Sick Sea Serpent was the real star of *Time for Beany*. He was one of those characters who trusted everyone, believing that goodness existed even in such scoundrels as Dishonest John. Not surprisingly, the Sea Serpent was usually the last of the show's characters to realize that old D. J. was profiting from schemes that took advantage of Beany and Captain Huffenpuff.

When "Cece" (as Beany frequently called him) discovered that his little pal was in trouble as a result of D. J.'s plotting, he suddenly roared, "I'm Comin', Beany Boy! I'm comin'!" Then Cecil proceeded to tear apart everything in sight until Dishonest John was defeated and Beany Boy had been saved from the villain's crooked machinations. After such a triumphant rescue, Cecil would noisily lick Beany's smiling face in an ardent (and his trademark) "slurp kiss." Following that sloppy show of affection would be a friendly exchange like this:

BEANY: Golly, Cece, you're the best friend a little kid like me ever had.
CECIL (*bashfully*): Aw, shucks, Beany Boy. Tweren't nothin' any red-
blooded American Sea Serpent wouldn't have did for his best lil pal.
[*Slurp! Slurp! Slurp!*]

The fact that Cecil was actually the most popular and well-developed character on *Time for Beany* was due to the show's creator. Bob Clampett had polished the characterization of Cecil during his own adolescence. He had already designed his Sea Serpent hand puppet and had been experimenting with the appropriate voice for the character. Cecil's voice was born on the day that young Bob's voice changed to its more mature and deeper tones. This was also about the time that Clampett's height dramatically increased. Like all adolescents experiencing puberty, he was extremely self-conscious about his new image. A slight variation on his new "grown-up" voice provided the proper sound for Cecil.

"...I crystallized Cecil's voice and personality at the very moment that I'd grown from a short, chubby youngster to a tall, skinny adolescent," Bob Clampett told interviewer Mike Barrier (in the fan magazine *Funnyworld*, issue number 12, summer 1970).

> I suddenly felt as if *my* neck was six feet tall ... and when I spoke it sounded to me as if my voice was coming from somebody else. A Sea Serpent is a thing apart. And that's exactly how I felt. Clumsy, unwanted, a minority of one, but with high hopes and great surges of new-found power.
>
> All the pains and pleasures, intense feelings and emotions of my own adolescence are ingrained in Cecil. So much of what I put into Cecil in my puppet show was deep-rooted emotion, which I am able to convey to other people. When you look at a Cecil gag you might say, "Oh, that's just funny." But there's a tear to it, too.

One of Cecil's recurring difficulties was his lack of the companionship of a female sea serpent (or "she" serpent), which had overtones of what most kids go through during the teenage years in trying to meet and then impress someone of the opposite sex. Bob Clampett applied this and other problems of youth to his serpentine brainchild until Cecil was actually his own alter ego. "In my daily puppet show," Clampett told Barrier, "I was able to develop Cecil's personality and changing moods much more slowly, and get the feeling of loneliness and sadness. And Cecil has great changes of pace."

Because of his close identification with the character and his practice as a teenager of letting the puppet speak the words that he was too shy or embarrassed to say, Clampett has almost always been the voice of Cecil. During the 1970s, many years after the final live telecast of *Time For Beany*, he still carried a Cecil hand puppet on his person when going anywhere that he might be called upon to speak. Cecil, needless to say, would always make his now "miniaturized" appearance and, as in the past, speak with the voice of Bob Clampett. At one such event, during which

Bob was presented with a gold statuette for his past work, Cecil feigned jealousy, loudly complaining, "Now just a darn minute, what the heck! Makes a Sea Serpent sore! Doggone you, Bob Clampett, I do all the work and you get all the awards." To which, Bob Clampett replied, "Well ... I had a hand in it."

Cecil the Sea Sick Sea Serpent originated nearly 25 years before the telecast of the first *Time for Beany* episode and before Bob Clampett's adolescence. The character was inspired by an event that occurred during Bob's highly impressionable childhood. Bob was always a creative youth and spent much of his free time drawing amateur comic strips and presenting puppet shows for the other kids in his neighborhood. In the summer of 1925, young Robert Clampett's mother had decided it would be best for her son not to view the silent motion picture that would inevitably directly influence the creation of Cecil. The film was, in her opinion, too fantastic for Bob's already wild imagination. But Bob, excited by the coming-attraction publicity for the movie, managed to get her to change her mind. The motion picture was *The Lost World*, released that year by First National.

Based on the novel by Sir Arthur Conan Doyle, *The Lost World* was the story in which boisterous Professor Challenger (played by husky and bearded Wallace Beery, with a more than subtle resemblance to the later Captain Huffenpuff) led an expedition to an isolated plateau in South America to find a world inhabited by living dinosaurs and an unexpected "missing link" (played by Bull Montana made up to resemble a prehistoric "apeman"). Challenger brought a live *Apatosaurus* (popularly called *Brontosaurus*) back to London, where it created havoc and eventually crossed London Bridge, which promptly collapsed under its 30-ton weight. The final scene in the picture showed the long-necked dinosaur swimming out to sea, presumably on a return trip to its prehistoric homeland, with Challenger watching forlornly.

The young Bob Clampett was totally enthralled by the prehistoric creatures in *The Lost World*, especially the "*Brontosaurus*," which came alive on the screen. Obviously the monsters in *The Lost World* were neither real nor alive. (In fact, they were miniature models animated a frame at a time by special-effects wizard Willis H. O'Brien.) Yet Bob knew they were three-dimensional creatures and not the product of drawn animated cartoons like the "Aesop Fables" shorts that were popular at the time, some of these featuring prehistoric animals.

Almost immediately after returning home from the movie house, Bob started to make sketches of his own humorous epilogue to *The Lost World*. First he designed a comical sea serpent who would greet the passengers on passing ships with his friendly "Howdy!" and receive the expected double-takes. He also drew a comic version of Professor Challenger, who would be the basis for the later Captain Horatio Huffenpuff. But the movement of that splendid "*Brontosaurus*" still seemed miraculous to Bob. His own sea serpent was so real and alive in his imagination that it necessitated more depth than the two-dimensional cartoon drawings could afford. When no one was able to supply him with a plausible explanation of how the film's dinosaur moved and breathed, he set out on his own to make his creature come to life in the simplest way possible.

Bob had been given a "Jocko" hand puppet by his aunt. Jocko was a monkey that reminded Clampett of the apish "missing link" he had seen in *The Lost World*. His problem of how to bring his sea creature to life had been solved. With the assistance of his mother, Bob began to work on his first Cecil hand puppet.

To begin, the two of them found an old sock. Bob and his mom cut and sewed the sock, then inserted a piece of cut cardboard to keep the newly formed mouth in place. In her sewing basket, Mrs. Clampett found appropriate buttons to become the puppet's eyes. Then Bob used Crayolas to color this first ever version of Cecil.

Thrusting his small hand into the newly born Cecil, Bob made him come to life. Already it had begun to assume its own (and Bob's) personality. Before long, Bob had built a prop boat constructed of cardboard. He took a Raggedy Andy doll and made it up to resemble Professor Challenger. The railing of his front porch served as a puppet stage, behind which Bob manipulated his puppets. With this arrangement the youthful performer entertained the local children, who delighted in watching the Cecil character take bites out of the miniature boat and chomp on the foliage that grew up alongside the porch.

About four years later Bob began to make Mickey Mouse dolls for Walt Disney, who gave them out at sales meetings and to all important studio visitors, as well as marketing them in the stores. During this time head doll designer Charlotte Clark taught Bob much about the construction of puppets, starting from extremely detailed paper patterns. Already Clampett was making improvements on his sea serpent character. But Cecil still had to wait for his screen debut.

Bob Clampett's professional career, primarily in the field of animated cartoons, began when he was just 16 years old. For many years Cecil was forced to remain in the background while Clampett devoted most of his working hours to Porky Pig, Bugs Bunny, and other Warner Bros. characters. Nevertheless the Cecil character was always in his thoughts, just waiting to be given "life."

Clampett began working as an animator for the Warner Bros. cartoon department early in 1931. He helped draw the very first in that studio's series of "Merry Melodies" sound cartoons, *Lady, Play Your Mandolin*, animated to music composed by Oscar Levant and Irving Caesar. Bob also helped make the early Harman-Ising "Looney Tunes" starring such characters as Bosko, the first black star of a series of cartoons. In his first weeks at Warner, Bob presented his idea for a musical sequence in which the advertisements on a streetcar came to life. This idea was utilized and became a highly successful and often-repeated formula. In 1936, Clampett was made a director at Warner Bros. and his 16 years with that studio was one of the prime creative forces behind the births of Bugs Bunny, Porky Pig, Elmer Fudd, Daffy Duck, Yosemite Sam, Beaky Buzzard, Sylvester the cat, and Tweety the canary. Bob first introduced such catch lines as "I tawt I taw a puddy tat!" and "Sufferin' succotash!", familiar to fans of Tweety and Sylvester.

All the while that Bob Clampett was making cartoons for Warner Bros., he was also experimenting with Cecil. Two of his Warner cartoons were suggestions of what was to come. In the first of these, a satire of Christopher Columbus's discovery of America made ten years before *Time for Beany* was launched on TV, Bob's storyboard showed the captain sailing toward what was listed on his map as a "sea serpent area." "That's silly," said the captain. "There's no such thing as a sea serpent!" (Captain Huffenpuff would often say this line during the early years of *Time for Beany*.) With that, an enormous head arose from the water and replied, "So, what am I? A brook trout?" As the sea serpent swam away, it sang, "I'm the biggest serpent in the C.C.C." A second Clampett cartoon from this same period. satirizing the 1940 Hal Roach hit film *One Million B.C.*, had a pet dinosaur lick its caveboy master's face in a way much like Cecil's later "slurp kiss," which Beany would always receive at least once per episode of *Time for Beany*.

Bob Clampett's (as well as Cecil's) first contact with television was as early as 1935 while on summer vacation from the Porky Pig studio. He visited the International Exposition in San Diego and its Palace of Science where a demonstration of that experimental new medium was in progress. Clampett was as awed by his first view of television as he had been ten years earlier when he saw the dinosaurs of *The Lost World* seemingly come alive on the screen. Imagine, he thought, having someone stand in one spot and instantaneously show up on a screen somewhere else. As always Clampett had his Cecil hand puppet in the glove compartment of his car. Several minutes later he was performing his very first Cecil telecast on that closed-circuit hookup. When people began to crowd around the tiny screen to watch as he put his puppet through every conceivable action, he knew that television was Cecil's medium. The immediacy of a puppet also eliminated any need for the time-consuming drawing of sketch after sketch, which was required for animated cartoons.

There was no doubt in Clampett's mind that television would be *the* next important medium of popular entertainment. Naturally his fellow animators at Warner Bros. thought that Bob's preoccupations of "playing with dolls," as they called his puppets, and with something as unperfected as this "television" gadget, were sheer folly. But Clampett ignored the derision, firmly believing that television would someday replace movies in popularity and that his "dolls" would be stars in that medium.

In 1938, while working at Warner Bros., Bob Clampett wrote gags for the black-and-white cartoon *Buddy's Lost World*, a spoof of the inspiring silent movie he had seen 13 years before with its own Mesozoic menagerie (and which featured the first "slurp kiss," here delivered by an *Apatosaurus*, which would later become the signature show of affection displayed by Cecil). That same year Bob set up his own puppet studio in a garage across the street from the studio and made a film of ventriloquist Edgar Bergen's dummy Charlie McCarthy, using a new twist on the animated-model technique employed in *The Lost World*. It was here that Bob developed Cecil's distinctive facial expressions.

Clampett was discontented with the standard puppets of the day, whose actions were limited mainly to vertically working mouths. Puppets and ventriloquists' dummies of the Charlie McCarthy variety had faces carved into but a single expression. None of the facial movements that made the cartoon characters so lively was possible with such puppets, so Bob began to experiment, learning new techniques which he would eventually incorporate into his Cecil puppet and which would allow the character myriad expressions. Thus, Cecil became the first puppet character to have "controlled multiple facial expressions."

In 1938, Bob also began to experiment with the format which would someday be adapted to *Time for Beany*. Since his background was in theatrical animated cartoons, he strove to give his puppet show all the freedom of a motion picture and obviate the extreme limitations of the traditional puppet stage. His characters would enter and exit from the wings as they would in a movie, rather than popping up from below the floor line as in most customary puppet shows.

Clampett had epic visions of adventures set in many colorful locales with spectacular storms, lightning and thunder, gale-force winds, underwater scenes, shipwrecks, volcanic eruptions, jungles, outer-space travel, and explorations of strange and wondrous lands. Working with one of his

Warner Bros. artists, he developed a system for producing a great number of multiple scenic backgrounds which could be set up and dismantled with incredible speed. Numerous miniature props and special effects were required to accommodate the storylines of the show. Ten years before the television premiere of *Time for Beany*, all the technical aspects of the show had been perfected.

The techniques Bob had devised in his garage studio were solely to be applied to film. His contract with Warner Bros. stipulated that the studio had first refusal rights on anything he created. After some test footage was shot to showcase Clampett's methods of puppetry, the film was screened for Leon Schlesinger, head of the animation wing at Warner Bros. Schlesinger laughed at the puppets' antics and admitted that the concept had great potential. He particularly liked Cecil. But Warner Bros. was equipped for cartoons and not puppets. "A shoemaker sticks to his last," Schlesinger told Clampett, which turned out to be the most welcome thing he could have said. Now Bob did not have to surrender his copyrights and trademarks on the characters to Warner Bros. Cecil would continue to be entirely his.

Bob Clampett continued to work on the Warner cartoons, in 1940 directing a color short featuring all kinds of ancient creatures, including armored dinosaurs and a panther-black sabretooth cat, in *Prehistoric Porky*, featuring its star in a "cave pig" role. Finally, after helping Bugs Bunny grow from a first rough sketch on a blank sheet of paper to box-office champion over Disney in the short subjects field, and following 16 very productive years, Bob Clampett left Warner Bros. to open his own studio. In 1948, with full copyright ownership of his puppet characters, he prepared for the official debut of Cecil. CBS and the *Los Angeles Times* set up an experimental television station on the top floor of the Pasadena Playhouse, a cultural theater, to train cameramen and performers for professional television.

Clampett was awarded a weekly children's program called *Cartoon Party* on which he would draw sketches of cartoon characters and feature special guests. All the while he observed what was occurring on the set until he was thoroughly knowledgeable about the technical aspects of the new medium. About the same time Ron Oxford, head of the new KFI television station, asked Clampett to do a half-hour program when that station first began telecasting in Los Angeles. KFI, an NBC affiliate, offered him 20 dollars a week as opposed to CBS's ten dollars, so Clampett began showing Cecil to the select few who owned television sets and to the many viewers who crowded in front of appliance stores with sets in their windows. Cecil was always the most popular feature of Bob's new program. Human characters who would appear on the same small TV stage with him included Jackie Gleason, Cliff (Charlie Weaver) Arquette, and All-American football star Tom Harmon, doing his sports news. Bob appeared on the station's opening-night premiere with movie stars Billie Burke (Mrs. Florenz Ziegfeld) and Adolphe Menjou, and the creator of *Jiggs and Maggie*, George McManus (who almost three decades earlier had appeared in the live-action parts of Winsor McCay's classic dinosaur cartoon *Gertie*).

Bob Clampett was now firmly implanted in the infant television medium. Later that year he interested a CBS executive in his idea for a show starring Captain Huffenpuff, a young boy character and, of course, Cecil. The executive liked Bob's idea but suggested that the preliminary drawings he had made of the boy character appeared a bit too young to be the "identification figure" for the age group he thought would most likely watch the program.

"Following the meeting with the CBS executive," Bob Clampett told the author during the early 1970s,

> I went to lunch on Wilshire Boulevard. And while I was sitting there a very appealing little boy walked in with his mother. He had on a striped turtleneck sweater and dark overalls with straps over the shoulders ... and a most winning smile. When I saw this little boy I immediately took a paper napkin and sketched him. He had a little yarmulke which I also sketched. And then, I don't quite know why, I added a propeller on top. I knew this was "my boy" and immediately began to think of the right name for him. When I went home that night I wrote down a list of different names. It struck me that because of his cap the best one was "Beany," and my mother agreed.

The little boy who would befriend a giant dinosaur-inspired sea creature had been named. (Luckily Clampett had added the propeller to the cap; otherwise the program might have been called "Time for Yarmulke.")

Time for Beany was sold to Paramount Television. It premiered as a syndicated series in 1950. Voice-over actor Daws Butler provided the voice of Beany. Other well-known talents to offer their voices to the series' characters included Stan Freberg and Jerry Colonna. Overnight it became one of the most popular children's programs on the medium. The *Saturday Evening Post* labeled it "the first successful Hollywood TV show."

Viewers of *Time for Beany* soon found that they could purchase a seemingly limitless array of merchandise bearing the images of Beany, Cecil, Captain Huffenpuff, and their friends.

Clampett also found that the public clamored to see his characters in person, expecting to meet a larger-than-life Cecil and *Leakin' Lena* as they appeared to be on television. They were, not surprisingly, disappointed to find everything in miniature. In order to carry out the illusion of reality (including full scale), Bob built a life-sized Cecil and company for personal appearances. The characters were also called upon to appear in the original (now excised) prologue to Arch Oboler's 3D movie *Bwana Devil* in 1952 and be seen alongside the film's star Robert Stack. When Cecil inflated a balloon to the point of bursting and Beany threatened to pop it, the theater audience predictably ducked for cover.

With the great success of *Time for Beany*, Bob Clampett expanded his television enterprises. New characters, always with the Clampett style of personalities and descriptive names, soon began to emerge on the black and white screen. Some of these characters starred in their own programs, such as *Thunderbolt the Wonder Colt*, featuring a horse with a split personality and a stage-struck lupine figure known as William Shakespeare Wolf. Critics regarded this show as a delightful satire of all superheroes.

In one spectacular adventure on *Time for Beany*, telecast in 1953, "J. Edgar You-Know-Who" commissioned Captain Huffenpuff to investigate such unnatural disturbances as freak electrical storms and the Sphinx of Egypt flying off into space. On a remote island Beany and Cecil discovered that the disturbances were caused by a fleet of flying saucers (which were subjects of recurring news items in the 1950s) that lifted off from the craters of three active volcanoes—Gotta Glow, Mona Glowa, and Boil Heights. Descending into the bowels of the Earth, the intrepid Beany and Cecil found that a race of alien monsters had been manufacturing the saucers by the hundreds, and that they were planning to use them to attack our planet. Fortunately, Cecil knew of a secret weapon which he called his 30-Second Men (twice as fast as Minute Men), consisting of robots, the giant gorilla Ping Pong and Pong's baby (played by a live chimpanzee), the Terrible Two-Headed Freep (Eddie and Freddie), not to mention a fighting mad Cecil.

For one scene Clampett, in this epic, had the following elements working for him simultaneously before the live cameras in a most complicated and believable fashion: A large armada of airborne saucers attacking numerous puppet characters; two human actors, one in a robot outfit, the other dressed as an ape; and one live trained baby chimpanzee. Needless to add, the chimp was capable of doing *anything* before the no-retake TV cameras and, on one show—just as the picture was discreetly fading to black—*did*.

Such spectacle was indeed impressive (and seemingly impossible to stage), especially since it was accomplished *live* without the benefit of film, tape, or retakes, as extravaganzas of considerably lesser scope would be done on television in later years. But then, Robert Clampett had been dealing with the impossible since he first gaped with wonder at those moving dinosaurs in *The Lost World.*

Bob Clampett and his puppets also appeared on national television with major stars like Bob Hope, Dean Martin, Bing Crosby, on Ed Sullivan's variety show and Ralph Edwards's *This Is Your Life.* For a while it seemed as though virtually every television program, including Groucho's *You Bet Your Life,* was making references to *Time for Beany.* Movie star James Stewart once phoned Clampett pleading that he not let Paramount change the show's air time so that he would not be forced to miss it. Actor Lionel Barrymore was also a great fan of *Time for Beany.* When producer Louis B. Mayer decided that TV was a threat to the motion-picture industry and forbade sets on his Metro-Goldwyn-Mayer studio lot, Barrymore sent his chauffeur to a local bar to watch the show and report on the plot developments. Everyone, it seems, loved *Time for Beany!*

After nearly a decade on TV as puppets, the Clampett characters made a successful transition to animated color cartoons. The first in this new series, "Beany and Cecil Meet Billy the Squid," was filmed in 1959 with original music by Bob and his wife Sody. The cartoons were distributed throughout the world by United Artists. This animated version, entitled *The Beany and Cecil Show,* had all the familiar characters, situations, puns, and much of the adult satire that had gone into the original puppet series. The cartoon show debuted over the ABC television network as a weekly series in January, 1962, running continuously for six years.

Nearly every child—and many older folks—in America knew the lyrics to the animated show's closing theme song:

> So come on, kids, wind up your lids,
> We'll flip again real soon
> With Beany Boy
> And Your Obedient Serpent in
> A Bob Clampett CartooOOOooon!

During the 1970s, Bob Clampett remained busy as ever, making TV commercials for top sponsors, and distributing his cartoons globally. He continued to take his Cecil puppet on speaking engagements at universities and various conventions, where fans would bombard him with questions about the Sea Sick Sea Serpent—that character inspired by a swimming dinosaur seen by a young Robert Clampett in 1925—and his colorful pals. Cecil's enormous popularity would even establish him as a kind of folk hero as far away as Israel.

But regardless of where Bob Clampett ventured, he would meet the parents of children who were now discovering his characters for the first time, mothers and fathers who remembered the original puppet show and longed for it to come back. For many adults could remember fondly those days when they put on their propellered Beany caps and huddled before primitive TV sets, anxious to hear the announcer say those magical words:

"And now, it's *Time for Beany!*"

DINOSAURS:
REAL VS. REEL

In 1997, to capitalize on the popularity and merchandising backlash of the mega-hit movie *The Lost World: Jurassic Park*, Starlog Entertainment, Inc., published, as part of its "Starlog Movie Series," a second one-shot magazine entitled *Dinosaur*.

The present author was commissioned by the Starlog company to write the following article comparing the fictional dinosaurs that have long lumbered and roared across the motion-picture screen to their real-life counterparts. Although the above title is the one used for the article itself, the one that appeared on the magazine's contents page was "The PC (Paleontologically Correct) Factor." It appears here through the courtesy of Anthony Timpone and Starlog Entertainment, Inc.

Dinosaurs—a specifically defined group of Mesozoic Era terrestrial animals—have been officially known to science for more than a century and a half. What we know of these fascinating animals, extinct for some 65 million years, is the product of research done by vertebrate paleontologists who study their collected fossilized remains (including fossil bones, skin impressions, eggs, and footprints). When enough fossil material is available for study, paleontologists are often able to reconstruct how these animals may have looked in life and deduce various things about their possible physiology and behavior.

The job of bringing dinosaurs to "life," however, has generally fallen within the province not of the paleontologist, but rather of the filmmaker.

For nearly a century, makers of motion pictures have met the challenge of bringing to life on screen creatures that no human being—extant or extinct—had ever seen "in the flesh."

To date, there have been virtually countless movies made about dinosaurs, ranging from *Prehistoric Peeps* (1905) to the more recent *Jurassic Park: The Lost World* (1997) and beyond. And yet, relatively few "reel" dinosaurs have displayed more than the most superficial resemblance to their "real" counterparts. Most movie dinosaurs, even those striving for a modicum of scientific verisimilitude, are embarrassingly inaccurate, often based upon outmoded information.

A good number of these movies are sheer fantasy, featuring impossible or made-up creatures (*e.g.*, *The Beast from 20,000 Fathoms*, in 1953, with its imaginary "Rhedosaurus," the Godzilla film series, *The Giant Behemoth*, 1959, and its "Paleosaurus," and *Gorgo*, 1961) or blown-up live lizards (*One Million B.C.*, 1940, *King Dinosaur*, 1995, and in the 1960 color remake of *The Lost World*) purporting to be dinosaurs. Some of these movies have featured dinosaurs portrayed by human actors wearing uncomfortable rubber suits, as in the original *One Million B.C.*, *Gorgo* and the Japanese *King Kong Escapes* (1968), the latter featuring a made-up theropod dinosaur called "Gorosaurus." In all such instances, however, the dinosaur's shape—being different from a human's—must be distorted or redesigned to conform with the person inside.

A primary reason for the lack of "paleontological correctness" in dinosaur movies is that most film producers, directors, and special-effects people are not concerned about scientific accuracy, tending to regard dinosaurs as monsters instead of real animals based in science fact. Roger Dicken, creator of the saurian puppets for *The Land That Time Forgot* (1975), based on the Edgar Rice Burroughs story, told this writer that he generally starts sculpting his dinosaur models without reference materials, imparting to the clay his personal impression of the creature. From that perspective, as with other kinds of "monsters," virtually anything goes. Still, some movies, even older ones, have occasionally been, in various ways, "on target."

One of the first dinosaur films of any kind was cartoonist Winsor McCay's animated short *Gertie* (1912). Though a comedy/fantasy, the film did contain some amazing accuracies that were ahead of their time. Gertie herself is an amiable *Apatosaurus* (a huge sauropod dinosaur once known as *Brontosaurus*). Until relatively recently, sauropods were generally thought to be swamp- or lake-bound animals too heavy to walk on land, requiring the buoyancy of the water to support their tremendous masses. Gertie, though living near a lake, was correctly depicted by McCay

This lizard, uncomfortably decorated with horns and dorsal sail, was unconvinc-
ingly passed off as a *Tyrannosaurus rex* in the 1960 color remake of *The Lost World*,
which wasted the talents of special-effects maestro Willis H. O'Brien. ©20th Century–Fox.

as a terrestrial animal who comfortably walks on legs and feet designed
to support great weight on land.

Coincidentally, McCay drew Gertie, not with the "traditional" box-
like head (based on another sauropod *Camarasaurus*) ubiquitous in most
early *Apatosaurus* restorations, but with an elongated head (resembling
another sauropod *Diplodocus*) not shown to be correct until 1978. (A box-
like head turned up on an *Apatosaurus* as recently as 1985's *Baby ... Secret
of the Lost Legend*, which I was hired to promote by Disney Studios. Other
modifications on "Baby," made by Isadoro Raponi and Ron Tantin,
included moving the nostrils from top of head to snout, so that the
dinosaur could more easily sniff flowers, and lengthening the forelimbs to
accommodate the human operator inside the rubber suit.)

Gertie depicted this Jurassic dinosaur coexisting with a Pleistocene
period woolly mammoth; in reality, the two creatures were separated by
well over 100 million years. This fostered the belief that many or all extinct

animals lived together in some vague, undefined "prehistoric era," an erroneous notion perpetuated by numerous other films (*e.g.*, *One Million B.C.*, *Fantasia*, in 1940, and *The Animal World*, 1956).

Considering what was known to paleontologists at the time, one of the best dinosaur movies ever made for accuracy is still *The Lost World* (1925 version). An entire Mesozoic menagerie was sculpted by Marcel Delgado for this silent classic, then brought to life via the stop-motion artistry of Willis O'Brien.

Delgado directly based all of his miniature creatures upon the artwork—mostly watercolor paintings then on display at New York's American Museum of Natural History—of Charles R. Knight who, from the late 1800s to middle 1950s, remained the premiere and most influential restorer of extinct life. Knight's art was supervised by a few of the most notable paleontologists of his era, and he worked from the bones up to create a fleshed-out finished drawing, painting or sculpture. Knight understood modern animals and applied that knowledge to his restorations of those long gone. His re-creations depicted dinosaurs as live animals and as the scientists then believed them to be. By today's standards, Knight's works are often dated, binding sauropods to watery environments, showing dinosaurs dragging their tails (we now know they didn't, though some films persist in portraying them this way), *etc.* In their day, however, Knight's restorations were correct. Consequently, the Knight-inspired dinosaurs of *The Lost World*, though tail-draggers, may be regarded as correct considering what was known at the time.

Generally, movie dinosaurs have been shown as one of a kind, apparently having no reason to exist other than to lumber into a scene to menace some hapless human or to engage another one-of-a-kind giant saurian "in mortal combat." *The Lost World*, however, featured groups of the same kinds of dinosaurs. After one *Apatosaurus* plunges off a cliff, another appears later. A prowling *Allosaurus* menaces a *Triceratops* family, complete with young. A *Triceratops* herd flees an erupting volcano (in the screen's first dinosaur stampede), and an *Allosaurus* group scavenges a sauropod that perished during the eruption. *The Lost World*, as would Delgado and O'Brien's masterpiece *King Kong* (1933), also portrayed dinosaurs as active rather than slow and sluggish animals, an idea fashionable for a while during the 19th century which then fell out of favor, not really catching on again until the late 1960s to early 1970s.

For *King Kong*, a one-dinosaur-of-a-kind species of movie, Delgado and O'Brien returned to Knight's original works, bringing to movie life some of the artist's most famous paintings. Outside of being grossly oversized (as demanded by producer Merian C. Cooper), the prehistoric

An *Apatosaurus* (the film realistically showed more than one) threatens actress
Bessie Love in the classic silent-film version of *The Lost World* (1925); model
sculpted by Marcel Delgado, animated by Willis O'Brien. ©First National.

creatures in *King Kong* were mostly "paleontologically correct"—again, for
their time. They did, however, perpetuate various notions now known to
be wrong, including having the dinosaurs drag their tails and making
Apatosaurus a swamp-dweller. Portraying this plant-eater (as well as the
aggressive *Apatosaurus* in *Lost Continent*, made in 1951) as an apparent carnivore certainly did *not* originate with Knight.

In attempting to reconstruct dinosaurs accurately, it is crucial to utilize up-to-date references, since new fossil discoveries continually lead to
more correct data. In designing the carnivorous dinosaur (or theropod)
Tyrannosaurus—often erroneously identified in print as an *Allosaurus*—
for *King Kong*, Delgado turned to a well-known painting of the "Tyrant
King" which Knight had done in the very early 1900s, when this dinosaur's
skeleton was just partially known. (With the recovery of additional specimens, Knight would produce more accurate restorations, though Delgado did not use them.) In his original painting, Knight had positioned
the eyes somewhat anterior to where they should have been and showed

about 10 extra feet of tail (which had been reconstructed following a skeleton of the comparatively longer-tailed and more completely known *Allosaurus*). The hands in this painting, as were those of the animated counterpart in *King Kong*, were shown as three-fingered (again, after *Allosaurus*).

For years, it was simply assumed that *Tyrannosaurus* had a two-fingered hand, though no complete forelimb of this dinosaur had yet been found. Because the hand of *Albertosaurus*, an older close relative of *Tyrannosaurus*, was known to possess two fingers, and as animals tend to lose (not gain) digits as they evolve, it was logically assumed that the hands of *Tyrannosaurus* were also two-fingered. Not until 1988 was a complete hand of this dinosaur found, confirming that it indeed had two fingers.

Most serious life restorations of *Tyrannosaurus* (including those in popular books) published since the 1920s have correctly shown this dinosaur with two small fingers per hand. Movies, however, have almost traditionally shown the hands as three-fingered (*e.g.*, *One Million B.C.*, *The Animal World*, *The Land Unknown*, 1957, and *Dinosaurus!*, 1960), often to the frustration of even the youngest paleo-minded members of the audience. Indeed, if one were to list the most common mistakes in dinosaur films (also TV-cartoon shows, comic books, toys, *etc.*), the three-fingered *Tyrannosaurus* hand would surely be near the top.

Reportedly, Walt Disney, when asked why the *Tyrannosaurus* in his classic cartoon feature *Fantasia* had three fingers (as would the mechanical one his company built for the 1964 New York World's Fair, later to reside at Disneyland Park), replied that three looked so much better. Disney's preference lingered after his passing, for the *Tyrannosaurus* in the more recent *My Science Project* (1985) is also three-fingered.

Movie makers without sufficient scientific knowledge have sometimes tried combining different kinds of dinosaurs to create a single animal. Stop-motion maestro Ray Harryhausen has stated that the title dinosaur in *The Valley of Gwangi* (1969) was a combination *Allosaurus/Tyrannosaurus*, while a scientist character in the American version of *King Kong vs. Godzilla* (1963) proclaimed Godzilla to be a hybrid *Tyrannosaurus/Stegosaurus*. The former example is somewhat loosely comparable to merging a bear with a tiger; in the latter, a tiger with a camel. Not understanding basic science has also resulted in portraying prehistoric creatures that are simply too big to live. Such massive behemoths as Godzilla, Gorgo, and Harryhausen's "Rhedosaurus," if alive in the real world, would have collapsed under their own weight long before stomping a single car or demolishing any building.

Some dinosaur movies were directly influenced by popular publications. Ellis Burman's creature designs for the programmer *Unknown Island*

Three *Ceratosaurus* individuals (presented as *Tyrannosaurus* dragging their tails in *Unknown Island*, 1948). (In reality, *Ceratosaurus* had a four-fingered hand while *Tyrannosaurus* had but two.) ©Film Classics.

(1948) were based on a series of Charles R. Knight paintings published in the February, 1942, issue of *National Geographic* magazine. Although Burman's intentions were honorable, the finished critters bore little resemblance to their inspirations (their shapes sometimes having to be altered to fit around the human performers portraying them) and sometimes proved inconsistent with the script. For instance, though dialogue suggested that these theropods were tyrannosaurs, they were clearly based on Knight's painting of the horned *Ceratosaurus*.

The Land Unknown was similarly magazine-inspired, this time by Rudolph F. Zallinger's Pulitzer Prize–winning mural which *Life* published in its September 7, 1953, issue as part of its series "The World We Live In." Unfortunately, Zallinger's dinosaurs, though prize winners, were not always that accurate; hence, the film's oddly proportioned *Tyrannosaurus*.

Movies such as the hit animated *The Land Before Time* (1988) and its sequels (plus knockoffs like Saturday morning TV's *Dink the Little*

Dinosaur series) offered their own inaccuracies. Despite obvious concessions to the cartoon format (imprecisely drawn and anthropomorphized dinosaurs, creatures from different times and places mixed together, *etc.*), these films strove for another kind of "p" (not paleontological) correctness by equating carnivory with evil, stupidity, and brutality. Generally just the herbivorous characters in these films are noble and can talk. Meat-eater "Sharp Tooth," a *Tyrannosaurus*, is a raging, roaring, virtually mindless monster focused solely on violence and devouring "Little Foot" and his lovable plant-eating pals. A more realistic first sequel to *The Land Before Time* than the one that got made might have been a single high-angle wide shot depicting the long-sought, isolated happy valley densely overpopulated with starving herbivores, their multiplying numbers unchecked by predators, the once lush vegetation depleted.

Many dinosaur films are inaccurate by virtue of their titles. *King Dinosaur* promised a *Tyrannosaurus* (depicted in the ads, not surprisingly, with three-fingered hands), but delivered only a green iguana lizard uncomfortably propped up, at least for its debut scene, on its hind legs. *When Dinosaurs Ruled the Earth* (1971), with its pluralized title, offers just one dinosaur, the horned *Chasmosaurus* (the marine reptiles, pterosaur, and lizard-like animal are not dinosaurs). And although Mesozoic Era reptiles did appear in *Legend of the Dinosaurs* (1977), none of them can be classified as dinosaurian.

The very successful *Carnosaur* (1993) also misled in its title, as no "carnosaur" appeared in the film. Even if producer Roger Corman knew that *Tyrannosaurus* is no longer classified with the Carnosauria, a fairly restricted group of large theropods, but rather with the more encompassing group Coelurosauria, he would probably have retained this very commercial title anyway. John Carl Buechler's Magical Media Industries hired the present writer to serve as *Carnosaur*'s "dinosaur consultant." Many suggestions proved moot, however, as some of the dinosaur designs were already in various stages of completion by the time I came on board, modified to accommodate either the mechanicals, cables, or human actors that would bring the film's creatures to "life."

Of course, the most successful dinosaur movie made remains *Jurassic Park* (1993), which has been praised for the authenticity of it dinosaurs. Indeed, when it comes to portraying dinosaurs as real animals based on current paleontological interpretations, this picture ranks among the highest. But, as would most of the movies preceding it, *Jurassic Park* made its own deviations from scientific accuracy, either for dramatic effect, or to satisfy the aesthetic tastes and dramatic instincts of director Steven Spielberg. At the risk of nit-picking, the following are some of those concessions:

Tyrannosaurus: Anatomical alterations (mostly in head and forelimbs) aside, there is no basis for the plot point that these two-fingered theropods only attacked what they could perceive moving.

Dilophosaurus: Besides being too small, there is no evidence that this theropod (or any dinosaur) sported a flaring, lizard-like collar or could spit venom.

Brachiosaurus: These sauropods did not chew their food, but swallowed it whole. Although some paleontologists believe sauropods could rear up tripodally to reach taller branches, relatively few of them believe this was true of *Brachiosaurus*, a massive animal with disproportionately short hindlimbs.

Velociraptor: The now common (and overused) term "raptor" refers to birds of prey, and has never really been used before to designate the theropod family Dromaeosauridae, to which *Velociraptor* belongs. (Some dinosaurs with names ending in "raptor," like *Eoraptor*, *Oviraptor*, and *Sinraptor*, are very different from *Velociraptor* and its kin.) The correct term is "dromaeosaurid," and the genus that appears in *Jurassic Park* is not the relatively small Mongolian *Velociraptor*, but apparently its larger North American relative *Deinonychus*. It was reported that, while the movie was filming, paleontologists discovered in Utah a very big dromaeosaurid which was promptly named *Utahraptor*. However, this genus is quite distinct from both *Deinonychus* and *Velociraptor*. And though scientists now believe at least some dinosaurs (like dromaeosaurids) were smarter than formerly believed, the most intelligent of them were probably no more so than today's ostrich or emu (neither of which has yet been observed opening a kitchen door).

For *Dinosaur Valley Girls*™ (1996), a campy comedy I wrote and directed, I insisted that the prehistoric animals—designed, made and brought to "life" by Thomas R. Dickens through his company Integrity Productions—be accurate. Dickens, as did Charles R. Knight, worked up from actual skeletal remains and also incorporated knowledge of living animals. His finished designs required approval by the movie's "dinosaur consultant," paleontologist and artist Gregory S. Paul. Emerging from this process were, in my admittedly biased opinion, some very accurate and up-to-date movie dinosaurs including the carnosaur *Allosaurus* and plated *Stegosaurus*, and, for the first time on any screen, the horned theropod *Carnotaurus*, armored sauropod *Saltasaurus*, and plant-eater *Camptosaurus*.

Why be concerned about accuracy in movies regarding animals gone for at least 65 million years? Dinosaurs were not imaginary monsters like dragons and vampires, but *real animals* subject to natural laws. More is known about dinosaurs today than has ever been known before, and the opportunity exists to re-create many of them with reasonable accuracy. Because there is no reason to portray modern animals in fanciful ways, the same can be said for dinosaurs.

Remember that it requires as much time and effort to create a paleontologically incorrect dinosaur as a correct one.

Dinosaurs in
Popular Culture

The third Dinofest™ event, "The World's Fair of Dinosaurs," was held in Philadelphia in April 1998. In conjunction with this event, and also to commemorate the new "Discovering Dinosaurs" exhibit at The Academy of Natural Sciences of Philadelphia, the Academy published the one-shot "Dinofest/Dinohall Collector's Magazine" entitled *Dinosaurs Invade Philadelphia*.

I was invited to write an article for this souvenir publication about dinosaurs in the popular culture. At first I was not too excited by this request, basically for two reasons: 1) I felt that I was just about "written out" on this topic, one of the most recent examples being a fairly long essay co-authored with paleontologist Michael K. Brett-Surman for *The Complete Dinosaur* (Indiana University Press, 1997), a major book he co-edited with paleontologist James O. Farlow; and 2) the article wasn't paying anything. I had long since passed the point of getting excited over seeing my name in print but not on a check.

Then I heard the names of some of the other contributors to this publication—including paleontologists John H. Ostrom, John R. Horner, Robert T. Bakker, Peter Dodson, Thomas R. Holtz, Jr., and Donald L. Wolberg. Knowing what prestigious company I would be in, how could I resist? The challenge, however, and what would make writing about this subject yet once again interesting to me, was finding another direction from which to approach it. That "new angle" proved to be associating the especially high waves of popular interest in dinosaurs with certain events in our history.

This article appears courtesy of Dinofest™ and Donald L. Wolberg.

Dinosaurs have occupied a special niche in our popular culture for almost as long as their fossil bones have been known to science—that is, more than a century. In fact, the public at large has enjoyed a long (and seemingly open-ended) love affair with these erstwhile creatures.

A frequently proposed explanation for this attraction of dinosaurs to non-scientists is that these animals were fantastic looking, sometimes gigantic in size, often frightening in appearance or dangerous in their behavior, and yet comfortably extinct. Equally important, dinosaurs (unlike the "fantasy" creatures some of them may have resembled, such as dragons and griffins) actually lived. In other words, dinosaurs are "real" and sometimes "scary monsters" who can do us no harm, and therein, somewhere, rests their appeal.

Today, dinosaurs are mainstream icons appearing in virtually every manifestation of our culture. They can be found in popular books, fiction, motion pictures, television shows, videotapes, parks, art, mechanical attractions, comic books, toys, games, model kits, postage and souvenir stamps, posters, trading cards, clothing, stationery, food, items for the home, just about anywhere their imagery can be utilized. They have even been the impetus for such events as Dinofest™, "The World's Fair of Dinosaurs." Although these animals have been extinct for some 65 million years, today may still be thought of as—at least in terms of media exposure—the age of dinosaurs.

Although dinosaurs always seem to be in the public eye, peaks in their popularity at various times seem to correlate with related events in the scientific community.

During the 1840s, after naming and describing the first dinosaurs known to science and coining the word "Dinosauria," the future knighted Richard Owen had the opportunity to see some of these creatures, at least as he envisioned them, fleshed out as re-creations of live animals. Owen's visions, though in many ways fanciful by today's standards, were brought into existence by the imaginative and "in-demand" sculptor Benjamin Waterhouse Hawkins, who created a menagerie of "life-sized" prehistoric figures for the Crystal Palace grounds in Sydenham, London. The figures, unveiled in 1854, created an immediate sensation and, for the first time in history, the public fell in love with dinosaurs.

Of course, this initial wave of dinosaur "consciousness" cannot be compared with some of the media blitzes of more recent years. Motion pictures, plastic assembly kits, and comic books did not exist in the mid-19th Century, but if they did, they might have exploited the concept of the dinosaur, Owen and Hawkins style.

In March 1853, less than a year before the opening of the Crystal

Palace exhibit, the first mention of a dinosaur appeared in a published work of fiction. Author Charles Dickens envisioned a *Megalosaurus* walking down a London street in the opening paragraph of his novel *Bleak House.*

There were a few attempts at marketing Hawkins's original imagery. These included a set of six wall posters depicting groupings of various prehistoric animals published in 1860 as "Waterhouse Hawkins' Restorations of Extinct Animals." A suite of miniature plaster-cast figures sculpted by Hawkins was sold through the famous Ward's catalogue of scientific supplies.

Perhaps at least unconsciously capitalizing on the public's interest in these fantastic animals, author Jules Verne, the "French Father of Science Fiction," saw the publication in 1864 of his fanciful novel *Voyage au centre de la terre* (English title: *A Journey to the Center of the Earth*), in which Mesozoic Era marine reptiles (genera also restored at Crystal Palace) are among the denizens inhabiting a world beneath the Earth's surface.

Things prehistoric, including dinosaurs, enjoyed a new popularity during the teen years of the 20th Century. By then, some of the classic dinosaurs—including *Tyrannosaurus, Triceratops, Apatosaurus,* and *Stegosaurus*—were well known based on fine fossil material. Some of the fossils had already been mounted for display at major natural history museums, while Darwin's theory of evolution was a quite controversial and emotional issue. During this time, dinosaurs became firmly established in the realm of popular literature and entertainment.

By 1912, the world was surely ready for its first real spate of dinosaur-related "things." That year, dinosaurs became threats in Sir Arthur Conan Doyle's novel *The Lost World* (which some literary detectives have argued is directly linked to the "discovery," that same year, of the fraudulent remains of "Piltdown Man"). Two years later, popular-fiction writer Edgar Rice Burroughs saw publication of *At the Earth's Core,* the first of many novels this American author would write featuring heroic characters encountering and inevitably fighting prehistoric creatures in various "lost worlds."

The year 1912 also saw the debut of the first classic character ever to appear on the silent-movie screen. Popular cartoonist Winsor McCay's *Gertie* (sometimes called *Gertie the Dinosaur*), starring an amiable *Apatosaurus,* charmed audiences, spawned a sequel, and inspired a counterfeit version. Dinosaurs, "cavemen" and other prehistoric creatures proved to be popular subjects in films produced during the next few years, this constituting the first (of many to come) "wave" of such movies.

Among these efforts was *Brute Force* (1913), directed by movie pioneer

D. W. (David Wark) Griffith, and featuring a life-sized, moving mockup of a *Ceratosaurus*, a horned meat-eating dinosaur. In 1914, Willis H. O'Brien pioneered the special-effects technique called "stop-motion animation" (animating a model by moving it a fraction of an inch in a sequence of such movements, then photographing each increment of movement on a succeeding frame of motion-picture film) with *The Dinosaur and the Missing Link*, the first in a successful series of prehistoric-themed comedy shorts. All such movies made during this time—either out of ignorance or for "dramatic license"—anachronistically portrayed dinosaurs and "cavemen" living at the same time.

During the 1930s, the public's awareness and craving for dinosaurs became greater than ever, mostly thanks to the advertising campaign of the Sinclair Refining Company. Launched early in the decade, the campaign aggressively used dinosaurs as a metaphor to emphasize the great age of the crude oils used in their products. Sinclair made dinosaurs available to the public via advertisements, billboards, models displayed at gas stations, and other items. Among the most popular of these were the stamps depicting ancient animals given away free at Sinclair gas stations for pasting in official Sinclair booklets. (The *Apatosaurus*, then still called "*Brontosaurus*," would become the company's trademark or symbol, eventually acquiring the more affectionate name of "Dino.")

Sinclair's most ambitious involvement with dinosaurs during this period involved A Century of Progress, the Chicago World's Fair of 1933–34. The oil company was highly visible at the Fair through the "Sinclair Dinosaur Exhibit," a free outdoor attraction located within walking distance of the still fairly new Field Museum of Natural History. The exhibit featured a group of full-scale dinosaur figures—some of them animated via internal motors—designed by P. G. Alen. The figures were all based upon murals at the Field Museum painted by the great Charles R. Knight (whose drawings, paintings, and sculptures, seen in many popular books, were mostly responsible for the public's concept of ancient animals from the late 1800s through mid–1950s).

The Fair featured other prehistoric attractions also, including "The World a Million Years Ago," a more sensational but less scientifically accurate re-creation of ancient life by the Messmore and Damon Company, which would play in various incarnations in the United States until as late as 1972. Visitors to the original attraction in 1933 were conveyed by a moving trackway past various tableaux featuring dinosaurs, pterosaurs, prehistoric mammals, and early forms of man. Clunky by today's standards, these figures, back then, were state of the art, amazing and delighting the people who came to view them.

Publicity photo for "The World a Million Years Ago," Messmore and Damon's popular attraction at A Century of Progress (1933–34), which featured a zoo of mechanical prehistoric creatures including this sabretooth cat (caveman not mechanical). Courtesy of the late Francis B. Messmore, Messmore and Damon.

With people more dinosaur-aware than in previous decades, new dinosaur product was required to satisfy their fascination. Frequently, lurid fantasy stories featuring dinosaurs appeared in cheaply produced "pulp" magazines. *Alley Oop*, V. T. Hamlin's newspaper comic strip featuring a caveman hero who rode a pet sauropod-like dinosaur named Dinny, would debut in 1933, and would be published for over half a century. The radio series *Ogg, Son of Fire*, featuring cavemen and dinosaurs, premiered on CBS in 1934. Both would offer some of the earliest collectible dinosaur premiums.

One of the most enduring and successful dinosaur-related icons to emerge from the 1930s, however, was the classic movie *King Kong* (1933). Although the main star of the film was a giant "prehistoric" gorilla, the island that this ape dominated was also populated by various dinosaurs and other Mesozoic reptiles. Special effects were by Willis O'Brien, who learned his craft via those relatively crude silent efforts, and had already triumphed with the 1925 production of *The Lost World*, based on Conan Doyle's novel. *King Kong* became an instant hit, spawning an entertaining but inferior sequel, *The Son of Kong*, made that same year. Countless revivals in theaters, on television, and later on home video firmly established the "giant monster" subgenre of fantastic films.

The 1940s, alas, offered no dinosaur fad, perhaps because the public's attention was diverted to the more immediate issues involving World War II and its aftermath. The Fifties, however, was another matter altogether.

The early 1950s saw several dinosaur-related events that happened at about the same time. In 1953, artist/writer/editor Joe Kubert's caveman hero Tor debuted in the comic book *1,000,000 Years Ago* (later retitled simply *Tor*). *King Kong* was rereleased to theaters in 1952, inspiring the making of a similar movie, *The Beast from 10,000 Fathoms* (1953), which had also been inspired by a story by Ray Bradbury published in *The Saturday Evening Post*. This film, about a giant prehistoric reptile revived from hibernation and then attacking a major city, would inspire a Japanese film, *Gojira* (1954). This movie would be released in the United States two years later as *Godzilla, King of the Monsters!* and would, in turn, launch a series of sequels and inspire numerous other non–Godzilla movies. Other movies featuring dinosaurs would also be released during this period, these including *The Animal World* (1956), a documentary, and such science-fiction efforts as *The Beast of Hollow Mountain* (1956) and *The Land Unknown* (1957).

Perhaps the most salient dinosaur-related imagery to reach the public during this time was the September 7, 1953, issue of *Life* magazine, which began its popular "The World We Live In" series. The cover, reproducing in full color a portion of a painting done by artist Rudolph F. Zallinger for Yale University's Peabody Museum of Natural History, was seen by millions of subscribers and people who happened to pass a display of magazines.

The 1950s proved to be even more productive regarding dinosaur output than even the Sinclair-dominated 1930s. Dinosaur movies, popular books, comic books (including what would become the several decades-running *Turok, Son of Stone* series), television shows, trading cards, and the first mass-produced dinosaur toys and model kits appeared in stores. Significantly, many of these items related more to children than to adults, who had been the target audience, than in previous decades. Children now were considered a commercially viable consumer group and target audience that would keep many manufacturers of dinosaur items in the financial black for years to come.

Life-sized model of the famous sauropod *Apatosaurus* made by Louis Paul Jonas
studios for Sinclair's "Dinoland," a well-attended attraction at the New York
World's Fair (1964). Courtesy Sinclair Oil Corporation.

The dinosaur boom of the 1950s did not really become extinct with
the culmination of that decade, but, though waning somewhat, more or
less segued into the 1960s, where it remained at a fairly consistent level.
Some of the old and familiar imagery was changing, following the death
in 1957 of artist Charles R. Knight and the emergence of British artist
Neave Parker and Czech artist Zdenek Burian. Comic books continued
to feature dinosaurs, as in the "War That Time Forgot" series in various
war-comics titles published by National Periodical Publications (DC
Comics). Sinclair returned to the arena of producing full-sized dinosaurs;
some were mechanical, made by Louis Paul Jonas for its "Dinoland"
exhibit at the New York World's Fair (1964–65). Dinosaur movies were
made in healthy numbers, including *One Million Years B.C.* (1967) and
The Valley of Gwangi (1969), both highlighted by stop-motion animation
effects by Willis O'Brien's protégé and successor Ray Harryhausen.

It should be stated that, for most of the late 1800s through late 1960s,
the public's awareness of "real" dinosaurs was largely based on what information was available in popular books. Although a small number of these

books were authored by paleontologists (*e.g.*, Dr. Edwin H. Colbert of the American Museum of Natural History), most such publications were written by freelance or staff writers with little knowledge of paleontology, and much of their text was considerably out of date. Newspapers or radio and TV news programs rarely announced new dinosaur discoveries then, while dinosaurs had become regarded by most paleontologists as evolutionary "dead ends" not worthy of much serious consideration. Moreover, the relatively few scientists who did work on dinosaurs had little if any involvement with the public, the results of their work found in the pages of scientific journals not generally accessible to lay people.

However, by end of the 1960s and beginning of the 1970s, much of that would change. In 1969, Professor John H. Ostrom of Yale University announced to the world a "new kind" of carnivorous dinosaur, the sickle-clawed *Deinonychus*, whose bones presented some quite wonderful (and newsworthy) implications: Perhaps dinosaurs were not the slow and sluggish, tail-dragging reptilian oafs as they had long been depicted. Some of them, like *Deinonychus*, must have been quite active creatures and were possibly even warm-blooded. Equally fascinating, some of them may have been directly ancestral to birds.

Ostrom's findings, followed by his further writings, and, more vocally, those of protégé Robert T. Bakker, led to what has been called the "Dinosaur Renaissance" of the early 1970s. Also an accomplished paleo-artist, Bakker often illustrated his ideas in drawings that said more to the public than did many a technical or popular article and book. Paleontologists began to study dinosaurs seriously again, and their work started to reach the public through the media.

A number of spectacular discoveries were made during the Seventies, such as the gigantic sauropod dinosaurs *Supersaurus* and *"Ultrasaurus"* found in Utah by "Dinosaur" Jim Jensen, the enormous "Texas pterosaur" *Quetzalcoatlus*, and the maternal duck-billed dinosaur *Maiasaura* described by John R. Horner and Robert Makela—all of which enjoyed media coverage.

As a result, the public became more dinosaur-aware during the 1970s than ever before, while dinosaurs themselves were being regarded in new and exciting ways. A popular book, *The Hot-Blooded Dinosaurs: A Revolution in Paleontology* (1976), by Adrian J. Desmond, persuasively brought many of the new ideas about dinosaurs to a general public in non-technical language. People began to crave more information about these animals, much of which was delivered in the form of books (some now written by professional paleontologists, but for a popular audience), and also in new and even greater waves of prehistoric paraphernalia.

Dinosaurs drew crowds through the 1980s, 1990s, and beyond. This mechanical *Tyrannosaurus rex*, made by the Kokoro Company and formerly distributed by Dinamation International Corporation, roared at visitors to "The Dinosaurs" (1988) exhibit at the State Museum of Pennsylvania, Harrisburg. Courtesy The Friends of the State Museum.

In 1990, when dinosaurs seemed to have achieved an all-time apex in popularity, Michael Crichton's science-fiction novel, *Jurassic Park*, about genetically engineered dinosaurs that run amuck in a theme park, became a nation-wide bestseller. Three years later, director Steven Spielberg's spectacular movie adaptation of Crichton's book became a megablockbuster featuring state-of-the-art special effects, earning more than $913 million in box office receipts, and boosting the world's love of things dinosaurian to unprecedented heights. A veritable flood of dinosaur merchandise relating to *Jurassic Park* would be eagerly purchased by the public and a spate of movies, toys, games, and other items—some related to the film, others not—would successfully follow in the movie's wake. A sequel, *The Lost World: Jurassic Park*, was released four years later, making back its cost in just a few days. At least one more sequel would be filmed.

During the past decade or so, the public's desire to see seemingly "live" dinosaurs has been met through the development of full-sized, state-of-the-art "animatronic" models, in a way extensions of the cruder mechanical figures produced during the early 1930s by companies like Sinclair and Messmore and Damon. The leading producer of such figures is Dinamation International Corporation, whose figures—made under the supervision of professional paleontologists like Robert T. Bakker, James I. Kirkland, and George Callison—appear world-wide to long lines of appreciative dinosaur lovers of all ages. Universal Studios, which released the *Jurassic Park* pictures, has recently followed suit, placing their own group of animatronic dinosaur figures in a permanent "Jurassic Park" setting at their theme park in Universal City, California. Clearly, dinosaurs have evolved from simply creatures reconstructed from fossil bones. They have transcended being mere items or products that come and go depending upon current trends. Indeed, they have become an integral and apparently permanent part of our popular culture.

INDEX

The following index consists of proper names and titles that appear in the text and in picture captions, the latter indicated by *italics*.